Our Prayers Rise Like Incense: Liturgies for Peace

Compiled and edited by Cindy Pile
Cover design: Frank Pauer
Editorial team: Holly Knight; Nancy Small; Michelle Balek, OSF; Mary Ellen Cummings, OSB;
    Lori Swanson Nemenz; Christine Obenreder; Nancy Phanco
Graphic Design: Lynch & Hagerty
Printing: Printing Technologies

©1998, Published by Pax Christi USA,
532 West Eighth Street, Erie PA 16502
814.453.4955
info@paxchristiusa.org
http://www.nonviolence.org/pcusa
ISBN 0-9666285-0-0

About Pax Christi USA

In a world that settles differences by armed violence and defines "justice" as "revenge," Pax Christi USA dares to break the cycle of violence by fostering reconciliation.

Pax Christi USA is the national Catholic peace movement of 14,000 members who are committed to the gospel imperative of nonviolence. Our membership includes over 550 religious communities; over 200 parish sponsors; over 140 bishops; over 130 Youth and Young Adult Forum members; approximately 500 Pax Christi local groups; and 18 regions that coordinate activities in their geographic areas.

The work of Pax Christi USA begins in personal life and extends to communities of reflection and action to transform structures of society. Pax Christi USA rejects war and every form of violence and domination. It advocates primacy of conscience, economic and social justice and respect for creation. Pax Christi USA commits itself to peace education and, with the help of its bishop members, promotes the gospel imperative of peacemaking as a priority in the Catholic Church in the United States. Through the efforts of all its members and in cooperation with other groups, Pax Christi USA works toward a more peaceful, just and sustainable world.

Pax Christi USA is a section of Pax Christi International, the Catholic peace movement.

Membership is open to all who support Pax Christi USA's statement of purpose. Regular membership is $35.00 per year, entitling the subscriber to Pax Christi USA's quarterly publication, *The Catholic Peace Voice*, and regular membership mailings. Full membership benefits are extended to those living on limited incomes who cannot afford the entire membership fee. For information about joining Pax Christi USA or to receive a catalogue of our publications, please call, write, e-mail or contact us via our World Wide Web site listed above.

Our Cry For Justice

It is the policy of Pax Christi USA to use inclusive language. However, some of the sources directly quoted in this manuscript did not use inclusive language and were left intact. Various terms that depart from traditional language usage also were incorporated in the book for the purpose of shifting people toward a more justice-based worldview. For example, the word "kin-dom" is often used as a replacement for the word "kingdom" as a means of moving away from the notion that God's reign will be reflected in principalities and powers and moving toward a notion that all will be family in the reign of God.

Introduction

A small group gathers in Indianapolis, Indiana to remember the brief life of JaRyan Cummings, another victim of gun violence. JaRyan's presence is felt strongly as the group visits the site of his murder and, with holy oil, they reconsecrate the ground where such a tender life was snuffed out.

Almost seventy people travel to our nation's only nuclear test site, located one hour outside of Las Vegas, to commemorate the bombing of Hiroshima and Nagasaki. They listen to the voices of the victims. They hear the cry of the earth. They make pledges. "Never again. Never again."

In Virginia many people come together to pray for the man who will be executed that evening and for the victim of his crime. The candle representing the victim is blown out. The candle representing the man who awaits death is left burning. As a sign of hope people light their own candles from that lone flame as they pray for an end to all forms of violence which exist in our world today.

A Pax Christi group in Florida holds a liturgy for the people of Haiti, a service that calls the congregation to listen to the cry of those who have endured years of oppression. Several members of the congregation have traveled to Haiti and have seen firsthand such brutality. One member wrote a poem about the killings. It is read during the Mass.

In San Francisco an interfaith coalition working for the rights of homeless people begins a public fast in support of these rights. They speak out against the criminalization of impoverished people. They bless, break and share bread, knowing that during the fast this will be their only nourishment as they seek justice for their sisters and brothers who are forced to walk the streets at night.

This book offers a variety of liturgies, some of which include eucharist, to be used for occasions when we as people of faith need to speak out boldly and clearly for justice and peace in our world. It is not a compilation of services designed by one person, however. The beauty of this book lies in the fact that it is comprised of liturgies which numerous groups throughout the country have already used in their own work for peace. It is fruit borne from standing for hours, holding vigil at military installations, the World Bank, the School of the Americas and the Indonesian Consulate. It is fruit borne from pounding the pavement on Good Friday as part of a contemporary Way of the Cross, which identifies the overwhelming number of crucifixions that continue to occur today. It is fruit borne from listening to the words of the martyrs and letting them sink deeply into not only our minds, but our hearts and souls.

Editing this book has been a gift, each prayer service I have received a treasure. I have been educated from reading some of the materials. I have wept while reading other selections. And in pouring over the hundred or so liturgies which I received, I have been filled with an abundant sense of hope and joy because of the faithful witness of all of you who seek to follow more closely Jesus, the human one, the nonviolent one, the Prince of Peace.

This book is an offering. I hope that you will use it as a resource for your ongoing work. The services can be used as are or adapted to meet your group's needs. General liturgical and music resources that might be of assistance in planning new services are listed in the back of the book.

May our prayers rise like incense then, our hands in supplication, as we continue to beseech our loving Creator who hears our prayers and answers them, sometimes in new and surprising ways. May our prayers rise like incense that we might trust more fully in the One who knew us before birth, who loves us with an everlasting, unconditional love. May our prayers rise like incense to the One Who is Holy so that, together, we might be empowered to continue the struggle to hasten the coming of God's reign of truth, justice, peace and nonviolent love. Oh God, hear our prayer!

Cindy Pile
Editor

Seasons of Peace

New Year Peace Meditation

Groups of people all over the world gather for one hour of simultaneous meditation and prayer for peace, beginning when the first part of the Earth turns into the new year. This time is 7 to 8 a.m. Eastern Standard Time on December 31. Pax Christi members in Chicago have been observing this ritual for the past several years, and have developed this service. It may be followed by a festive breakfast.

Luminaria (candles inside paper bags) line the walkway to the house. People enter quietly into the room and sit on the floor, a chair, or a pillow. Meditative music may be playing in the background. Lights should be out except for candles around the room and the Christmas tree lights. One large candle is in the center of the floor, surrounded by evergreen branches.

(Incense is lit)

Introduction and Guided Meditation

(Everyone sits)

Leader:
Every year since 1979 small groups of people all around the world have agreed to meditate and pray for peace for one hour at exactly the same time, the time that the Earth first begins to turn toward the new year. At this very moment, all around this beautiful blue planet, which is in so much need of healing and peace, people of many faiths and traditions are gathering to meditate as one, in the belief that the power of many communities united can indeed help to bring peace to our world.

Put yourself in a comfortable position, with your back straight and your muscles relaxed. You may want to lean lightly against the wall or furniture. Close your eyes. Take a deep breath in and, as you exhale, let your muscles relax even further. Breathe slowly in...and out...Now open your eyes and look at the candle in the center. Know that this is the same fire that burns at the center of the earth beneath us...it is the same fire that flares forth from our sun...and this flame contains the power and energy of healing, of compassion, of peace beyond all telling...Let the flame tell you about itself, of what it can do when people allow it to burn in their hearts...Now close your eyes and let this flame come into your own heart. Feel it spreading its light and warmth throughout your whole body...Let the energy of the flame spread beyond the margins of your body and rise up into this room...see it merge with all the other flames rising up from the other people in this circle.

And now let us together send our united flame out from this house to connect with the flame of energy from the other groups in (name your city) who are meditating...Let this flame spread further still to connect with flames rising up from all parts of (name your state)...And let it connect with flames from many people gathered in places all over the United States...and expand to include flames in other parts of the Western Hemisphere: Canada, Central America, the Caribbean, South America...Then spread across the waters to the flames rising from places in Asia, Australia, Africa, and Europe...Let the image come before you of the entire Earth encircled with the glow of this healing and loving energy...

We'll now enter into our silent meditation. After about 20 minutes, we will intersperse the silence with more guided meditation, poetry, and blessing. Then we will conclude with a sign of peace and each person can make a toast to the new year.

(The following three readings are suggested examples. Or you can invite guests to bring their favorite peace prayer, song, or poem to share.)

First Reading

"The New Genesis" by Robert Muller (adapted) (From *The Way of Peace,* c. Pax Christi USA.)

And God saw that all nations of the Earth, black and white, poor and rich, from North and South, from East and West, and of all creeds, were sending their emissaries to study together, to think together, and to care together for the world and all its people...And God said, "It is good."

And God saw that humans were loving the whole Creation, the stars and the sun, the day and the night, the air and the oceans, the earth and the waters, the fishes and the fowl, the flowers and the herbs, and all their human sisters and brothers...And God said, "It is good."

And God saw that humans were suppressing hunger, disease, ignorance and suffering all over the globe, providing each human person with a decent, conscious and happy life, and reducing the greed, the power and the wealth of the few...And God said, "It is good."

And God saw that humans were living in harmony with their planet and in peace with one another, wisely managing their resources, avoiding waste, curbing excesses, replacing hatred with love, greed with contentment, arrogance with humility, division with cooperation, and mistrust with understanding...And God said, "It is good."

And God saw that soldiers of peace were separating the combatants of quarreling nations, that differences were being resolved by negotiation and reason instead of arms, and that the leaders of nations were seeing each other, talking to each other and joining their hearts, minds, souls and strength for the benefit of all humanity...and God said, "It is good."

And God saw that people were destroying their arms, bombs, missiles, warships and warplanes, dismantling their bases, and disbanding their armies...And God said, "It is good."

And God saw humans changing their institutions, beliefs, politics, governments and all human entities to be servants of God and the people. And God saw them adopt as their supreme law, "You shall love God with all your heart, all your soul, all your mind and all your strength. You shall love your neighbor as yourself. There is no greater commandment than these."...And God said, "It is good."

(Several minutes of silence)

Second Reading

"Let There be Light" by Frances W. Davis (From *Grant us Peace,* a joint project of PCUSA and the Liturgy Training Publications 1-800-933-1800. c. 1991 Archdiocese of Chicago. Reprinted with permission of American Peace Society, Washington, DC.)

Let there be light
Let all the nations gather
Let there be understanding
Let them be face to face

Open our lips
Open our minds to ponder
Open the door of concord
Opening into grace

Perish the sword
Perish the angry judgment
Perish the bombs and hunger
Perish the fight for gain

Sacred is our love
Sacred is the deaths of martyrs
Sacred is their holy freedom
Sacred is your name

Your kin-dom come
Your spirit turn to language
Your people speak together
Your spirit never fade

Let there be light
Open our hearts to wonder
Perish the way of terror
Sacred is the world God made

(Several minutes of silence)

Third Reading

By Mary Rogers, adapted from the Gaelic (From *Earth Prayers*, p.172, edited by Elizabeth Roberts and Elias Amidon. c. 1991, Harper San Francisco, a division of Harper Collins Publishers.)

Deep peace of the running wave to you,
of water flowing, rising and falling,
sometimes advancing, sometimes receding...
May the stream of your life flow unimpeded!
Deep peace of the flowing air to you,
which fans your face on a sultry day,
the air which you breathe deeply, rhythmically,
which imparts to you energy, consciousness, life.
Deep peace of the flowing air to you!

Deep peace of the quiet earth to you,
who, herself unmoving, harbors the movements
and facilitates the life of ten thousand creatures,
while resting contented, stable, tranquil.
Deep peace of the quiet earth to you!

Deep peace of the shining stars to you,
which stay invisible till darkness falls
and discloses their pure and shining presence
beaming down in compassion on our erring world.
Deep peace of the shining stars to you!

Deep peace of the watching shepherds to you, of unpretentious folk, who, watching and waiting, spend long hours out on the hillside, expecting in simplicity some Coming of Lord.
Deep peace of the watching shepherds to you!

Deep peace of the God of Peace to you,
who swift as the wave and pervasive as the air,
quiet as the earth and shining like a star,
breathes into us Peace and Spirit.
Deep peace of the God of Peace to you!

Sign of Peace

New Year Toast

Each person receives a glass of sparkling wine or grape juice. Standing in a circle, each has the opportunity to express his/her hope for the new year.

(The origination of the new year peace meditation is unknown. This specific service was created by Jack and Judy Speer, regional coordinators for Pax Christi Illinois).

"I Have A Dream"
Martin Luther King, Jr. Day

Call to Prayer

"I Have a Dream" by Martin Luther King, Jr. (*excerpts adapted*) (From *Let the Trumpet Sound: The Life of Martin Luther King, Jr.* by Stephen B. Oates, c. 1982 Published by Harper Collins.)

I have a dream today.

I have a dream that one day, down in Alabama with its vicious racists, with its governor having his lips dripping with the words of interposition and nullification, that one day, right there in Alabama, little black boys and black girls will be able to join hands with little white boys and white girls as sisters and brothers.

I have a dream today.

I have a dream that one day every valley shall be exalted, every hill and mountain shall be made low, the rough places will be made plain, and the crooked places will be made straight, and the glory of God shall be revealed, and all flesh shall see it together.

This is our hope. This is the faith that I go back to the South with. With this faith we will be able to hew out of the mountain of despair a stone of hope. With this faith we will be able to transform the jangling discords of our nation into a beautiful symphony of brotherhood. With this faith we will be able to work together, to pray together, to struggle together, to go to jail together, to stand up for freedom together, knowing that we will be free one day...

When we allow freedom to ring, when we let it ring from every village and every hamlet, from every state and every city, we will be able to speed up that day when all of God's children, black and white, Jews and Gentiles, Protestants and Catholics, will be able to join hands and sing in the words of the old Negro spiritual, "Free at last! Free at last! Thank God almighty, we are free at last!"

Song

"My Blood" *(By the Neville Brothers, c. 1980 Neville Music (BMI)/SAIB Music (ASCAP).)*

Reading

"Faithful Witness: The Testimony of Scripture and of Martin Luther King Jr." *(Compiled by Dan Buttry and Ken Sehested for the Baptist Peace Fellowship of North America, PO Box 280 Lake Junaluska, NC 28745 704/456-1881.)*

Reader 1:
World peace through nonviolent means is neither absurd nor unattainable. All other methods have failed. Thus we must begin anew.

Reader 2:
The harvest of righteousness is sown in peace by those who make peace. (James 3:18)

Reader 1:
The ultimate weakness of violence is that it is a descending spiral, begetting the very thing it seeks to destroy. Instead of diminishing evil, it multiplies it. Through violence you murder the hater, but you do not murder hate. In fact, violence merely increases hate...Returning violence for violence multiplies violence, adding deeper darkness to a night already devoid of stars. Darkness cannot drive out darkness; only light can do that.

Reader 2:
Do not be overcome by evil; but overcome evil with good. (Romans 12:21)

Reader 1:
Violence leaves society in monologue rather than dialogue.

Reader 2:
You shall not hate your kin in your heart, but you shall reason with your neighbor, or you will incur guilt yourself. (Leviticus 19:17)

Reader 1:
Love is the most durable power in the world...Love is the only force capable of transforming an enemy into a friend.

Reader 2:
For if while we were enemies, we were reconciled to God through the death of Jesus, much more surely, having been reconciled, will we be saved by his life. (Romans 5:10)

Reader 1:
There are some things within our social order to which I am proud to be maladjusted and to which I call upon you to be maladjusted. I never intend to adjust myself to segregation and discrimination. I never intend to adjust myself to mob rule. I never intend to adjust myself to the tragic effects of the methods of physical violence and to tragic militarism. I call upon you to be maladjusted to such things.

Reader 2:
Do not be conformed to this world but be transformed by the renewal of your mind, that you may prove what is the will of God, what is good and acceptable and perfect. (Romans 12:2)

Reader 1:
Any religion that professes to be concerned with the souls of men (and women) and is not concerned with the slums that damn them, the economic conditions that strangle them and the social conditions that cripple them is dry-as-dust religion.

Reader 2:
But if you have the world's good and see neighbors in need, yet you close your heart against them, how does God's love abide in you? (1 John 3:17)

Reader 1:
One of the tragedies of humanity's long trek has been the limiting of neighborly concern to tribe, race, class or nation...Our world is a neighborhood. We must learn to live together as brothers (and sisters), or we will perish as fools. For I submit, nothing will be done until people put their bodies and souls into this.

Reader 2:
If you love those who love you, what credit is that to you? For even sinners love those who love them. And if you do good to those who do good to you, what credit is that to you? For even sinners do the same. And if you lend to those from whom you hope to receive, what credit is that to you? Even sinners lend to sinners, to receive as much again. But love your enemies, and do good, and lend, expecting nothing in return; and your reward will be great, and you will be children of the Most High. (Luke 6:32-35)

Reader 1:
I am convinced that if we are to get on the right side of the world revolution, we as a nation must undergo a radical revolution of values. We must rapidly begin the shift from a "thing-oriented" society to a "person-oriented" society. When machines and computers, profit motives and property rights are considered more important than people, the giant triplets of racism, materialism and militarism are incapable of being conquered.

Reader 2:
What causes wars, and what causes fighting among you? Is it not your passions that are at war in your members? You desire and do not have; so you kill. You covet and cannot obtain; so you fight and wage war. (James 4:1-2)

Reader 1:
We must accept finite disappointment, but we must never lose infinite hope. Only in this way shall we live without the fatigue of bitterness and the drain of resentment.

Reader 2:
In the world you have tribulation; but be of good cheer, I have overcome the world. (John 16:33)

Reader 1:
Now let us rededicate ourselves to the long and bitter but beautiful struggle for a new world.

Reader 2:
We exhort you, brothers and sisters, admonish the idlers, encourage the fainthearted, help the weak, be patient with them all. See that none of you repays evil for evil, but always seek to do good to one another and to all. Rejoice always, pray constantly, give thanks in all circumstances. May the God of peace sanctify you wholly; and may your spirit and soul and body be kept sound and blameless at the coming of Jesus Christ. He who calls you is faithful, and he will do it. (I Thess. 5:14-18, 23-24)

Questions for Silent Reflection

(Prayer leader introduces. You may wish to play instrumental music in the background while people spend time in reflection. You may also wish to hand out a sheet with these questions.)

1) In what ways do your attitudes toward people of other racial or ethnic groups differ from those of your parents?
2) Do you have friends of other races? If so, how did you get to know them?
3) How often do you see the stereotype of people of color linked with poverty and vice versa?
4) What privileges do you have because of your skin color?
5) Dr. King spoke of racism, materialism and militarism all being interwoven. Where do you see the connections?

Rededication to the Prophet's Dream

Leader:
Is there something that has come out of these reflections to which you would like to rededicate yourselves? After each rededication, please respond:

All:
To the dream we rededicate ourselves.

Closing Prayer

"Celebrating Our Diversity," prayer card by Cyprian Lamar Rowe *(From Pax Christi USA.)*

All:

Beloved God, Creator of the just and the unjust, Lover of all humankind, share your eyes of love so that we will see beauty in all creation. Let us, God, as we pass this way make it a way that sings the glory of all your creation and celebrates the infinite variety of your divinity in all and through all.

Help us, O God, to understand that the violence of "isms," whether racism or sexism or anti-Semitism or heterosexism or militarism, is a violation of your creative will.

Help us to understand, God, that we have neither knowledge nor power to know the infinite designs of worlds where by your grace we may inhabit. Help us to explore the heights and depths of our need to love and be loved, to understand that what we hate is often our sense of incompletion. We shout against creations that we cannot love because we fear and do not understand.

We need to understand because we need to bow before them as being godly as we too are godly.

Help us, God, and in the spirit of Mary, Mother of the afflicted, let us stand by the cross of our own humanity, loving it and knowing that dying to hatred is the only path to salvation. In the name of our Loving Brother, Jesus Christ. Amen.

(Prepared by Tricia Sullivan for a Pax Christi Youth & Young Adult Forum Retreat.)

Ash Wednesday Service

This prayer service is designed to be held at a military installation, or at some site that brings violence and death into our world. Bring palm leaves and symbols of the many good things that are being consumed by our country's commitment to war-making to burn in the ash-making ritual. These symbols can be made of cardboard. Some suggestions: school buses, school books, medicine bottles, food, houses, etc. Also bring a large container to burn these items in, such as a garbage can, and bowls with which to distribute the ashes.

Opening Song
"Turn to Me" *(By John Foley, SJ, c.. 1975, John Foley, SJ, and New Dawn Music.)*

Opening Prayer
Leader:
We gather this morning at the start of the season of Lent to repent of our sins, our personal sins and the sins of our nation, of our government. We come to renounce the idols in our own lives, the hatred and fear which divide us, the apathy and despair which keep us from continuing the struggle for a better world, and to renounce the idols of nuclear weapons that our government continues to build in our names. Be with us, God, this day. Show us your mercy and your love. Forgive us our sins, though they be many, and bring us to new life that we might follow you more closely as makers of justice and peace in our world. Amen.

First Reading
Wisdom 15:7-13

Second Reading
(By Archbishop May)

When a weapons manufacturer says we must build weapons because we need jobs, it is troubling indeed...unemployment is not an excuse to make war or things of war.

Third Reading
(From *The Companions of Jesus* by Jon Sobrino, SJ, c.1990, Orbis Books.)

There is a deep conviction in Latin America that idols exist in this world. Puebla spoke of them and also Archbishop Romero in his last pastoral letter of 1979...Liberation theology has done what is not done elsewhere, and developed a theory of idols. As has been said so many times, but needs repeating because it continues to be a horrific reality, idols are historical realities, which really exist, which pass for divinities, and reveal themselves with the characteristics of divinity. They claim to be ultimate reality, self-justifying, untouchable, offering salvation to their worshipers even though they dehumanize them. Above all, they require victims in order to maintain their power. These idols of death were identified in El Salvador by Archbishop Romero as the idol of wealth, making capital an absolute–the first and most serious of idols and the originator of all the others–and the doctrine of national security. Then he added a serious warning to the popular organizations, that they should not become idols themselves and never adopt a mystique of violence, even when violence became legitimate. So idols exist, and as Archbishop Romero chillingly said, you cannot touch them without being punished. "Woe to anyone who touches wealth. It is like a high tension cable that burns you." This is what happened to the six Jesuits and so many others.

Shared Reflections

Repenting of Our Sins

Leader:
Let us now repent of our sins and of the sins of our government—the sin of continuing to build weapons that can annihilate us all, weapons that are already killing poor people as funds spent on bombs and missiles leave millions without homes, food, healthcare and education. Let us pray.

Litany of Repentance
(From *The Fire of Peace*, c. 1992, PCUSA.)

Reader:
We ask forgiveness for our complicity in the violence now unleashed in our world and we repent of the violence in our own hearts. Please respond: Forgive us, we pray.

For hardness of heart.........forgive us, we pray.
For wasting our gifts
For wanting too much
For wounding the earth
For ignoring the poor
For trusting in weapons
For refusing to listen
For exporting arms
For desiring dominance
For wanting to win
For lacking humility

For failing to risk
For failing to trust
For failing to act
For failing to negotiate
For failing to hope
For failing to love
For our arrogance
For our impatience
For our cowardice
For our pride
For our silence

That we learn compassion.........change our hearts.
That we embrace nonviolence
That we act with justice
That we live in hope
That we might be strong
That we do your will
That we might be peace.

Song
"Unless a Grain of Wheat" *(By Bob Hurd, c. 1984, Bob Hurd, Published by OCP.)*

Burning of Palms/Symbols

Leader:

Let us not be shy. Let us not turn away from God's invitation to change our ways. I invite you to now come forward and burn not only holy palms but the symbols of the many things which are being consumed on our sacrificial altar to the idol of national security. We repent of the many ways that we have allowed such violence to continue.

(Start the fire with some newspapers, then have people bring their palms and their symbols forward to burn.)

Distribution of Ashes

Leader:

The idols which we have renounced, the sins of which we have repented have now been transformed into ashes, symbol of our common birth, our common humanity, our common destiny, symbol of our desire to follow you, Jesus, more closely that we might announce the Good News that we are all one. Please come forward to be marked with the sign of our repentance, the sign of our hope for humanity and of our commitment to being bearers of peace, justice, truth and love to all we meet.

(A few people come forward to put the ashes in bowls and then walk around the circle, marking those gathered with the ashes. As they make the sign of the cross on people's foreheads, they say: "Repent of violence and hatred and believe in the Good News of liberating love." Others pour the ashes which remain in the garbage can on the ground in the sign of the cross.)

Commissioning of Those Taking Ashes to the Employees and Police

(The leader invites those who are choosing to commit civil disobedience to come forward and be commissioned. The leader invites people to extend their hands over this group as s/he speaks a few words of blessing.)

Final Blessing

Leader:

Let us go forth now, marked with the sign of our faith, forgiven and blessed by our merciful God and our crucified Savior, and empowered by the Spirit to be instruments of peace. Amen.

Action

(Those who feel called to commit nonviolent civil disobedience approach either employees of the military installation if they are nearby, or the police, and offer them ashes, inviting them to join the group in repenting of our nation's sins. The rest of the group remains holding vigil in either prayerful silence or begins singing appropriate songs.)

(Adapted from an Ash Wednesday Service and Action held at Lawrence Livermore Labs, located 45 miles outside of the San Francisco Bay Area in California.)

Lenten Reflections on the Cross

In creating the environment, simplicity and lack of visual distraction are key. Put a plain, wood cross in the center of a circle of those gathered or at the front of a worship space, perhaps draped in red or purple cloth or simply there. Readings can be passed around the circle so that many of those gathered can take part or a team of readers (anywhere from two to ten) can split the readings as seems appropriate and comfortable. The pace of the readings is slow and measured with plenty of time for silence and reflection, both on the words and on the cross which binds them and us to the story of Jesus' passion until they are part of a single, on-going story.

Call to Prayer

"Were You There" *(Or any other appropriate song that can begin instrumentally to set the mood. Tune: Were You There, Afro-American Spiritual, Harmony by Robert J. Batastini, c. 1987 G.I.A. Publications, Inc.)*

Reading

"The Good Friday Reproaches" (From *All Desires Known,* by Janet Morley, pp. 43-45, c. 1988, 1992 Morehouse Publishing, P.O. Box 1321 Harrisburg, PA 17105 (in the U.S.) SPCK Holy Trinity Church Marlebone Road London NW1 4DU (in the U.K.).)

All:
Holy God, holy and strong, holy and intimate, have mercy on us.

O my people, what have I done to you?
How have I offended you? Answer me.

I brooded over the abyss, with my words
I called forth creation: but you have brooded on destruction,
and manufactured the means of chaos.

O my people, what have I done to you?
How have I offended you? Answer me.

I breathed life into your bodies, and carried you tenderly in my arms:
but you have armed yourselves for war, breathing out threats of violence.

O my people, what have I done to you?
How have I offended you? Answer me.

I made the desert blossom before you, I fed you with an open hand:
but you have grasped the children's food, and laid waste fertile lands.

O my people, what have I done to you?
How have I offended you? Answer me.

I abandoned my power like a garment, choosing your unprotected flesh:
but you have robed yourselves in privilege, and chosen to despise the abandoned.

O my people, what have I done to you?
How have I offended you? Answer me.

All:

Holy God, holy and strong, holy and intimate, have mercy on us.

I would have gathered you to me as a lover, and shown you the ways of peace:
but you have desired security, and you would not surrender yourself.

O my people, what have I done to you?
How have I offended you? Answer me.

I have torn the veil of my glory, transfiguring the earth:
but you have disfigured my beauty, and turned away your face.

O my people, what have I done to you?
How have I offended you? Answer me.

I have labored to deliver you, as a woman delights to give life:
but you have delighted in bloodshed, and labored to bereave the world.

O my people, what have I done to you?
How have I offended you? Answer me.

I have followed you with the power of my spirit, to seek truth and heal the oppressed:
but you have been following a lie, and returned to your own comfort.

O my people, what have I done to you?
How have I offended you? Answer me.

All:

Holy God, holy and strong, holy and intimate, have mercy on us.

(Allow time for silent reflection.)

Reading

Oscar Romero (From *A Lent Sourcebook: The Forty Days,* Book Two: Tuesday of the Third Week of Lent to Holy Thursday, p.179 (excerpted from The Violence of Love by Oscar Romero, compiled & translated by James R. Brockman c. 1988 Chicago Province of the Society of Jesus, Harper-Collins Publishers).)

For the church, the many abuses of human life, liberty and dignity are a heartfelt suffering. The church, entrusted with the earth's glory, believes that in each person is the Creator's image and that everyone who tramples it offends God. As the holy defender of God's rights and of God's images, the church must cry out. It takes as spittle in its face, as lashes on its back, as the cross in its passion, all that human beings suffer...They suffer as God's images. There is no dichotomy between humans and God's images. Whoever tortures a human being, whoever abuses a human being, whoever outrages a human being abuses God's image, and the church takes as its own that cross that martyrdom.

All:

Holy God, holy and strong, holy and intimate, have mercy on us.

(Allow time for silent reflection.)

Reading

We are complicit in the crucifixion when…

…we allow brutal welfare cuts that punish the poor for their poverty

…we allow unconstitutional laws to strip the homeless of their basic human rights

…we are silent in the face of continued preparations for nuclear war in the wake of the devastation of Hiroshima and Nagasaki

…we scapegoat the "strangers" in our midst, forgetting that we are called to reach across boundaries to include society's outcasts in our communities

All:

Holy God, holy and strong, holy and intimate, have mercy on us.

(Allow time for silent reflection.)

Reading

Dom Helder Camara (From *Peacemaking: Day by Day,* Feb 12, p.17 c. 1985 Pax Christi USA.)

We must have no illusions. We must not be naive. If we listen to the voice of God, we make our choice, get out of ourselves and fight nonviolently for a better world. We must not expect to find it easy; we shall not walk on roses, people will not throng to hear us and applaud, and we shall not always be sure of divine protection. If we are to be pilgrims of justice and peace, we must expect the desert.

All:

Holy God, holy and strong, holy and intimate, have mercy on us.

(Allow time for silent reflection. Gently introduce "Hold Us in Your Mercy" as the sung response for the prayers that follow.)

Sung Response:

"Hold Us In Your Mercy" (*Hold Us In Your Mercy: A Penitential Litany,* text: Rory Cooney / music: Gary Daigle / c. 1993, GIA (found in the newest *Gather* book).)

(Sing refrain through at least twice, fade to instrumental and then to silence as the prayer is concluded.)

Prayer

(Adapted from "Prayers for Good Friday," by Linda Murphy in *A Triduum Sourcebook*, pp. 40-45, Ed. Gabe Huck & Mary Ann Simcoe, c. 1983, Archdiocese of Chicago/Liturgy Training Publications.)

Reader 1:

Brothers and Sisters, let us lift up our prayers in the same spirit we lift up the cross: proclaiming Jesus as the way that leads us beyond ourselves, the truth that cannot be silenced, and the life that will not be entombed.

Sung Response:

Hold Us in Your Mercy…verses 1-3

Reader 2:

For our earth, with its lavish but limited resources, and its enthralling but fragile beauty… For all who lead nations, who hold power of destruction or apply pressures of opinion… For those who develop and disburse our world's resources… For those who shape society's laws and mold our lifestyles…

(Begin instrumental here.)

Reader 1:
Gracious and loving God, we have heard your crucified Son give his dearest ones to one another and we believe that he gives us to one another in much the same way. Pour out your kindness on this dispersed and often divided family that calls itself your church, harmonize our efforts and gather us into the joy and peace of your house.

Sung Response:
Hold Us in Your Mercy...verses 4-6

Reader 2:
For ourselves when, like Pilate, we turn away from truth and accommodate injustice... For ourselves when, with Peter, we defensively deny what we cherish most dearly... For every form of rejection and unbelief let us ask pardon as we pray to you, God...

(Begin instrumental here.)

Reader 1:
Merciful and compassionate God, we know that you have dispatched armies of prophets to reclaim our faithfulness. Carry us past the confusing crossfire of denial and dogma and enable us to love freely and fearlessly.

Sung Response:
Hold Us in Your Mercy...verses 7-9

Reader 2:
For men and women handcuffed by unemployment... For children scourged by poverty and prejudice... For the elderly whose lives are crowned with thorns of indifference and disrespect... For all who will die uncomforted or pass from our company unremembered... For every human sorrow and lack we seek comfort and pardon as we pray to you, God...

(Begin instrumental here.)

Reader 1:
All-seeing and ever-present God, no person slips through cracks in your perception and no event is slurred in the impeccable precision of your eternity. Make us all count to one another as seriously as we do to you; let not one of us given into your Son's care be lost, but bring us all to a share in his glory.

Sung Response:
Hold Us in Your Mercy...verses 10-11 (And conclusion, gradually fading to quiet.)

All:
Holy God, holy and strong, holy and intimate, have mercy on us. Amen.

(End in silence.)

(Developed by Kate McMichael and Theresa Hausser, liturgists and pastoral ministers at St. Boniface Catholic Community, San Francisco, for Good Friday 1997.)

15

Holy Thursday Liturgy "I Have Given You An Example, That So You Also Should Do" (Jn. 13:15)

Lent is an important season for those of us who call ourselves Christian. It is a time to focus on the meaning of discipleship, of what it truly means to walk the same path as Jesus, whose journey ended upon a cross. It is a time to take an honest look at how we are responding to the invitation to be disciples of Christ. This Lenten prayer service, with its focus on discipleship, is designed to be a resource for small groups who wish to remember and share in the tradition of the first disciples, whose feet were washed by Jesus and who ate and drank with him on the night before he died.

All are invited to bring food to share. Candles are placed around the room where the service is to be held, preferably enough to hold the service by candlelight. Chairs and/or pillows are arranged in a circle around a table, on which is placed the food, a loaf of bread, a cup of wine or grape juice, a pitcher (or several if it is a large group) filled with warm water, a basin, several towels, and two candles. It is recommended that the parts of the service designated as "leader" be shared by different people in the group. The service begins when all are seated and quiet.

Call to Worship

Leader:
God came to Moses in the burning bush and said, "Take off your shoes, for the place upon which you are standing is holy ground." (Ex. 3:5) As we begin our prayer this evening, I invite you to remove your shoes in that same spirit, honoring the holy ground upon which we walk and the presence of the holy in each one of us gathered here. (All remove shoes.)

Gathering Song

(Suggested Songs: "Lord, When You Came" by Cesar Gabarain, c. 1981, Oregon Catholic Press; "We are Many Parts" by Marty Haugen, c. 1980, by GIA Publications; "The Circle's Larger" by Colleen Fulmer, c. 1989, by Colleen Fulmer; and "God Beyond All Names" by Bernadette Farrell, c. 1990, by Oregon Catholic Press.)

Penitential Rite

Leader:
God of our journeys, you beckon us to follow, but sometimes we turn away in fear. God, have mercy.

All:
God, have mercy.

Leader:
God dwelling among us, you tell us that we are to see your face in every sister or brother we meet, but sometimes we refuse to look...Christ, have mercy.

All:
Christ, have mercy.

Leader:
God of infinite patience, you show us that you are with us on the road, not only at the destination, yet we fail to trust in your abiding presence. God, have mercy.

All:
God, have mercy.

Leader:
Ever-loving God, we long to be a people who walk in your ways. Humble us, that we might exalt you. Inspire us with a faith which does not count the cost. In your name, we pray.

All:
Amen.

First Reading
John 13:33-35

Silent Response

Second Reading

"Making God's Love Visible" by Mary Evelyn Jegen, SND (Adapted, from *Words of Peace*, c. Pax Christi USA.)

It is an astonishing truth that we shy away from our vocation to make visible God's own response to violence. It is God who wants to express love, justice, mercy and forgiveness in us. "This is the love I mean, not our love for God, but God's love for us" (1 John 4:10).

We can do this only as children of God. It is the intimacy of our relationship to God that makes us bold, hopeful, able to take risks and seek a company of sister and brother believers.

We are to make God's love visible. We learn how as disciples of Jesus; we act our way into his astonishing way of thinking. It begins by paying attention to people without exception, paying attention to their specific joys, hopes, and pains, and also to their vague but overwhelming fears and anxieties that cannot even find expression in words.

For Jesus, making God's love visible meant his own active concern for John and Judas, for women and men, for children, widows, tax collectors, soldiers, even executioners-his own. For us, making God's love visible means active concern for each person in our family, for the unemployed, the addicts, and the people around the world.

The whole thrust of Jesus' good news is about seeking the best for each and every one, because we are, after all, one family: God's. Jesus talked about the reign of God as a party where we all sit together and God serves the dinner (Luke 12:37). It was just one of Jesus' inventive ways of trying to get across the truth that we are connected by love, and that we refashion broken connections only by love...

More than ever, as militarism and terrorism tighten their grip on our way of life, we need to support each other in the risk of unconditional love, translating it into concrete actions in the social and political arena as well as in our interpersonal relationships. Only in this way can we make our contribution to breaking the spiral of violence; only in this way can we enlarge and encourage our hope, can we be children of God, and disciples of Jesus who is our pioneer in faith.

Shared Reflection
(All are invited to share their reflections on the above readings.)

Litany for Peace
(*From* The Fire of Peace, c. *1992, Pax Christi USA.*)

Reader 1:
Let us pray to Jesus that we may be set free from the chains of violence and war. Jesus, by your cross and resurrection...

All:
Deliver us.

Reader 1:
by your nonviolence and love...
by your witness to truth...
by your passion and death...
by your victory over the grave...
from the desire for power...
from the conspiracy of silence...
from the negation of life...
from the worship of weapons...
from the celebration of killing...
from the slaughter of the innocent...
from the extermination of the weak...
from the nightmare of hunger...
from the politics of terror...
from a false peace...
from relying on weapons...
from the spiral of armaments...
from plundering the earth's resources...
from the despair of this age...
from global suicide...

Reader 2:
by the light of the Gospel...

All:
Give us peace.

Reader 2:
by the good news for the poor...
by your healing and wounds...
by faith in your word...
by a hunger and thirst for justice...
by the coming of your reign...
by the outpouring of the Spirit...
by reconciliation of enemies...
by gentleness and nonviolence...
by the truth that sets us free...
by prophecy and witness...
by persecution because of your name...
by the power of love...

All:
Lamb of God who takes away the sins of the world, have mercy on us. Lamb of God who takes away the sins of the world, have mercy on us. Lamb of God who takes away the sins of the world, grant us peace.

Ritual of Footwashing

Leader:
Before us waits a pitcher of water, a basin, a towel. They remind us of our baptism into the Christian community. Water poured forth upon us, washing away our complacency, readying us for a journey in the footsteps of Jesus, who followed his faith to the cross. These symbols remind us, too, of the example of Jesus on the final night of his life. Gathered with those he loved, Jesus taught us that the posture of the Christian community begins on bended knee.

After washing Peter's feet, Jesus said, "I have given you an example, that so you also should do." (John 13:15) Following the example of Jesus, we now prepare ourselves to wash the feet of each other. We cradle the feet of our neighbor in our hand, these weary feet which have stumbled over rocks of injustice, hatred and despair. Rocks which slow us down and impede our journey toward peace. These faithful feet that have kept on walking, hastening the vision for which Jesus gave his life, summoning joy enough to join in the dance of possibility. We gingerly pour water upon these Christian feet, washing away fear, doubt and the temptation to run when the going gets tough. We wash away the dust of hatred, apathy, despair and defeat which sometimes settles in as an uninvited guest. We tenderly dry these feet, wrapping them in a living, loving mantle of community.

Jesus has given us this example, telling us that we should do the same. So let us.

(The leader takes the pitcher, basin and towel and washes the feet of one of the group members. They, in turn, wash the feet of the leader and pass the pitcher, basin and towel to their neighbor. The washing continues until all have had their feet washed. Suggested music: "A New Commandment" by Michael Ward, c. 1989, by World Library Publications; "The Lord Jesus" by Gregory Norbert, c. 1973, by Benedictine Foundation of Vermont; "Digo 'Si' Senor" by Donna Pena, by GIA Publications.)

Prayer Over Gifts at the Table

Reading:
First Corinthians 11:23-26

Leader:
And so we gather to remember, as Jesus taught us. We remember with grateful hearts the abundance you promise us, God, and we thank you for the bountiful feast before us. *(Lifting bread.)* We remember, too, that each of us, like the grains of wheat in this bread once scattered in the field, have been brought together around this table by our common passion for peace. Like this loaf, God has kneaded us with strong and loving hands, sometimes gently, sometimes with great vigor, working hard to get rid of all the lumps.

All:
God has set us to rise, and we've risen.

Leader:
At times, we've been pounded down, made humble, brought back to the earth which once cradled our seeds.

All:
And each time we've risen, like leaven that cannot be kept down, we have risen!

Leader:
Before us, waits a loaf of bread. One loaf, waiting to nourish us if only we would break it...

All:
For it is in the breaking that we recognize God dwelling among us.

Reader 1:
God breaks open and creates a space for peace when we dare to speak truth to power.

Reader 2:
God breaks apart and makes room for new growth when we witness against oppression and suffering.

Reader 1:
God breaks through and wraps us in longing arms when we believe that we are God's beloved.

Reader 2:
God breaks in, through walls of hatred, fear, and despair, when we proclaim the vision for which Jesus gave his life.

Leader:
As we break this bread, we remember the body of Jesus, broken for a vision that he would not betray. We remember the brokenness of our world and pray that we, as peacemakers, might be agents of healing.

All:
We open ourselves to your transformative power, O God. Mingle this bread with your hope and our flesh, that we might be your body broken for a world which cries out for peace.

(As the bread is shared among the group, a song is sung. Suggested songs: "We Remember" by Marty Haugen, c. 1980, by GIA Publications; "Ubi Caritas" by Laurence Rosania, c. 1992, by Oregon Catholic Press; and "Song of the Body of Christ" by David Haas, c. 1989, by GIA Publications).

(After all have eaten the bread, the leader continues.)

Leader:
(Lifting cup) We remember, too, that like this cup we are united by our common thirst for justice. Like these grapes, God has gathered us together and pressed us, squeezing hard to remove layers of stubborn resistance.

All:
As Jesus transformed water into wine, so are we transformed to be God's lifeblood.

Leader:
God pours us out, as sweet wine/juice upon a thirsty world...

All:
As milk and honey to refresh those whose eyes and spirits are downcast.

Leader:
Before us waits the cup of God's passion. One cup, overflowing with God's love and grace, if only we would drink it.

All:
For it is in the drinking that we savor the sweetness of God's reign.

Reader 1:
A time when kindness and faithfulness shall be one, where justice and peace shall kiss...

Reader 2:
A place where all people are seated together to savor wisdom's feast...

Reader 1:
A time when swords have been beaten into plowshares, spears molded into pruning hooks...

Reader 2:
A place where all live in peace upon God's holy mountain.

Leader:
As we drink this cup, we remember the blood of Jesus, poured out upon the seeds of nonviolence which he sowed in courage, tenderness, and eternal love. We remember the blood which is spilled each day at the hands of violence, and we pray that we, as peacemakers, might create a way for peace.

All:

We open ourselves to your transformative power, O God. Mingle this wine/juice with your hope and our flesh, that we might be your blood, poured out upon a world which thirsts for justice.

(The song continues as the cup is shared among the group.)

Closing Prayer

(From *The Fire of Peace* by Pax Christi USA.)

All:

Oh God, we believe that peacemaking means planting seeds even though we may never see the flower, and that it means never losing sight of the vision promised by You. We hold fast to Your word that one day swords will be beaten into plowshares. May we, as peacemakers, stake our lives on that promise. We ask this through your life-giving Spirit. Amen.

Song of Sending Forth

(Suggested Songs: "Jerusalem, My Destiny" by Rory Cooney, c. 1990, by GIA Publications; "God of Abraham" by Bernadette Farrell, c. 1990, by Oregon Catholic Press; "Against the Grain" by Donna Pena c. 1989, by GIA Publications; and "The Isaiah Song" by Michael Ward, c. 1985, by World Library Publications).

(The service ends with a sharing of the meal.)

(Prepared by Nancy Small, National Coordinator of Pax Christi USA.)

Way of the Cross: Good Friday Peace Walk

For the past 15 years Pax Christi Metro New York has organized this Good Friday Witness where over 1,000 people join in the largest public Christian peace witness in New York City. The Good Friday Way of the Cross is a modern-day enactment of the Stations of the Cross, witnessing for peace and justice in the streets of our cities.

Station #1: Jesus is Condemned to Death
Theme: United Nations / People In Countries Ravaged By War

Leader:
We adore you, O Christ, and we praise you.

All:
By the power of your holy cross, help us to change the world.

Scripture:
Luke 23:13-21

Statement:
By Pax Christi Fordham University (adapted)

Reader 1:
War and violence ravish our world. In Burundi, Zaire, N. Ireland, Israel, East Timor and Albania, guns and bombs rend the fabric of life, condemning our brothers and sisters to death. Christ was condemned to die by the leaders of Rome in cooperation with the leaders of the Jewish people. Similarly, everywhere on earth people are condemned to death by the latter day Romans such as ethnic groups, dictators, invested capital and political expedience.

Reader 2:
The cruel realities of war are often initiated and created by non-military agents. The World Bank and the International Monetary Fund, working for the benefit of multinational corporations, often contribute as much to building an atmosphere for violence as do armies and generals. The violent attitudes of neo-colonial development and economic manipulation are as cruel as mortar shells and machine guns. The distorted aims of the World Bank and IMF build situations where war is ripe.

Reader 1:
In an age where wars are perpetually fought around the globe, we need to summon the highest part of our humanity and we need to look to Christ as the peaceful answer to strife and violence. We must take to heart Christ's radical message of nonviolence and peace. Only by following humanity's more divine impulses to humility, love and respect for one another, can an end be found to our ceaseless wars.

Response:
Jesus, have mercy.

Song:
"Bring Forth the Kingdom" *(By Marty Haugen, c. 1986, GIA Publications, Inc.)*

(Walking Chant: "Ubi Caritas," Text: Taize Comm., 1978 / Tune: Jacques Berthier, c. 1979, Les Presses de Taize.)

Station #2: Jesus is Made to Carry His Cross

Theme: Homophobia / People With AIDS

Leader:
We adore you, O Christ, and we praise you.

All:
By the power of your holy cross, help us to change the world.

Scripture:
Matthew 27:27-32

Statement:
By Pax Christi Westchester (adapted)

Reader 1:
Since HIV/AIDS was first recognized in 1981, between 900,000 and 1.2 million Americans are estimated to have been infected. The epidemic's greatest impact has been on young adults. Among men 25 to 40 years old, AIDS is the number one killer and it is the number three killer of young women. This has grave repercussions. It is anticipated by the year 2000, AIDS will have caused 125,000 to 150,000 American children to become orphans. These statistics are a small percentage of the 28 million worldwide who have become HIV infected, with six million already dead.

Reader 2:
How can we respond to this appalling situation? Today, we contemplate Jesus carrying his cross almost two thousand years ago. Are we able to see him now in the faces of countless AIDS victims, including thousands of innocent children? As a church that is deeply committed to health care and to defense of the poor, are we doing all that we can to educate vulnerable populations in the area of AIDS prevention? Are we even aware of the multitudes of AIDS victims who languish in developing countries without hope of adequate medical treatment? Are we as individuals willing to work against discrimination toward HIV infected persons and to become advocates with legislators for assistance to the poor who cannot afford the promising new medicines being discovered?

Reader 1:
Let us pray. Jesus, the poor one, you bear the burden of all people. Carrying the cross, you carry all of us, particularly our sisters, brothers and children who are infected with AIDS. We renew our promise to live under no other sign of power than the sign of the cross.

Response:
We take up the burdens others carry and reject all that hinders us from following Jesus on the way of the cross.

Song:
"Lord, Let Me Walk" (By Jack Mittleton, c. 1975, World Library Publications, Inc.)

Station #3: Jesus Falls the First Time
Theme: People Whose Human Rights Are Denied

Leader:
We adore you, O Christ, and we praise you.

All:
By the power of your holy cross, help us to change the world.

Scripture:
Psalm 22:6-7, 16

Statement:
By Pax Christi St. Vincent Ferrer (adapted)

Reader 1:
Jesus has fallen under the weight of the cross. Alas, today He falls again and again through-out our world, in the form of the down-trodden, the inarticulate, the disadvantaged victims of giant oppressors of human rights. These oppressors are those powerful members of local, national, and international governments, as in China , Indonesia or Serbia, whose laws reflect the hardening of their hearts towards the masses. They are the unscrupulous employ-ers who exploit their workers in order to maximize and maintain their incredible profits. They are the gambling and drug kings who capitalize on the weaknesses of others. They are the arms dealers who thrive on conflict. They are the porno kings and queens who poison our children, and ultimately our society in the name of entertainment. We become the oppressors when we sit back complacently and do nothing to speak out against injustice in all its forms.

Reader 2:
But beware, oppressors, for Exodus 22 verses 20-26 warn that God's wrath will flare up and destroy us for molesting and oppressing those who are different from us, for infringing on the rights of the widow and the orphan, for extortion. God is compassionate and hears the poor. Take heart, cross-carriers. Learn from Jesus. Endure, stand firm, and have strong faith, until the changes come-for God is compassionate and hears the cry of the oppressed. (By Cynthia Addison-Bernadine.)

Response:
Hear our cry, Jesus.

Song:
"The Cry of the Poor" (By John B. Foley, SJ, c. 1978, 1991, John B. Foley, SJ and New Dawn Music)
(Walking Chant: "Jesus, Remember Me." Text: Luke 23:42, Music: Jacques Berthier and the Community of Taize, c. 1981, Les Presses de Taize.)

Station #4: Jesus Meets His Afflicted Mother
Theme: Children Who Are Abused Or Neglected / Abortion

Leader:
We adore you, O Christ, and we praise you.

All:
By the power of your holy cross, help us to change the world.

Scripture:
Luke 2:34-35

Statement:
By Pax Christi St. Andrews (adapted)

Reader 1:

There is no greater love than that of a mother for her child. We can only imagine the pain and grief in Mary's heart as she watched the son she had given birth to and raised carrying the cross on the way to Calvary.

Reader 2:

Children grow up to treat others as they have been taught. If they are raised with love, they grow up loving; if they are raised with violence or treated violently, they grow up to repeat the pattern. The violence, abuse, and destruction of young and unborn children reveal our society's lack of care for God's greatest gift-the gift of life-the gift of the child. If we are not to value such a precious gift, what then are we to value? Each child born into this world deserves to be raised with total reverence.

Reader 1:

Abuse, abandonment, domestic violence, poverty, sexual exploitation, lack of respect, and lack of child support are all in direct contrast to God's will. Therefore, let us rectify these conditions. Let us begin at the most basic level-in the home, in school, in church, in the neighborhood. Let us reach out to women and children in need. Let us call upon fathers to take shared responsibility for the care, guidance and protection of the children they bear. Let us be constantly vigilant for the rights of the unborn, for neglected and abused children.

Reader 2:

Jesus identified with the smallest among us. John Paul II once said that, "The Son of God did not come in power and glory...but as a child, needy and poor, fully sharing our human condition in all things, but sin. He also took on the frailty, and hope for the future, which are part of being a child." In Luke's Gospel, Jesus says, "Let the children come to me. Do not hinder them; for to such belongs the Reign of God." To fulfill the command of Jesus, we must let the children come to us for "Whoever receives this child in my name, receives me."

Response:

Jesus, help us to welcome you.

Song:

"Gather Us In," v. 1, 2, 4. (By Marty Haugen, c. 1982, GIA Publications, Inc.)

Station #5: Simon of Cyrene Helps Jesus Carry His Cross

Theme:

People Who Are Hungry; Connection To Weapons Industry

Leader:

We adore you, O Christ, and we praise you.

All:

By the power of your holy cross, help us to change the world.

Scripture:

Luke 23:26

Statement:

By Pax Christi Long Island (adapted)

Reader 1:

Usually poets and generals do not look at the world through the same lens. So, when they agree, maybe we should listen.

First, the poet. Here are the first few lines of a poem called simply "Arms," by Manuel Arce of Guatemala:

You have a gun
And I am hungry

You have a gun
Because
I am hungry

You have a gun
Therefore
I am hungry

Now the general. His name was Dwight David Eisenhower, and this is what he said, after almost eight years as president of the United States:

"Every gun that is made, every warship launched, every rocket fired signifies, in the final sense, a theft from those who hunger and are not fed, those who are cold and are not clothed."

The poet and the general have both grasped the heart of the matter: the unbreakable cause-and-effect link between weapons spending and hunger.

Reader 2:
As the poet put it, "You have a gun/Because/I am hungry." Too often in our times, the weapons that nations buy are aimed at the poor, because they are poor and, therefore, presumed dangerous and desperate for change. To protect themselves from the desperation of their own people, governments buy weapons. To protect American society from the hunger and aspiration of the Third World, the United States maintains a military far larger than any rational analysis of the threat could possibly justify.

Reader 1:
As the general said, weapons spending devours billions that could otherwise be available to alleviate hunger. As long as our world spends $600 billion or more each year on weapons, people will continue to starve. One estimate is that the diversion of even a tenth of that arms spending into food programs could end world hunger.

Reader 2:
Even after the end of the Cold War, the U.S. spends about $265 billion a year on the military. In contrast, Russia spends $60 billion and China $30 billion. The Center for Defense Information estimates that the American government is spending at the rate of $8,117 per second. America's total military spending is estimated at $963 per citizen, compared with $429 in Russia and $24 in China. Not content to do all that spending ourselves, we have become the world's greatest exporter of arms, helping other nations to imitate our profligate weapons spending.

Reader 1:
And what good does all that spending do for America? Bread for the World reports that poverty among children is far worse in the United States than in any other industrialized nation. An estimated 21.5% of American children are poor, compared with 13.5% in neighboring Canada, for example.

Reader 2:
It is not, of course, the mere cost of the weapons that causes hunger. It is also their use. One United Nations study reported that a massacre in one area of the Sudan cut the number of livestock from 1.5 million to 50,000. That meant the loss of most of the region's milk supply. And all over the world, the dangers of mine fields keep farmers from harvesting grain fields. The deadly rain of artillery fire drowns out the soft rain that coaxes food from the ground. The bottomless appetite of war machines upsets the balance of farm markets, taking food out of the mouths of children to put into the hands of soldiers.

Reader 1:

So let us remember, as the poet and the general remind us, that the true cost of all our spending on "national security" is international hunger. Let us pray.

Response:

Come, O Jesus!

Reader 1:

That like Simon, we might help carry the cross by working to divert the billions of dollars poured into United States defense industries to the elimination of degrading housing, crumbling schools and the drug wars in our streets, we pray

Response:

Come, O Jesus!

Reader 2:

That we might help carry the cross by ensuring that our nation sends food, medicine and constructive help to impoverished countries, instead of exporting expensive weapons systems, we pray

Response:

Come, O Jesus!

Reader 1:

That we might help carry the cross by continuing to protest the use of our tax dollars for the maintenance of a war machine that further marginalizes the poor, we pray

Response:

Come, O Jesus!

Reader 2:

That we might help carry the cross by choosing a simpler lifestyle, according to the Gospel, and learn to share our substance with the destitute, we pray

Response:

Come, O Jesus!

Reader 1:

And let us say

Response:

Amen!

Song:

"Gather Your People" (By Bob Hurd, c. 1991, Oregon Catholic Press.)

(Walking Chant: "Salvator Mundi" Text: Taize Community, 1978, Tune: Jacques Berthier, c. 1979, Les Presses de Taize.)

Station #6: Veronica Wipes the Face of Jesus

Theme:
People Living Without Homes

Leader:
We adore you, O Christ, and we praise you.

All:
By the power of your holy cross, help us to change the world.

Scripture:
Matthew 25:37-40

Statement:
By Pax Christi Holy Cross

Reader 1:
Oh no, not another one! I can't ride the bus or drive my car without another one of "THEM" coming to bother me. Look, I feel like saying, "I give to organizations; I really understand the problems of the homeless-just don't bother me okay!" But here he comes and now there he is, and he looks at me. It's that look I can't stand. It's a penetrating look that I can't escape. I don't want to be disturbed from the hamster wheel of my own mind...that look is upsetting me so...I don't even hear the words he says. That look that sears my soul...but it is a gentle look. It shouldn't be a gentle look...if it were an angry look I could get angry too and turn away feeling justified, like the good Pharisee that I am. A quarter-all this over a quarter! But it's the principle that counts, at least that's what I keep telling myself. And as I put my head down and reach in for that quarter, I know that when I come back up from my careful search I'm going to have to look into those eyes. And so I do, and he smiles, and he says, "God bless you; thank you; have a great day"...for what...for my helping him with a quarter, for my wiping his face? No, it is he who has wiped my face. It is he who has penetrated my heart. It is he who from a space deep inside him has allowed me, has invited me into his Holy of Holies, into a paradise that I don't even know. All in a look? Yes, in a look. And then he trudges away and I go away. And I don't even know his name. Or do I?

Response:
God of Mercy, Hear our prayer.

Song:
"Blest Are They" (Tune, David Haas; Vocal arrangement by David Haas and Michael Joncas, c. 1985, GIA Publications, Inc.)

Station #7: Jesus Falls the Second Time

Theme:
People Who Are Victims Of Racism and Cultural Biases

Leader:
We adore you, O Christ, and we praise you.

All:
By the power of your holy cross, help us to change the world.

Scripture:
Hebrews 5:7-8

Statement:
By Sisters of St. Joseph Nonviolence Group

Reader 1:
Racism...It courses through the blood of all of us-all of us who call ourselves American. It courses through us as individuals, as families, as persons in relationship. It courses through the organizations we run and the systems we control. So much of our energy is spent in denial of our racism and cultural bias. Yes, it is so easy to focus on the discrimination in other places and deny our own, right here and now. Let us, today, listen to the voices of some of our own sisters and brothers-our fellow Americans.

Reader 2:
My name is Kim Sumo. I am an Asian American. I suffer from the increase in racially motivated violence in our country against those of us of Asian ancestry. We are scapegoated for the failures of your economic system. You talk about how well our kids do in school. You don't say anything about our kids who don't do well. You talk about what good business people we are. But then you red line all communities from us except the African American community. You say, "Go ahead and build your business on the backs of African Americans. It's the American Way." Then you present the problems of the cities as a conflict between Africans and Asians. We built your railroads and we spent time in your concentration camps. We know what's still happening. I am your sister. Welcome me in.

Reader 3:
My name is Roberto Sanchez. I am proud of my Hispanic American heritage. Yet, you develop 'English only' campaigns to exclude us. You write immigration laws that leave us carrying cards in an apartheid-like system. You call us 'aliens' as if we were from another world. All of us are suspect when we apply for a job. We work in fields and are sprayed with poisons that are on the food you eat, but you won't listen to us for your benefit or our benefit. You love to present urban problems as a struggle between African Americans and us. And then you fail to provide us both with a 'safety net' to ensure equitable access to basic human needs, health care and education. I am your brother. Welcome me in.

Reader 4:
My name is Mary Running Cloud. I am a Native American. We are many nations and we have treaties with you. Our concern is for our legal rights contained in these treaties. You grant yourself religious freedom but fail to protect our traditional religious practices. You have tried all kinds of assimilation practices. You desecrate our religious places and bury your nuclear waste there with our bones. You pretend we are honored by the 'tomahawk chop' of the Atlanta Braves and by Chief Wahoo of the Cleveland Indians. We are committed still to sovereignty in Hawaii, to sovereignty in Alaska and to sovereignty for our 300 nations within the continental United States. We are your brothers and sisters. Welcome us in.

Reader 5:
My name is Kaseem Davis. I am an Afro-American. The economic disparity between the median income of European Americans and us is wider now than it was 10 years ago. You have demonized the African American community and the result is genocide. You present our young men as street savages and our young women as having babies just to earn welfare. Your Justice Department is 15 times more likely to prosecute an African American elected official than a European American elected official. You have even tried to cut down our very souls by burning our churches. I am your brother. Welcome me in.

Reader 1:
My name is Sister. I am a European American. We find it so easy to doubt the experience of people of color. When a person of color says a situation is racist, our first response is "prove it." Our racist tapes play even when we don't expect them to, soothing stereotypes into our ears and blasting stereotypes into our minds. I've tried ignoring these tapes; they don't ignore well. I've tried erasing them. I've tried being liberal and pretending they don't exist. But these tapes are with all of us who are white. You may not have mine, but you have your own. We need to acknowledge them and confront them with the true experience of people of color-the suffering Christ who is still falling under the weight of the cross.

Response:
Amen!

Song:
"Against the Grain" (Words and music by Donna Pena. Arranged by Marty Haugen., c. 1989, GIA Publications, Inc.)
(Walking Chant: "Ubi Caritas")

Station #8: Jesus Meets the Women of Jerusalem

Theme:
Women's Suffering

Leader:
We adore you, O Christ, and we praise you.

All:
By the power of your holy cross, help us to change the world.

Scripture:
Luke 23:27-29

Statement:
By Pax Christi Staten Island (adapted)

Reader 1:
In this Gospel reading, Jesus describes an apocalyptic moment, a time of no hope-like the days immediately following the crucifixion. Yet even as the disciples hid, a few women overcame their fear and ventured out to Jesus' tomb. There they gained the first news of the triumph of the Cross, God's promise fulfilled in the light of the resurrection. Then they went forth proclaiming God's greatness.

The first evangelists, these women are sometimes called. Since the birth of the Christian Church women have been announcing the gospel through their leadership and love. Please join us in a litany to honor some of these faith-filled women.

Litany

Reader 2:
Julian of Norwich, joyful mystic who drew wisdom-seeking pilgrims from afar. Response: Our being proclaims your greatness, O God.

Reader 1:
Dorothy Day, who saw homeless and hungry people and without asking for permission started the Catholic Worker movement. Response: Help us win justice and equality in the church.

Reader 2:
Sarah, who laughed at first, but responded to God's call by giving miraculous birth to Isaac, Abraham's son. Response: Our being proclaims your greatness, O God.

Reader 1:
The Mothers of the Disappeared in Latin America, who witness to injustice, shaming violent regimes into telling the truth. Response: Help us win justice and equality in the church.

Reader 2:
Catherine of Siena, who counseled popes while bringing peace and reunification to the church. Response: Our being proclaims your greatness, O God.

Reader 1:
Hildegard of Bingen, a Doctor of the church who glorified God through the art of music. Response: Help us win justice and equality in the church.

Reader 2:
Ita Ford, Dorothy Kazel, Maura Clarke, and Jean Donovan, who gave their lives as martyrs for the people of El Salvador. Response: Our being proclaims your greatness, O God.

Reader 1:
Mary Magdalene, passionate follower of Jesus, who bravely kept watch in the shadow of Good Friday. Response: Help us win justice and equality in the church.

Reader 2:
Brigid of Kildare, not officially a bishop, but a woman who led the Irish church into a renaissance of charity and justice. Response: Our being proclaims your greatness, O God.

Reader 1:
When called by God, Mary said, "Here I am." She agreed, in perfect fidelity, to give her life to God's service. Is there a better definition of Christian ministry? And haven't women in the church been doing the same for centuries? Clearly, God can call women-and women can respond. Now it is time for ordained Christian ministry, including the Catholic priesthood, to be opened to all God's people. To women as well as men. In hope and expectation of that day, let us continue the litany by singing Mary's Magnificat.

Song:
"Holy is His Name" (By John Michael Talbot, c. 1980, Birdwing Music/Cherry Lane Music. Administered by EMI Christian Music Publishing. Available from Oregon Catholic Press-in the 1997 Music Issue.)

Station #9: Jesus Falls the Third Time

Theme:
People Harmed By The Military, Including Military Personnel

Leader:
We adore you, O Christ, and we praise you.

All:
By the power of your holy cross, help us to change the world.

Scripture:
Matthew 24:9-13

Statement:
By Pax Christi Downtown Brooklyn (adapted)

Reader 1:
The generations living now have been affected by continuous global wars and witnessed their horrors. Let us have a moment of silence to reflect on this legacy of violence. (Moment of silence.)

Response:
Oh God our Redeemer, we acknowledge our active and passive participation in the destruction of your peace.

Reader 1:
With this history, how do we endure? How do we go forward and not repeat? How do we break the cycle of strife, destruction and dehumanization of all people all over the world? For the strength to know who we are, let us pray.

Response:
Loving God, never let us forget that you are God. That you made us, that we belong with You as a child belongs with a loving parent. That all the Earth's people are Your children.

Reader 2:
We share our experiences of war so that others will know its dehumanizing effect on soldier and civilian victim alike. A current example is that Gulf War veterans have succeeded in getting the United States government to recognize the damage done to them by the chemical weapons used during combat. Another example is the work of people who are engaged in a courageous campaign to remove the landmines in South East Asia-weapons that continue to kill civilians. Others travel to Iraq annually to bring relief to the civilians who continue to suffer from the aftermath of the Gulf War.

We all must take responsibility for counseling others to understand that no one is less human than we are. We are all children of God. Let us respond to the "near occasions of grace" whenever we can by reminding our children, our students and one another of that simple truth.

Song:
"Walking the Ways of Peace" (By Jesse Manibusan, c. 1994, Two by Two, 510/523-3370)

Station #10: Jesus is Stripped of His Garments

Theme:
People Who Are Victims Of Economic Injustice

Leader:
We adore you, O Christ, and we praise you.

All:
By the power of your holy cross, help us to change the world.

Scripture:
Psalm 22: 14-18

Statement:
By Pax Christi Queens (adapted)

Reader 1:
Almost two thousand years later, we continue to divide the garments and cast lots for the raiments that are not rightfully ours. Aware of this disgrace, our bishops composed the Pastoral Letter, Economic Justice for All. In it, they wrote "Economic decisions have human consequences and moral content; they help or hurt people, strengthen or weaken family life, advance or diminish the quality of justice in our land...The pursuit of economic justice takes believers into the public arena, testing the policies of government by the principles of our teaching...This letter calls us to conversion and common action, to new forms of stewardship, service and citizenship."

How well have we responded to that call? Let us examine four key principles of Economic Justice for All in the face of current circumstances.

Reader 2:
The economy exists to serve the human person, not the other way around.

Reader 3:
The stock market has been breaking historic records practically every day...(however) Where profits are reinvested, they more often go for machines that replace workers or to move production to places where labor costs are lower and regulations lighter. (Center Focus, Center for Concern, Spring 1996.)

Reader 2:
Economic life should be shaped by moral principles and ethical norms.

Reader 3:
There is a spiritual problem at the heart of our current economic situation...
(It is that) those who have more than they need rest comfortably while those who lack basics struggle and suffer. (Center Focus, Center for Concern, Spring 1996.)

Reader 2:
Economic choices should be measured by whether they enhance or threaten human life, human dignity, and human rights.

Reader 3:
Military spending is "off the table" in budget cutting now, and is scheduled to increase, while funding for housing, social safety net programs, education and health care are being slashed. (NETWORK Connection, November/December 1996.)

Reader 2:
The moral measure of any economy is how the weakest are faring.

Reader 3:
Economic forces, family disintegration, and government action and inaction have combined to leave more than a fifth of our children growing up poor in one of the richest nations on earth. (A Decade after Economic Justice for All, USCC, 1995.)

Reader 1:
The political debate has become ugly and incivility prevails in the media and public forums. Concern for the common good and for the poor and powerless is lost in partisan bickering. Against this trend, we must shout out in prayer. (NETWORK Connection, November/December 1996.)

Response:
"A Psalm on Behalf of the Poor" (adapted) (By Miriam Therese Winter, WomanWord: A Feminist Lectionary and Psalter, Women of the New Testament, c. 1990, Medical Mission Sisters. Published by Crossroad Publishing Company.)

Reader 2:
Helpless are the poor, Shaddai, for the poor do not have access to the bounty of the earth.
Response: Clothe people everywhere with the will to share the earth's abundance.

Reader 3:
Without hope are the poor, Shaddai, when promises all trickle down to nothing but despair.
Response: Clothe people everywhere with the strength to transform possibilities into reality.

Reader 2:
How long must the poor cry out to You and wait to receive an answer? How long can we keep faith in You, so silent to our need?

Response:
Clothe people everywhere with the wisdom to recognize that Your response is present in our actions.

Reader 3:
May the morning star bring hope to all in the midst of destitution. May evening find the poor at rest in Your everlasting arms.

Song:
"God of Day and God of Darkness" (Text by Marty Haugen / Music from the Sacred Harp, 1844, c. 1985, GIA Publications, Inc.)

(Walking Chant: "Jesus, Remember Me")

Station #11: Jesus is Nailed to the Cross

Theme:
Our Ravaged Earth

Leader:
We adore you, O Christ, and we praise you.

All:
By the power of your holy cross, help us to change the world.

Scripture:
Mark 15:22-24

Statement:
By Morris County, New Jersey Pax Christi groups (adapted)

Reader 1:
We the people of the Earth, rejoice in the beauty and wonder of the lands, skies, water, and life in all its diversity. Earth is our home. God has made us stewards of our home, not only for our immediate use, but for all humankind, for all generations to come. We therefore call for an increase in consciousness about the impact of our choices and activities on this Earth which God has so generously provided.

Reader 2:
Let us admit that government alone cannot secure our environment. As citizens of the world, let us accept responsibility in our personal, occupational, and community lives, to protect the integrity of the Earth. In covenant with each other and on behalf of the whole Earth community, let us commit ourselves to the following principles and action:

- All life is sacred.
- Each human being is a unique and integral part of the Earth's community of life and has special responsibility to care for life in all its diverse forms.
- Each human being has the right to a healthful environment and access to the fruits of the Earth. Each also has a continual duty to work for the realization of these rights.
- Economic development, to be sustainable, must preserve the life-support system of the Earth.

Reader 1:
Therefore, concerned that every person shall have food, shelter, pure air, potable water, and all that is necessary to enjoy the full measure of God's providence, let us work for more equitable access to the Earth's resources.

Let us also work for the enactment of laws on the local, regional, national, and international level that protect the environment and promote their observance through educational, political, and legal action. Most of all, let us learn to live on the Earth with consciousness and intentionality, and not just surrender to custom. We need to take responsibility for creating a future in which life can continue in its incredible variety and beauty.

Reader 2:
Let us pray. For lacing our children's water with the bitter gall of industrial waste and carelessly causing leukemia and cancer...

Response:
Forgive us, O God.

Reader 1:
For crucifying our innocent neighbors on the cross of land polluted by our greedy exploitation...

Response:
Forgive us, O God.

Reader 2:
From the results of our cowardice that caused us to build nuclear arsenals and threaten all future generations with radioactive by-products of our folly...

Response:
Deliver us, O God.

Reader 1:
From the specter of biological weapons capable of destroying all that you have held so precious as to sacrifice your life...

Response:
Save us, O God.

Song:
"O Healing River" (Traditional Baptist Hymn, Arranged by Michael Joncas, c. 1982, GIA Publications, Inc.)

Station #12: Jesus Dies on the Cross

Theme:
Victims Of The Death Penalty/Criminal Justice System

Leader:
We adore you, O Christ, and we praise you.

All:
By the power of your holy cross, help us to change the world.

Scripture:
Mark 15: 33-37

(Silence, all kneel.)

Statement:
By Manhattan Mennonite Fellowship (adapted)

Reader 1:
"My God, my God, why have you forsaken me?" The Sacred Head, already sinking toward death, straightens one last time and yells for God. The weight is too great to bear: the sin of the whole world-of a battered creation, of hardened hearts, of unforgiving spirits, of refusing to believe that there is enough love to go around.

Reader 2:
As believers in a Crucified Christ we dare to say that in his death our sins are dead. We confess Christ as the last scapegoat, the ultimate sacrifice, the final death for sin.

Reader 1:
There can be no more deaths to pay for sin. To kill someone for the evil they have done is to insist that the death of Christ was not enough. From the vantage point of Christian faith, the state does not have a right to take human life. To do so is to feed the vicious circle of an eye for an eye and a tooth for a tooth. Gandhi warns us that such systems of retributive punishment led to a whole human race that is eyeless and toothless.

Reader 2:
It is not only through the death penalty but in much of the conduct of the criminal justice system that retribution and revenge seem to have the last word. We tell ourselves that by making prisoners-most of them guilty of wrongdoing, but many of them also victims-scapegoats, we exorcise evil from our midst. Yet we know it is not so.

Reader 1:
It is not that there isn't evil in the world: its weight crushed Jesus. But we believe that in Jesus' death the great reverse began. A willing, undeserved death for others' evil; the breaking of the vicious circle, the offer of restoration in place of retribution.

Response:
Jesus, remember us, when you come into your Glory.

Song:
"Were You There?" (Tune: Were You There, Afro-American Spiritual, Harmony: Robert J. Batastini, c. 1987 GIA Publications, Inc.)

(Walking Chant: "Salvator Mundi")

Station #13: Jesus is Taken Down From the Cross

Theme:
People Living With Addictions

Leader:
We adore you, O Christ, and we praise you.

All:
By the power of your holy cross, help us to change the world.

Scripture:
John 19:31-38

Statement:
By Pax Christi Greenwich Village (adapted)

Reader 1:
As Jesus is taken down from the cross, we are reminded that he suffered and died to free us from our sins and addictions. Jesus said, "Forgive them, for they know not what they do." Would Jesus, then, treat drug addiction as a crime or as a sickness to be healed? How would Jesus respond to the 3.6 million people who are addicted to drugs in the United States? Would he create "three strikes and you're out" laws for even nonviolent drug users? We can say, "Of course not!" Yet this is what is happening! Minorities are particularly affected by bias in sentencing. African Americans and Latinos constitute almost 90% of offenders sentenced to state prison for drug use. From 1986-1991, the number of African American women incarcerated for drug offenses increased 828%, resulting in broken homes and child foster care.

Reader 2:
We have built more and more prisons, creating a quickly evolving prison industrial complex, which has become a societal addiction in itself. The world's highest incarceration rate has see-sawed in recent years between the United States and Russia, with both far outdistancing other nations. The prison population continues to grow at an unprecedented rate. State corrections officials expect that their 1994 inmate population will rise 51% by the year 2000. Can we imagine how spending for prisons will affect budget cuts in health, education, and housing?

Reader 1:
As people of God, we need to examine all of our addictions, both personal and societal, and free ourselves from them. Jesus asks each of us to take his pierced body down from the cross, and in so doing, to let go of all the addictions that are nailing us down.

Response:
God, hear our prayer.

Song:
"Precious Lord, Take My Hand" (Words and Music by Thomas A. Dorsey, 1932, c. 1938, Hill & Range Songs, Inc. Renewed by Unichapel Music, Inc.)

Station #14: Jesus is Placed in the Tomb

Theme:
Victims Of The Nuclear Weapons Industry

Leader:
We adore you, O Christ, and we praise you.

All:
By the power of your holy cross, help us to change the world.

Scripture:
John 9:40-42

Statement:
By Pax Christi Bronx (adapted)

Reader 1:
In a little-known story from the Acts of the Apostles, a silversmith named Demetrius is angry that the Christians Paul and Alexander are converting so many people to Christianity in their area. Why is he angry? Let's listen to his story and find out.

Reader 2:
It was during this time that a rather serious disturbance broke out in connection with the Way. A silversmith named Demetrius, who employed a large number of craftsmen making silver shrines of Diana, called a general meeting of his own men with others in the same trade. "As you men know," he said, "it is on this industry that we depend for our prosperity. Now you must have seen and heard how not just in Ephesus but nearly everywhere in Asia this man Paul has persuaded and converted a great number of people with his argument that gods made by hand are not gods at all. This threatens not only to discredit our trade, but also to reduce the sanctuary of the great goddess Diana to unimportance. It could end up taking away all the prestige of a goddess venerated all over Asia, yes, and everywhere in the civilized world."

Reader 1:
After this speech, "the whole town was in an uproar," and the mob threatened to harm the Christians. Why? Because Paul's message threatened this town's economic survival. If people turned to Jesus, there would be no more reason to have silver statues of Diana; the economy would collapse.

Reader 2:
We have our own silver gods now: the silver gods of nuclear destruction. We are still afraid to follow Jesus' way of nonviolence, because of the effect it would have upon our lifestyle. We must continue to ask ourselves-what do we depend upon for our prosperity? Is it a way of life or a way of death?

At this station, Jesus is laid in a tomb. It seems, sadly, that this world continues to worship not the Jesus who is resurrected but the Jesus who is in the tomb. Why do we love death so much that we continue to venerate it as our god? Nuclear weapons are gods of death.

Reader 1:
The silversmiths in the apostles' time were worried about how Christianity affected their way of life. Here at the end of the 20th and beginning of the 21st Century, Jesus' nonviolent way still disturbs us, still should affect our way of life. Jesus is no longer in the tomb. He conquered death and embraced life. May our countries embrace life, too. May we not profit by death but by life. No more weapons! We lay down our arms and we do not study war anymore!

Response:
Jesus, may we listen only to your word and follow your way.

Song:
"Down By the Riverside" (public domain)
(Walking Chant: "Ubi Caritas)

Station #15: The Resurrection of Jesus Christ

Leader:
We adore you, O Christ, and we praise you.

All:
By the power of your holy cross, help us to change the world.

Scripture:
Matthew 28:1-8

Statement:
By Washington Square United Methodist Church

Reader 1:
We'd like to share with you "A Psalm of the People Rising," which is an adaptation of Miriam Therese Winter's "A Psalm of Women Rising." We'd like you to speak the words of the psalm with us as a call-and-response psalm. After every short phrase that we call out, please respond "The people are rising!" For this is what we believe to be one meaning of Christ's resurrection in the here and now: that each one of us here who has or seeks to overcome any manner of adversity or oppression embodies the spirit of our Brother Jesus, the Risen Christ, the Risen Christa. To paraphrase the poet Maya Angelou:

They may ground us in the dirt with their bitter, twisted lies, but by the healing grace and power of God still like dust we rise.

Reader 2:
Everywhere, the people are rising.
Everywhere, the people are rising, rising from the dead.

From our silence...

All:
The people are rising!

Reader 1:
From our bondage...
From exclusion...
From exploitation...
From violence...
From our guilt...
From all affliction...
From all addiction...
Against all odds...

All:
Everywhere, the people are rising.
Everywhere, the people are rising, rising from the dead.

Reader 1:
Like the sun...

All:
The people are rising!

Reader 1:
Like the moon...
Like a kite...
Like an eagle...
Like the tide...
Like a prayer...
Just like incense...
Just like bread...
Just like Jesus...

All:
Everywhere, the people are rising.
Everywhere, the people are rising, rising from the dead.

Reader 2:
Into hope...

All:
The people are rising!

Reader 2:
Into freedom...
Into speech...
Into power...
Into love...
Into significance...
Into the future...

All:
Everywhere, the people are rising.
Everywhere, the people are rising, rising from the dead.

Reader 1:
Across the nation...

All:
The people are rising!

Reader 1:
Around the world...
Across false boundaries...

All:
Everywhere, the people are rising.
Everywhere, the people are rising, rising from the dead.
(Adapted by Robin Small-McCarthy.)

Song
"I Am the Bread of Life" (By Suzanne Toolan, c. 1970, GIA.)

Following the 15th Station
An Act of Nonviolent Civil Disobedience

It is now common practice for people to add a fifteenth station. "Jesus is raised from the dead," to the traditional fourteen. This is in recognition that the events of Good Friday and Easter Sunday cannot be understood fully except in relation to each other. It is a sign that God is with us, even in the face of so much potential destruction and annihilation, a sign of our hope and strength against such heavy odds. In ending the Way of the Cross with a fifteenth station we actively anticipate the Resurrection.

With this in mind, you are invited to continue today's peace witness by participating in the civil disobedience action that is planned or by accompanying those who will be arrested.

(Adapted from The Good Friday Peace Walk developed by Pax Christi Metro NY.)

Easter Morning Prayer

Create a festive atmosphere. Place the Paschal candle as well as some incense in a prominent place ready to be lit. Cover the table the candle sits on with white cloth, and perhaps drape green cloth or a variety of bright cloths and/or scarves over the table and around the flowers. Surround the candle and table with Easter lilies and/or an array of colorful flowers.

Lighting of the Paschal Candle and Incense
Leader:
Christ is Risen!

All:
Alleluia, alleluia!

Leader:
He has given birth to the dream.

All:
Let us give birth to the dream.

Opening Song
"Morning Hymn" (By David Haas, C. 1987, SUMMIT HILL 88998.)

Dramatic Reading
A Prayer for the Dawning of the New Millennium
(Designed by Paula Dodd-Aiello (adapted))

Reader 1:
I saw a new heaven and a new earth; for the first heaven and first earth had passed away and the sea was no more. And I saw the holy city, new Jerusalem, coming down out of heaven from God...and I heard a voice from the throne saying, "Behold, the dwelling of God is with God's people. God will dwell with them and they shall be God's people, and God will be with them. God will wipe away every tear from their eyes, and death shall be no more, neither shall there be mourning nor crying nor pain anymore, for the former things have passed away. And the One who sat upon the throne said, 'Behold, I make all things new.'" (Revelations 21:1-5)

Reader 2:
I say to you, today, my friends, that in spite of the difficulties and frustrations of the moment, I still have a dream. It is a dream deeply rooted in the American dream. (Martin Luther King, Jr.)

Reader 3:
Lift up your eyes upon / This day breaking for you. Give birth again / To the dream. (Maya Angelou)

All:
Risen Christ, let us lift up our eyes upon this day breaking for us. Let us give birth again to the dream.

Reader 1:
The Rock cries out to us today, you may stand upon me,
But do not hide your face. (Maya Angelou, Random House)

Reader 2:
God is the source of my hope. With God alone for my rock, my safety, my fortress, I can never fall. Rest in God, my safety, my glory, the rock of my strength. (Psalm 62)

Reader 3:
The rock cries out to us today, you may stand upon me,
But do not hide your face. (Maya Angelou)

All:
Risen Christ, let us lift up our eyes upon this day breaking for us.
Let us give birth again to the dream.

Reader 1:
I have a dream that one day every valley shall be exalted, every hill and mountain shall be made low, the rough places will be made plain, and the crooked places will be made straight, and the glory of God will be revealed, and all flesh will see it together. (M.L. King, Jr.)

All:
Risen Christ, let us lift up our eyes upon this day breaking for us.
Let us give birth again to the dream.

Reader 2:
This is our hope…With this faith we will be able to hew out of the mountain of despair a stone of hope. With this faith we will be able to transform the jangling discords of our nation into the beautiful symphony of (sisterhood and) brotherhood. With this faith we will be able to work together, to pray together, to go to jail together, to stand up for freedom together, knowing that we will be free one day… (M. L. King, Jr.)

All:
Risen Christ, let us lift up our eyes upon this day breaking for us.
Let us give birth again to the dream,

Reader 1:
Let us have the courage to believe in the bright future and in a God who wills it for us-not a perfect world, but a better one. The perfect world, we Christians believe, is beyond the horizon, in an endless eternity where God will be all in all. But a better world is here for human hands and hearts and minds to make. (*The Challenge of Peace: God's Promise and Our Response, #337*, c. 1983, United States Catholic Conference, Washington, DC. Used with permission. All Rights reserved.)

All:
Risen Christ, let us lift up our eyes upon this day breaking for us.
Let us give birth again to the dream.

Reader 2:
Be thou our vision this day, O God. We seek Thy vision not for tomorrow, nor for some future day when we are more worthy and more prepared to know and understand. We seek Thy vision this day. ("Meditations of the Heart" by Howard Thurman.)

Reader 3:
Accompany us then on this vigil and you will know what it is to dream! You will then know how marvelous it is to live threatened with Resurrection! To dream awake, to keep watch asleep, to live while dying and to already know oneself resurrected!" ("Threatened with Resurrection" by Julia Esquivel)

All:
Risen Christ, let us lift up our eyes upon this day breaking for us. Let us give
birth again to the dream.

Celtic Alleluia

(c. 1985, Fintan O'Carroll and Christopher Walker, OCP)

Prayers of Thanksgiving

(Leader invites people to offer thanks for the new life they have experienced in their lives and for the dreams to which they are helping to give birth. The response after each petition is: "Thanks be to God. Alleluia, alleluia!")

The Prayer of Jesus

Gospel reading: John 20: 11-18

Closing Prayer

(Adapted from *All Desires Known* by Janet Morley.)

Leader:

O God, Bringer of New Life, you chose as your first witness a woman, a voice that is not always heard. Grant that, as Mary of Magdala first faithfully announced the resurrection to the other disciples, we too may have courage to persist in proclaiming your liberating word in the power of Jesus Christ, the Crucified and Risen One. Amen.

Passing of the Peace

Closing Song:

"Lord of the Dance" *(Text: Sydney Carter, c. 1963, Stainer & Bell, Ltd, London, England. Administered by Hope Publishing Co.) (Have some people who like to dance start to lead a circle dance. Perhaps end with an Easter brunch.)*

(Adapted from several sources, especially a morning prayer created by Paula Dodd-Aiello for a Bay Area Pax Christi regional assembly.)

Prayer Service in Remembrance of Archbishop Oscar Romero

On a table in the center of the circle place a bowl of seeds, several clay pots containing soil and a bowl of water.

Opening Song

"Who Speaks for Me?" (By Tom Paxton, Hogeye Records, 847/475-0260.)

Reading

John 12:23-26 (Followed by silent meditation.)

Dramatic Reading

Speaker 1:

Archbishop Oscar Romero of San Salvador, El Salvador was a voice for the voiceless, a voice for the poor and oppressed of his country. For that reason, he had received many threats to his life, and he knew he could be killed at any time.

Speaker 2:

On March 23, 1980, he preached a powerfully prophetic homily. "Brothers, you who are of the same people as we are, you are killing your very own peasant brothers (and sisters). An order to kill coming from a man must be overridden by the law of God which says: Thou shall not kill! No soldier is obliged to obey an order against the law of God...No one must carry out an immoral law... it is now time that you regain your conscience and obey your conscience before obeying a sinful order."

Speaker 3:

"The Church, the defender of the rights of God, of the law of God and human dignity...cannot remain silent." He then pled with the men of the Salvadoran army: "In the name of God, therefore, and in the name of this suffering people whose lamenting reaches the heavens with more and more tumult every day, I beseech you, I beg you, I order you in the name of God: stop the repression!" (Excerpts taken from The Voice of the Voiceless, UCA Publishers.)

Speaker 1:

On March 24, 1980, Archbishop Romero was scheduled to celebrate a mass at 6 p.m. at a hospital chapel. The mass was announced in the newspaper and some of the Archbishop's friends wanted him to let someone else preside, for his own safety.

Speaker 2:

But in the Gospel reading for that day we hear that unless the grain of wheat falls to the earth and dies, it remains only a grain. But if it dies, it bears much fruit. So Archbishop Romero went ahead with his plans to preside at the mass. In his homily he said: "You just heard Christ say that it is necessary not to love oneself so much that you protect yourself from getting involved in the risks that history demands of us... the person who, because of love of Christ, gives everything to the service of others will live as the grain of wheat that dies, but only apparently...if there is a harvest, it's because the grain dies, sacrificing itself in the earth, and in doing so, producing the harvest."

Speaker 3:
"This...Eucharist is an act of faith. With Christian faith we know that at this moment the wheat host is changed into the body of Christ, who offered himself for the world's redemption, and in this chalice the wine is transformed into the blood that was the price of salvation. May this body...and this blood sacrificed for humans nourish us also, so that we may give our body and blood to suffering and to pain-like Christ, not for self, but to teach justice and peace to our people..." (Excerpts from the Violence of Love by Oscar Romero, compiled and translated by James R. Brockman, c. 1988, Chicago Province of the Society of Jesus, Harper-Collins Publishers.)

Speaker 1:
At that moment a shot rang out.

Speaker 2:
Archbishop Romero was standing behind the altar, facing the people. He slumped to the floor behind the altar, at the foot of the large crucifix. The congregants were stunned for a moment; some crouched in the pews. Several nuns and other people ran to him, and turned him onto his back. He was unconscious, gasping, blood pouring from his mouth and nose. The bullet had entered his left breast and lodged in this back.

Speaker 3:
Blood was turning the violet vestment and white alb red as the people carried him from the chapel to a small truck outside. Down the drive, down the street, down the hill it went, five minutes to the Policlinica hospital. In the emergency room, he lay on a table, still gasping, still bleeding, still unconscious. In a few minutes he stopped gasping and died.

(Silent meditation.)

Planting of Seeds

Speaker 4:
Oscar Romero said that if he was killed, he would rise in the Salvadoran people. He said his blood would be a seed of freedom. He was martyred during Lent; during the time of the Spring equinox, when the earth's northern hemisphere wakens from the death of winter and when the seeds of the green plants sprout into new life. Let us pray over these seeds. Please extend your hand over them as together we say:

All:
Life-giving God, bless these seeds, symbol of those things in our lives and in our world which seem to be dying, symbol of all that needs to be transformed into the new life of God's reign of justice, peace and nonviolent love.

Speaker 4:
Let us pass this bowl of seeds around the circle. As it reaches each of you, please pray out loud or in silence for the things in your own life and in the life of our world that need new life and transformation. Let us pray with confidence that Oscar Romero is with us now and lends his voice to our prayers.

(Pass the bowl around. When it has gone all the way around return it to the center of the circle.)

Speaker 4:
Now as a sign of hope, as a sign of our faith in the life that lies latent in the darkest of nights, in all deaths, all situations of violence, injustice and pain-the new life that we hope and struggle for-please come forward and plant a seed in one of these pots.

(People come forward and plant seeds in the pots in the middle of the circle. When people are finished all say the following.)

All:
Unless the seed falls to the ground and dies, it remains a seed. But if it dies, it bears much fruit. "That is what we are about. We plant the seeds that one day will grow. We water seeds already planted, knowing that they hold future promise. We lay foundations that will need further development. We provide the yeast that produces effects far beyond our capabilities. We cannot do everything and there is a sense of liberation in realizing that. This enables us to do something and to do it very well. It may be incomplete, but that is the difference between the master builder and the worker. We are workers, not master builders, ministers, not messiahs. We are prophets of a future that is not our own." *(Archbishop Romero's Prayer of Hope)*

Speaker 4:
Let us now bless one another for the journey with this water.

(Pass the bowl of water around and invite each person to bless the next person, making the sign of the cross on their forehead, saying, "Through the death and resurrection of Jesus Christ, and the intercession of Oscar Romero, may you be raised up to new life and bear much fruit.")

(Conclude by watering the seeds with water from the cup.)

Song
"O Healing River" *(by Michael Joncas, c. 1982, G.I.A. Publications, Inc.)*

(Adapted from an evening prayer service planned by Jack and Judy Speer of Pax Christi Illinois for a local campus ministry.)

War Tax Resistance Day Vigil

This vigil can be held outside of an IRS office if people wish to hold a "legal" gathering or inside the office if people wish to risk nonviolent civil disobedience. For the vigil you will need blank tax forms placed in a bowl and your own blood, if you so desire, to pour over the forms, as well as symbols of life-giving vocations in which you are involved such as pictures of your children, schoolbooks, medical instruments, canned food, AIDS prevention material, etc. Before you begin the vigil, you may want to pass out flyers and/or hold signs letting people know how their tax dollars are being spent.

Creation of Altar

(Place a cloth on the ground or a table. On one side of the table place items of death-blank tax forms in a large bowl. If people want to they can pour their blood over the forms. On the other side of the table place items of life that represent the various works people do, as well as aspects of their lives (family, community, etc.).)

Reading:
Deuteronomy 30:11-20

(Silent reflection.)

Reading:
(Compiled from "Where Your Income Tax Money Really Goes," a flyer produced annually by the War Resisters League, 339 Lafayette St., New York, NY 10012 212/228-0450.)

According to the United States Federal Budget for Fiscal Year 1997, 52 percent of your tax dollars pays for war. Twenty-two percent, $286 billion, pays for current military spending which includes money allocated for the Department of Defense ($247 billion) plus other "defense" portions from other parts of the budget. Spending on nuclear weapons (without their delivery systems) amounts to about one percent of the total budget. Thirty percent, $377 billion, covers past military expenses which include veterans' benefits plus 80 percent of the interest on the national debt. If there had been no military spending, most (if not all) of the national debt would have been eliminated. Analysts differ on how much of the debt stems from the military, estimates range from 50 percent to 100 percent.

In 1996, without a request from the Pentagon, Congress added $7 billion to the military budget. This money could have bought annual health care for 1.3 million people and doubled the Center for Disease Control funding and provided vocational education for 15 million people and tripled funding for safe and drug-free school programs. Or, it could have doubled annual salaries for 190,000 first-year school teachers and doubled funding to fix unsafe bridges. Or that $7 billion could have paid for eight years of summer youth employment and training for 550,000 more youth. $7 billion is only two percent of current military spending-imagine what we could do with the other 98 percent. (These figures are from the Center for Defense Information, Defense Monitor, August 1995.)

(Silent reflection.)

Song:
"Choose Life" *(By Colleen Fulmer, c. 1985, Loretto Spirituality Network.)*

Reading:
Micah 4:2b-3 ("For from Zion shall go forth instruction...") and Matthew 25:34-36

(Silent reflection.)

Reading:
(From "Civil Disobedience" by Henry David Thoreau, in Nonviolence in America: A Documentary History, edited by Staughton Lynd and Alice Lynd, c. 1995, Orbis Books.) (Adapted)

Henry David Thoreau served a night in jail, in 1846, for refusing to pay the Massachusetts poll tax. He believed that the war with Mexico, then going on, was intended to spread slavery; and that those who wished to do more than wish Godspeed to the right as it went by them (as he put it) would have to put their bodies in the way

"I meet this American government, or its representative, the State government, directly, and face to face, once a year-no more-in the person of its tax-gatherer; this is the only mode in which a man situated as I am necessarily meets it; and it then says distinctly, recognize me; and the simplest, the most effectual, and, in the present posture of affairs, the indispensablest mode of treating with it on this head, of expressing your little satisfaction with and love for it, is to deny it then. My civil neighbor, the tax-gatherer, is the very man I have to deal with-for it is, after all, with people and not with parchment that I quarrel-and this tax-gatherer has voluntarily chosen to be an agent of the government. How shall he ever know well what he is and does as an officer of the government, or as a man, until he is obliged to consider whether he shall treat me, his neighbor...as a neighbor and well-disposed man, or as a maniac and disturber of the peace.

"I know...that if one thousand, if one hundred, if ten men whom I could name-if ten honest men only-aye, if one HONEST man, in this State of Massachusetts, ceasing to hold slaves, were actually to withdraw from this copartnership, and be locked up in the county jail therefore, it would be the abolition of slavery in America. For it matters not how small the beginning may seem to be: what is once well done is done forever...

"Under a government which imprisons any unjustly, the true place for a just man is also a prison...If any think that their influence would be lost there, and their voices no longer afflict the ear of the State...they do not know by how much truth is stronger than error, nor how much more eloquently and effectively he can combat injustice who has experienced a little in his own person. Cast your whole vote, not a strip of paper merely, but your whole influence. A minority is powerless while it conforms to the majority...but it is irresistible when it clogs by its whole weight. If the alternative is to keep all just men in prison, or give up war and slavery, the State will not hesitate which to choose. If a thousand men were not to pay their tax-bills this year, that would not be a violent and bloody measure, as it would be to pay them, and enable the State to commit violence and shed innocent blood. This is, in fact, the definition of a peaceable revolution....If the tax-gatherer, or any other public officer, asks me, as one has done, 'But what shall I do?' my answer is, 'If you really wish to do anything, resign your office.' When the subject has refused allegiance, and the officer has resigned his office, then the revolution is accomplished."

(Silent reflection.)

Song:
"Passionate God" *(By Colleen Fulmer, c. 1985, Loretto Spirituality Network.)*

Shared Reflections
(Share reflections on the readings and/or what it was that brought people to the IRS office to protest war taxes.)

Petitions
(Invite people to share any prayers they might have.)

The Prayer of Jesus/Final Blessing
(Depending on how you decide to hold this vigil, people might be arrested during the service or, if you want to continue the entire service, you may have to move the vigil to another location.)

(Adapted from a "Tax Day Liturgy and Action" developed by Peter Stiehler from the San Bruno Catholic Worker in San Bruno, California.)

International Earth Day Service

It is suggested that this liturgy be held out-of-doors. Begin with silence and an invitation to breathe slowly in and out, to take in the beauty and mystery of creation that surrounds us. You will need sage or a smudge stick to burn for the purification ritual.

Greeting of the Four Directions

By Andy Dufner, SJ *(Face each direction as it is called into awareness.)*

All:
Come, God of the NORTH, God of the earth.
We invoke you and call you.
You bring us the stars, stones,
High mountains and fields of grain.
Send forth your strength.
Be here now!

Come, God of the EAST,
We invoke you and call you.
Whirlwind, God of the birds that fly,
God of the rising sun, of all there is to know.
Send forth your light.
Be here now!

Come, God of the SOUTH, God of Fire.
We invoke you and call you.
You bring us the warmth of summer.
Send us your fire.
Be here with us now!

Come, God of the WEST, God of water.
We invoke you and call you.
You bring us feelings of care and love.
You bring us the cleansing rain, the rivers, the sea.
Send forth your soothing love.
Be here with us now!

Come, God of the Center,
Spirit of our hearts and our lives.
We invoke you and call you.
You bring us power, creativity, adventure.
You bring us laughter and tears.
You are our hope, it is you we long for.
Send forth your Spirit.
Be here now!

Opening Song

"Song at the Center" *(By Marty Haugen, c. 1993, GIA.)*

First Reading

Genesis 1-2:4

Call to Prayer

(From *Environmental Sabbath: Earth Rest Day,* c. 1990, U.N. Environment Program.)

Leader:
We who have lost our sense and our senses-our touch, our smell, our vision of who we are; we who frantically force and press all things, without rest for body or spirit, hurting our earth and injuring ourselves: we call a halt.

We want to rest. We need to rest and allow the earth to rest. We need to reflect and to rediscover the mystery that lives in us, that is the ground of every unique expression of life, the source of fascination that calls all things to communion.

We declare a Sabbath, a space of quiet: for simply being and letting be; for recovering the great, forgotten truths, for learning how to live again.

A Prayer of Sorrow

(From *Environmental Sabbath: Earth Rest Day,* c. 1990, U.N. Environment Program.)

Reader 1:
Our response will be: We have forgotten who we are.

All:
We have forgotten who we are.

Reader 1:
We have forgotten who we are. We have alienated ourselves from the unfolding of the cosmos. We have become estranged from the movements of the earth. We have turned our backs on the cycles of life... We have forgotten who we are.

Reader 2:
We have sought only our own security. We have exploited simply for our own ends. We have distorted our knowledge. We have abused our power... We have forgotten who we are.

Reader 1:
Now the land is barren. And the waters are poisoned. And the air is polluted... We have forgotten who we are.

Reader 2:
Now the forests are dying. And the creatures are disappearing. And the humans are despairing... We have forgotten who we are.

Reader 1:
We ask for forgiveness. We ask for the gift of remembering. We ask for the strength to change.

All:
 Help us remember who we are.

Cleansing Ritual

(The prayer leader lights the sage or smudge stick and passes it around the group, inviting people to purify themselves by drawing the smoke to their bodies).

(Pause for a moment of silence.)

A Prayer of Gratitude

(From *Environmental Sabbath: Earth Rest Day,* c. 1990, U.N. Environment Program.)

Reader 1:
Our response will be.

All:
We rejoice in all life.

Reader 1:
We live in all things. All things live in us.

All:
We rejoice in all life.

Reader 2:
We live by the sun. We move with the stars.

All:
We rejoice in all life.

Reader 1:
We eat from the earth. We drink from the rain. We breathe from the air.

All:
We rejoice in all life.

Reader 2:
We share with the creatures. We have strength through their gifts.

All:
We rejoice in all life.

Reader 1:
We depend on the forests. We have knowledge through their secrets.

All:
We rejoice in all life.

Reader 2:
We have the privilege of seeing and understanding. We have the responsibility of caring.
We have the joy of celebrating.

All:
We rejoice in all life.

Reader 1:
We are full of the grace of creation.
We are graceful.
We are grateful.
We rejoice in all life.

All:
We rejoice in all life.

Song

"The Blue, Green Hills of Earth"
(By Kim Oler, c. 1986, Hendon Music Inc., a Boosey and Hawks Company.)

A Prayer of Healing

(From Environmental Sabbath: Earth Rest Day, c. 1990, U.N. Environment Program.)

Reader 1:
Our response will be.

All:
We join with the earth and with each other

Reader 1:
To bring new life to the land. To restore the waters. To refresh the air.

All:
We join with the earth and with each other

Reader 2:
To renew the forests. To care for the plants. To protect the creatures.

All:
We join with the earth and with each other

Reader 1:
To celebrate the seas. To rejoice in the sunlight. To sing the song of the stars.

All:
We join with the earth and with each other

Reader 2:
To recall our destiny. To renew our spirits. To reinvigorate our bodies.

All:
We join with the earth and with each other

Reader 1:
To create the human community. To promote justice and peace. To remember the children.

All:
We join with the earth and with each other

Reader 2:
We join together as many and diverse expressions of one loving mystery: for the healing of the earth and the renewal of all life.

All:
Amen.

Closing Song

"Holy Ground" *(By Christopher Beatty, c. 1982/1986, Birdwing Music (a division of The Sparrow Corp) and BMG Songs, Inc. and Cherry Lane Music Publishing Co., Inc.)*

(Adapted from resources put out by the United Nations Environment Program.)

"Am I a spy in the land of the living, that I should deliver men to Death?"

"We Will Not Kill:" International Conscientious Objector Day

Opening Song
"Prayer for Peace" (By David Haas, c. 1987, GIA.)

Poetry Reading
"Conscientious Objector" by Edna St. Vincent Millay

I shall die, but that is all that I shall do for Death. I hear him leading his horse out of the stall; I hear the clatter on the barn-floor. He is in haste; he has business in Cuba, business in the Balkans, many calls to make in the morning. But I will not hold the bridle while he cinches the girth. And he may mount by himself: I will not give him a leg up. Though he flick my shoulders with his whip, I will not tell him which way the fox ran. With his hoof on my breast, I will not tell him where the black boy hides in the swamp. I shall die, but that is all that I shall do for Death; I am not on his pay-roll. I will not tell him the whereabouts of my friends nor of my enemies either. Though he promises me much, I will not map him the route to any man's door. Am I a spy in the land of the living, that I should deliver men to Death? Brother, the passwords and the plans of our city are safe with me; never through me shall you be overcome.

Responsive Scripture Reading
(Paraphrased from Matthew 5.)

Reader 1:
"When he saw the crowds, Jesus went up on a mountainside and sat down. His disciples came to him, and he began to teach them, saying: 'You have heard that it was said to the people long ago, 'Do not murder, and anyone who murders will be subject to judgment.'"

All
God, we have heard the commands instructing us not to kill, and we affirm them as a community of faith, professing that it is a sin to kill or to support killing. We refuse military service, believing that it violates your commandments.

We confess that we have been a murderous people and that we have justified killing and war, often in your name. We stand convicted and we commit ourselves to conscientious objection. We will not kill.

Reader 2:
Jesus continued teaching, saying, "But I tell you that anyone who is angry with brother or sister will be subject to judgment."

All:
God, we see that it is not only those who bear arms who murder but your words encourage us to search out the hate and violence which we carry inside of us and among our community.

We repent of the hate and fear and injustice which lead to war and death. Not only will we refuse to kill, but we will examine ourselves and our conscience, seeking to turn from the destructive path of violence.

Reader 3:
Jesus pressed the people further, saying, "You have heard that it was said, 'Love your neighbor and hate your enemy.' But I tell you: Love your enemies and pray for those who persecute you, that you may be children of your Father and Mother in heaven. God causes the sun to rise on the evil and the good, and sends rain on the righteous and unrighteous."

All:
God, you not only command us not to kill, but you invite us to love. We will go beyond refusal to kill and will seek to bring peace to our world by loving those who would be our enemies. Through the love of God, the fallen nature which leads to war will be redeemed and we, our Church and our community, will seek peace and pursue it.

We recognize that conscientious objection to military service is an expression of our faith not because Jesus said "do not murder" but because he said, "Love your enemies and pray for those who persecute you."

Song
"Power of Love" *(By Bob Hurd, c. 1984, OCP.)*

Stories of Conscientious Objectors
Reader 1:
Many conscientious objectors have been sainted for their loyalty to God. St. Maximilian was a young Roman, the son of a veteran. He was a Christian and when ordered to join the Roman military at Theveste in Numidia in 296 A.D., he refused, saying, "My army is the army of God, and I cannot fight for this world. I have already said it, I am a Christian." For his faith and conscientious objection, he was condemned and executed. (Taken from "The Catholic Peace Tradition" by Ronald G. Musto.)

(Pause for a moment of silence.)

Reader 2:
During the war with Persia in 298 A.D., there was a centurion in Tangier by the name of Marcellus. He too was a conscientious objector-one of the earliest known military conscientious objectors. During a celebration of Emperor Maximilian's birthday, he threw down his military belt in public and declared, "I serve only the eternal king, Jesus Christ." He, too, was condemned and executed. (Taken from "The Catholic Peace Tradition" by Ronald G. Musto.)

(Pause for a moment of silence.)

Reader 3:
One of the best known conscientious objectors to become a saint was St. Martin of Tours. Martin was born in what is now Hungary in 316 A.D. He was the son of a military tribunal, but he tried to avoid military service. He was in chains when he finally took the military oath. When he turned 22, he became a Christian. He applied for a discharge, telling his commander, "I am a soldier of Christ. It is not lawful for me to fight." Fortunately, Martin was not executed and he eventually became bishop of Tours. It is interesting to note that the feast day of this military conscientious objector falls on November 11-Veteran's Day in the United States. (Taken from "The Catholic Peace Tradition" by Ronald G. Musto and "Conscientious Objection: Catholic Perspectives" by Gordon Zahn.)

(Pause for a moment of silence.)

Recognition and Affirmation of Conscientious Objectors in the Congregation

(If there are any conscientious objectors among you, take this opportunity to recognize and affirm their faithful witness-those who served in Civilian Public Service camps or performed 1-W alternative service, those who were imprisoned and those who emigrated. Affirm also those who have refused to register for the draft or pay war taxes. Recognize all who are committed to following the dictates of their consciences and seeking peace, regardless of the cost.)

Prayer

St. Martin of Tours Prayer for COs (From *The Fire of Peace,* c. 1992, Pax Christi USA.)

All:

Blessed Martin of Tours, as a soldier in the Roman army you opened your heart to the nonviolent message of Jesus and refused to bear arms.

Comfort and strengthen young people of the United Stated Armed Forces who for reasons of conscience cannot participate in war. May we imitate your example and always follow the law written on our hearts. Give us the courage to obey the dictates of conscience in all circumstances, even when the voice within conflicts with the law of the land.

Enable all who refuse to bear arms to feel our love and support. Inspire our government leaders to grant amnesty to all conscientious objectors. Amen.

Benediction

Hebrews 13:20-21

Closing Song

"Whispering Peace" *(By Jesse Manibusan, c. 1992, Two by Two 510/523-3370.)*

(Adapted from a liturgy prepared specifically for this book by John David Thacker of the National Interreligious Service Board for Conscientious Objectors.)

A Pentecost Celebration: Lives Made One in Spirit

Two pitchers, one filled with wine or grape juice, two chalices and a basket of bread should be arranged on a table. You will need two prayer leaders and four readers. If you are including a potluck dinner as part of this celebration, bring appropriate dishes.

Gathering Song

"Send Us Your Spirit" *(By David Haas, c. 1981, 1982 GIA.)*

First Reading

Acts 2: 1-18

Call to Prayer

Leader 1:
Loving God, we gather on this day of Pentecost. In the days of old You poured out Your Spirit upon Your disciples gathered in fear, filling them with courage and passion to go forth and speak to people of all nations and races, that unity might be established between all who inhabit this earth. You poured out Your Spirit upon all humankind, empowering those who were young and those who were old to envision a new world where justice and peace would flourish. We ask that You pour out Your Spirit anew upon those of us gathered here today, that we might be healers of the wounds that divide us from one another, making us one in Your Spirit, that we might be dreamers and visionaries, witnesses to Your reign, a reign that we know calls us to...

All:
Act justly, to love tenderly and to walk humbly with one another and with our God.

Sung Response:
"What Does the Lord Require?" *(By Jim Strathdee, c. 1986, Desert Flower Music.)*

Second Reading: Isaiah 58:3-11

All:
Yes, God calls us to act justly.

Sung Response:
"What Does the Lord Require?"

Third Reading: Ruth 1:8-18

All:
Yes, God calls us to love tenderly.

Sung Response:
"What Does the Lord Require?"

Fourth Reading: John 13: 1-5, 12-15

All:
Yes, God calls us to walk humbly with one another and with our God.

Sung Response:
"What Does the Lord Require?"

"Reflect on a single promise that you can make, to the people of God, the human community."

Cup of Promise

Leader 2:

What does all this mean-how do we embody, give flesh to high ideals so that they are something lived, not mere words on a page that we admire and enshrine, but do not allow to touch us? I invite all of you to reflect on a single promise that you can make, in word and deed, to the people of God, the human community. Then come forward, pour the wine which is before us into the pitcher and if you so desire, articulate your promise.

(Allow time for people to reflect in silence. Then when all have finished pouring the wine or grape juice from one pitcher into the other pitcher and stating their promise, the two leaders fill the chalices from the pitcher and then invite the group to pass the chalices around).

Leader 2:

We now share this cup to signify our willingness to share the burden of not only making these promises, but of keeping them as well. Since there are some of us who may not wish to partake of this wine, I invite you to simply hold the cup for a moment when it comes around and drink in spirit.

(Pass the cup around. Suggested music "Here's to the Day" by Milton Brasher-Cunningham & Billy Crockett, c. 1990 Radar Days Music/ASCAP-on the Billy Crockett Album "Any Starlight Night," or "This is Our Room" by Jesse Manibusan, c. 1993, Two by Two, 510/523-3370. Do whatever is necessary to insure that music accompanies the whole of the ritual-either sung or taped or instrumental.)

Gathering at Table

Leader 1:

Jesus was a man of deep insight-he realized that for all his power to keep a crowd spell-bound by his words, he reached them most concretely in the breaking of bread, in the sharing of a cup of wine, in gathering at table-as the teacher has done let us do also...

(Break the bread and share it and then, if you so choose, have a potluck dinner.)

Words of Gratitude

Leader 2:

Having broken bread together, please now offer any prayers of thanksgiving you might have.

(Allow time for people to express prayers of gratitude.)

Blessing/Sending Forth

Leader 1:

We have shared a cup of promise, we have broken bread. We have lifted our hearts in prayer and our voices in song. We have shared our stories-and we know we have many more stories to share. As we come to the end of this celebration, let us share one more story, for it is our story...

Song:

"This is Our Room" *(By Jesse Manibusan, c. 1992, Two by Two 510/523-3370.) (Use the entire song. Play the song underneath the narrative, then conclude with song and verse.)*

Leader 2:

So may we go forth, women and men of boldness and courage, to be faithful to the promises we have made, to live what we believe, to give what we can give-Amen, Alleluia!

(Adapted from Pentecost liturgy created by Kate McMichael and Theresa Hausser for St. Boniface Catholic Community in May 1996.)

Declaring Our Interdependence

Place a loaf of bread in a central place to be used for the agape meal.

Opening Song

"Sing Out, Earth and Skies" *(Text: Marty Haugen; tune, SING OUT 77 77 with refrain; Marty Haugen, c. 1985, GIA.)*

Reading

Excerpts from "On the Pulse of Morning" by Maya Angelou, Random House

Each of you a bordered country,
Delicate and strangely made, proud,
Yet thrusting perpetually under siege.
Your armed struggles for profit
Have left collars of waste upon
My shore, currents of debris upon my breast,
Yet, today I call you to my riverside,
If you will study war no more.

We Ask For Forgiveness

Leader:

This is a new day breaking for us and so we gather to declare not our independence, but our interdependence. We were all created by the same God and share the same destiny. We are all one with the earth, with the rock, the river and the tree. But we have abused this gift of unity, as our nation makes war with other countries, pointing missiles at them, pretending that we do not need their kinship and we punish and scapegoat those who are different, those who are impoverished, because they were not independent like us, not able to pull themselves up by their own bootstraps. Yet, in the midst of our perversion of a true and healthy sense of independence, the Word of God comes to us like a sharpened sword, cutting away our defenses and excuses and calling us to repentance.

Reading

"The Human Condition: A Litany" *(Source unknown.)*

I. In The Beginning

Reader 1:

In the beginning of Creation, when God made heaven and earth, the earth was without form and void; with darkness over the face of the abyss, and a mighty wind that swept over the surface of the waters. God said, "Let there be light," and there was light; and God saw that the light was good...

All:

And God created us: in the image of God were we created.

Reader 1:

You eternal separator of light and darkness, creator of form out of the formless, meaning and substance out of the void; bridger of the abyss and tamer of the heedless wind...

All:

If you really meant to make us in your image, then teach us how to fulfill it before it is too late.

"We have abused this gift of unity, pretending that we do not need kinship."

Reader 1:
Formlessness and void once more threaten to overtake us. The abyss widens; the destructive winds of bitter human passion blow mightily again.

All:
Let us live out the image of your intention, so that light may shine again.

II. A Plea
Reader 2:
From brassy patriotism and a blind trust in power,

All:
Deliver all nations, O God.

Reader 2:
From public deceptions that weaken trust, from self-seeking in high political places...

From divisions among us of class or race, from wealth that will not share and poverty which results from military might...

From neglecting rights, from overlooking the hurt, the chained, and the needy...

From a lack of concern for other peoples, from narrowness of national purpose, from failure to welcome the vision of peace...

All:
Deliver us, O God.

(Invite those gathered to add their own petitions.)

Agape Meal

Leader:
Having been forgiven by our loving God, as a sign of our interdependence let us break the bread that is before us and share it, that it might unite us more fully to one another and to all those who cry out for justice. (Leader passes the loaf of bread around so all can break off a piece to eat.)

Song

"One Bread, One Body" *(By John B. Foley, SJ, c. 1978, John B. Foley, SJ, and North American Liturgy Resources.)*

Declaring Our Interdependence

(Excerpts from The Declaration of a Global Ethic, 1993 Parliament of the World's Religions.)*

Leader:
Strengthened by this meal, together we declare that:

All:
We are interdependent. Each of us depends on the well-being of the whole, and so we have respect for the community of living beings, for people, animals, and plants, and for the preservation of the Earth, air, water and soil.

We take individual responsibility for all we do. All our decisions, actions, and failures to act have consequences.

We must treat others as we wish others to treat us. We make a commitment to respect life and dignity, individuality and diversity, so that every person is treated humanely, without exception...

We consider humankind our family. We must strive to be kind and generous. We must not live for ourselves alone, but should also serve others, never forgetting the children, the aged, the poor, the suffering, the disabled, the refugees, and the lonely. No person should ever be considered or treated as a second-class citizen, or be exploited in any way whatsoever...

We commit ourselves to a culture of nonviolence, respect, justice and peace. We shall not oppress, injure, torture, or kill other human beings, forsaking violence as a means of settling differences.

We must strive for a just social and economic order, in which everyone has an equal chance to reach full potential as a human being. We must speak and act truthfully and with compassion, dealing fairly with all, and avoiding prejudice and hatred...

Earth cannot be changed for the better unless the consciousness of individuals is changed first. We pledge to increase our awareness by disciplining our minds, by meditation, by prayer, or by positive thinking. Without risk and a readiness to sacrifice there can be no fundamental change in our situation. Therefore we commit ourselves to this global ethic, to understanding one another, and to socially-beneficial, peace-fostering, and nature-friendly ways of life.

Sending Forth

Leader:
Let us go forward to live out this ethic.

All:
Thanks be to God!

(Created by Cindy Pile.)

* Reprinted from *A Global Ethic The Declaration of the Parliament of the World's Religions* edited by Hans Kung and Karl-Josef Küschel. Copyright 1993 by the Council for the Parliament of the World's Religions, Chicago. Reprinted by permission of The Continuum Publishing Company.

Reclamation of the Elements: Hiroshima/Nagasaki Memorial Service

For the final part of this liturgy-the blessing of each other and the land-you will need a large bowl of water and several palm leaves or branches from fir trees.

Desecration of the Elements

Opening Reading

Jeremiah 4:23-29

Litany of the Elements

Earth:
Earth I am.

Fire:
Fire I am.

Wind:
Wind I am.

Water:
Water I am.

Earth:
I am the earth-ravaged and raped-barren, infertile, dying. Violated by humanity's hatred of humanity, hatred of those who have a different vision.

Voice 1:
Welfare parasite!

Voice 2:
They're taking our jobs!

Voice 3:
You're just a woman!

Voice 4:
Illegal alien!

Voice 5:
Homo!

Earth:
Words of violence, words of fear.

All:
For this the earth shall mourn!

Earth:
And now I lie pockmarked with craters which run deep into the very core of my being, eternal stigmas bearing witness to your death machines. And millions of people lie dead, their life's breath extinguished. In Hiroshima, in Nagasaki, hundreds of thousands unable to be laid to rest in my bosom. I could not embrace them! My people, I longed to gather you to myself, to shield you, to protect you. But all that remained of your humanity was a black, charred mass.

All:
The cities are forsaken. No one dwells in them.

Fire:
I am fire, the fire which burned and mutilated those bodies! My flames, my tongues of red, orange and yellow leapt into the darkened sky, singeing whoever crossed my path. I cried out, "Stop the killing! Stop the killing!" I was not made for death. Use me for warmth, for cooking, for comfort and companionship, but let not my flames envelope the children. But my pleas were answered by silence and by a great explosion over the city of Hiroshima, and over the people of Nagasaki. I burned babies, my flames scorched mothers carrying babes-seared old and young alike so that their faces were distorted and disfigured. Clouds of smoke drifted over the condemned city...

All:
For thus says God, "The whole land shall be a desolation."

Wind:
What of me, what of wind? I am no longer the one who brings gusts of cool air on a stifling hot day. I am the wind of destruction, rushing through lands, sweeping through towns, seeking death. I seek to kill. I blast people to their death, catapulting them into buildings of concrete, blowing them into houses of stone. I wreak havoc. I killed with a vengeance that day, those days-and many days since. I am a hurricane of fatality! I bring a sentence of death to all who cross my path!

All:
I looked on the mountains, and lo, they were quaking and all the hills moved to and fro.

Water:
I am water, pure, clear, running. I bring refreshment, revival, new life, but have been desecrated by war and violence.

All:
I looked, and lo, the fruitful land was a desert.

Water:
The earth has become a desert. The bomb does not need me. The Bomb does not need my rushing rivers and flowing streams to grow and be nurtured. The Bomb is fed by hatred, by malice. Where am I to go then? To the eyes of those who cry out in anguish and pain.

Voice 1:
Save us, we are dying!

Water:
Tears gushing from the eyes of the old who are abandoned, streaming from the eyes of people of color, from those who are poor and homeless, cries from those who lived, who live, in Hiroshima and Nagasaki. I, too, cry out-for new life, for birth. I pray that my streams will once again run in the desert.

All:
I looked on the earth. It was waste and void, and to the heavens. They had no light.

Song

"God Save the People" *(By Stephen Schwartz, c. 1971 The Herald Square Music Company & New Cadenza Music Corporation, Hal Leonard Publishing Corporation.)*

Shared Thoughts and Prayers

Voice 2:
Let us pause for a moment of silence and then please name people who have died and places that have been destroyed by the abuse of the elements.

(Moment of silence, naming of people and places.)

All:
("Song of the Cranes" by Children's Peace Opera, in *Peace: A Dream Unfolding*, ed. Penney Kome and Patrick Crean, c. 1986, Somerville House Books Ltd.)

For ever and ever, for ever and ever
We sing out, We cry out
All nature is one
For ever and ever, for ever and ever
Peace on earth, peace on earth
This is our hope, this is our prayer
Peace on earth, peace on earth
This is our hope, this is our prayer

Reclamation of the Elements

Chant

"Earth I Am" *(Can be chanted in any manner.)*
Earth I am. Fire I am. Wind and Water and Spirit I am.

Reading

Earth
(Excerpt from letter written by Chief Seattle to the president of the United States, 1854.)

Every part of this earth is sacred to my people. Every shining pine needle, every sandy shore, every mist in the dark woods, every clearing, and humming insect is holy in the memory and experience of my people. The sap which courses through the trees carries the memories of the red people.

The white people's dead forget the country of their birth when they go to walk among the stars. Our dead never forget this beautiful earth, for it is the mother of the red people. We are part of the earth and it is part of us.

Reading

Fire
(Exodus 3:1-8 by Peter Ediger)

In the 20th century people were tending to their business as usual. And in the middle of the century a raging fire appeared on the earth: first in Hiroshima, then Nagasaki, then the islands of the Pacific and continuing in the desert of Nevada. And some people asked, "Why is this fire raging on the earth? Will it consume us all?"

And the God of Creation appeared saying, "My people! My people!" And the people said, "Here we are!"

The God of Creation said, "Take off your shoes. The earth you are on is a holy place. Now therefore, I am sending you to go to your soul and say 'Let my Creation live! Let my Creation live!'"

Reading

Wind
(Excerpt from letter written by Chief Seattle to the president of the United States, 1854.)

The Indian prefers the soft sound of the wind darting over the face of a pond and the smell of the wind itself, cleansed by a midday rain or scented with the piñon pine.

The air is precious to the red people, for all things share the same breath–the beast, the tree, the woman and the man they all share the same breath…The wind that gave our grandparents their first breath also receives their last sighs. And the wind must also give our children the spirit of life. And if we sell you our land, you must keep it apart and sacred, as a place where even the white people can go to taste the wind that is sweetened by the meadow's flowers.

Reading

Water
(Isaiah 35:6-7)

Blessing of Each Other and the Land

Litany of the Spirit

Spirit:
I am Spirit. I come to the earth in wind and fire and water. I come to renew the face of a tired and weary land. I come to bring hope to those whose hearts are heavy. I say to the people of Hiroshima and Nagasaki

Voice 3:
"Never again!"

Spirit:
I say to the homeless people on the streets of our cities, to the immigrants from many countries, to people of all colors,

Voice 4:
"Your voice has been heard!"

Spirit:
And to the people of Northern Ireland, the Middle East, East Timor, Central America, the Nevada Test Site,

Voice 5:
"Take heart, for I bring freedom, truth, and liberation!"

Spirit:
I am Spirit, present in the elements, in the land which first belonged to our Native American sisters and brothers, in the rushing wind and the raging fire, in clear, sparkling water. I breathe my life into all of nature. Let the desert bloom and the waters of life flow. And cry. Cry tears of joy. Cry freedom, cry truth, cry never again-and remember.

Voice 1:
As a sign of our belief in the waters that will flow, as a sign of our belief in new life, in justice, peace and liberation, please come forward and bless yourselves, one another and the land by dipping the palm fronds into this font of water.

(All come forward to the font of water to participate in the blessing.)

Closing Poem
Song of the Cranes

All:
For ever and ever, for ever and ever
For ever and ever, for ever and ever
Only tears of joy shall we cry
For ever and ever, for ever and ever
The roots of trees grow deep, hold tight
For ever and ever, for ever and ever
We sing out, We cry out
All nature is one
For ever and ever, for ever and ever
Peace on earth, peace on earth
This is our hope, this is our prayer
Peace on earth, peace on earth
This is our hope, this is our prayer
For ever and ever, for ever and ever
With faith and love we cannot fail
For ever and ever, for ever and ever
Truth is marching in
For ever and ever, for ever and ever
Filled with love that comes from above
For ever and ever, for ever and ever
Truth is marching in

(Created by Cindy Pile for August Desert Witness, 1989, a gathering sponsored by the
Nevada Desert Experience each August at the Nevada Test Site.)

Hiroshima/Nagaskai: Never Again

Set up an "altar," a focal point where several pictures of the victims of Hiroshima and Nagasaki are displayed. Have flowers available that people will later place around the pictures.

We Remember The Past

Opening Reading

"Gathered at the River" by Denise Levertov (From *Peace: A Dream Unfolding*, edited by Penney Kome and Patrick Crean, c. 1986, a Somerville House Book published by Sierra Club Books, San Francisco.)

As if the trees were indifferent...
A breeze flutters the candles, but the trees
give off a sense of listening, of hush.

The dust of August on their leaves
but it grows dark, green is something
known about, not seen.

But summer twilight takes away only color,
not form. The tree-forms, massive trunks
and the great domed heads, leaning in
towards us, are visible,
a half-circle of attention.

They listen because the war we speak of,
the human war with ourselves,
the war against earth, against nature,
is a war against them.

The words are spoken of those who survived awhile,
living shadowgraphs, eyes fixed forever
on witnessed horror,

Who survived to give testimony,
that no one may plead ignorance.
"Contra naturam" The trees,
the trees are not indifferent.

We intone together, NEVER AGAIN,
we stand in a circle, singing, speaking,
making vows, NEVER AGAIN,
remembering the dead of Hiroshima, Nagasaki...

Song

"Cry of Ramah"
(By Colleen Fulmer, c. 1985, Loretto Spirituality Network.)

"I knew being near the master this morning I would never lend my talents toward building vehicles of death again."

Reading

A verse by Michiko Ogina (age 10 at time of bombing) (adapted) (From *Peace: A Dream Unfolding*)

Under a fallen house my sister was madly crying
The beam would not move a bit
Even a soldier had gone saying,
"Nothing can be done."

I noticed a person coming like an arrow.
Like a woman it looked.
She's naked, she's discolored.
Why mamma! Now I felt free from danger.

Our neighbor tried with all his might.
But the beam would not move a bit.
"You must give up, nothing can help it."
So saying, he went away, too, pitying us.

The flame flared up!
Mamma's face went ashy pale.
Mamma looked down at my sister,
Sister's small eyes looked up from under.

Mamma's eyes followed the beam,
She fit her right shoulder to the beam;
"Yo, heave, ho, yo heave ho"
She endeavored with might and main.

Crack! Crack! Crack!
Free did legs of my sister become.

But down did Mamma drop
Never to get up.

Mamma was bombed at noon.
When getting eggplants in the field.
Short, red, crisp her hair stood.
Tender and red her skin was all over.

Peeled off was the skin over her shoulder
That once lifted the beam off my sister.
Constant blood was spurting
From the sore flesh appearing.
Soon Mamma began to struggle
With pain and agony
With pain and agony
She left the world for heaven that evening.

Song

"Cry of Ramah" *(Refrain only.)*

(Moment of silence.)

Reading

"A Silent Flash of Light" by Setsuko Thurlow
(*From* Peace: A Dream Unfolding.)

I heard no explosion. Miles out of the city, people apparently heard a thunderous roar. But like all survivors close to the hypercentre, I heard nothing. There was just the silent flash. The moment I saw it I tried to duck under a desk. But I had a sensation of floating. Together with the building, my body was falling...Lying in the rubble I couldn't move and I knew I was faced with death. Mysteriously I never had a feeling of panic. I felt calm. After awhile I started to hear my classmates. In weak voices they were asking for God...

My clothes were tattered and covered with blood. I had cuts and scratches all over me, but all my extremities were there. I looked around me, even though it was morning the sky was dark, as dark as twilight. Then I saw streams of human beings shuffling away from the center of the city. Parts of their bodies were missing and strips of flesh hung like ribbons from their bones...

The strangest thing was the silence. It is the most unforgettable impression I have. You'd think people would be panic-stricken running, yelling. They moved in slow motion like figures in a silent movie, shuffling through the dust and smoke. I heard thousands of people breathing the words "water, give me water." Many simply dropped to the ground and died.

(Moment of silence.)

We Confront the Present

Song
"I Shall Be Released" (By Bob Dylan, c. 1974, Columbia Records.)

69

We Hope for the Future

Reading:
"Machines of Destruction" by Mike Kennedy, SJ

wooden beams
stored in a long roman room
wooden beams
carried to a room
where a man lay
in his own blood
day's beginning
i had been making wooden beams
for years
this day I had trudged
and brought
these two carefully
carved beams
and would be making
two more trips
for the other criminals
wretched beings
not deserving of my fine work
so i stood in this room
and asked the guard
to whom i deliver
this first set of beams
he pointed
to the man
lying in his own blood
i approached him
and tried to see
if he had the strength
to carry these beams
i got him to sit up
they had really worked him
over last night
i was about to leave the room
when he uttered
help me
help me stand
so i took him by the arms
and lifted him up
being this close
when i looked into his face
i recognized the rabbi
who had been teaching
here of late
sharp currents of anger
flowed through me
why are you here?
what have they done to you?
where are all your followers?
i looked into his eyes
he didn't say anything

but that was enough for me
i began to loathe
that i ever fashioned
these wooden beams
to be used so destructively
i leaned against his shoulder
i could feel my hammerings
this vehicle for execution
inside of him
i could see
other strange vehicles
of death inside of him
i looked closer
and i saw large
spear-like missiles
landing
with huge explosions
of light
screams of terror
were in this master
here i had brought him
this vehicle of death
representing
all the vehicles of death
through the centuries
i wanted to get away
from the master
to tear myself from him
but i saw tens of thousands
of war machines
all different sizes
i saw torture chambers
i saw the vehicles of death
that humans could invent
so they could destroy another
and i was the one
who cooperated
with this system
of death
i knew
being near the master
this morning
i would never
lend my talents
toward building
vehicles of death again
and i left him
with shame
but knowing
i was going
to walk a different path

70

Placing of Flowers
(Place the flowers next to the pictures of the victims of the bombing of Hiroshima and Nagasaki.)

Song
"Down by the Riverside" (public domain)

Reading
(Excerpt from *Lightning East to West* by Jim Douglass, c. 1983, Crossroad.)

Faith is a belief in a Reality, and a transformation, through which it is possible for us to live deeply enough to choose new life rather than nuclear death. A lived faith will stop the Bomb.

The decision to act in faith is always at hand. We live alongside the steady preparation for nuclear holocausts, as unseeing as were the onlookers of Nazi genocide. Yet the decision to act on faith is more possible for us in a liberal capitalism than it was for those who lived in fear alongside the barbed wire fences and guard towers in Europe in the forties. Because they didn't act, they gave up hope for the rest of their world. Despair at political change comes from the heart. Given hearts rooted in faith, barbed wire fences can themselves become openings to the belief that there is hope for our world.

Closing Prayer
By Dom Helder Camara (From *The Desert is Fertile*, c. 1974, Orbis Books.)

All:
Let us open our eyes. Let us begin at once to fight our selfishness and come out of ourselves, to dedicate ourselves once and for all, whatever the sacrifices, to the nonviolent struggle for a more just, more human world. Let us not put off the decision till tomorrow. Let us begin today, now, intelligently and firmly.

Let us look about us and recognize our brothers and sisters who are called like us to give up their ease and join all those who hunger for the truth and who have sworn to give their lives to make peace through justice and love.

Let us not waste time discussing who shall be our leader. What is important is for us to unite and go forward, remembering that time too is our enemy.

Let us give the best of ourselves to helping create moral pressure for freedom to bring about the necessary change. Let us gather information on the situations we wish to change. Let us spread this information by all reasonable means at our disposal and let the information be truthful, able to stand up to criticism and disturb the consciences of all good people.

Let us through all this stand firm without falling into hatred, let us be understanding without conniving at evil. Amen.

Closing Song
"Imagine" *(By John Lennon, c. 1971, Capital Records.)*

(Prepared by the Julia Occhiogrosso from the Las Vegas Catholic Worker.)

St. Francis Day Prayer

Opening Song

"Peace Prayer" *(By John B. Foley, SJ, c. 1976, John B. Foley, SJ, and North American Liturgy Resources.)*

First Reading

Universal Kinship-Francis' most famous insight. *(Reading from SFO Rule, Par. #18 (adapted).)*

Moreover all people should respect all creatures, animate and inanimate, which 'bear the imprint of the Most High,' and they should strive to move from the temptations of exploiting creation to the Franciscan concept of universal kinship.

Reflection

"Universal kinship" implies "integrity of creation" with a Franciscan flavor, for in kinship is how Francis believed all things should ideally be. He understood all things to be in relationship one to another as brother and sister-because all creatures have one Father and one Mother. Thus each and every part depends on the other, and the whole depends on God. Therefore all creatures form one family, and human beings are an integral part of the family.

And Francis' relationship with nature did have a family-like quality to it. A cricket kept him company for eight days. The lark and the falcon announced for him the time of office. Flowers consoled him. He was thankful that the sun gave him light. He walked reverently upon stones because of the One called the Rock. Also, a pheasant would not leave Francis' side when the Saint was sick but would force its way in under the brothers' habits to hide.

(Brief silent meditation.)

Response

Job 36:22-37:5 *(Alternate sides)*

Side 1:
Look, by reason of such power God is supreme,
what teacher can be compared with God?
Who has ever told God which course to take,
or dared to say to God, "You have done wrong?"

Side 2:
Turn your mind rather to praising God's works,
a theme that many have sung:
a sight that everyone can see,
that one may gaze on from afar.

Side 1:
Yes, the greatness of God exceeds our knowledge,
the number of God's years is past computing.
God it is who keeps the raindrops back,
dissolving the showers into mist,
which otherwise the clouds would
spill in floods over all.

Side 2:
Thanks to them God nourishes the nations
with generous gifts of food.
And who can fathom how God spreads the clouds,
or why such crashes thunder from God's tent?

Side 1:
God spreads out the mist, wrapping it about,
and covers the tops of the mountains.
God gathers up the lightning in hand,
choosing the mark it is to reach;
the thunder gives warning of its coming:
wrath overtakes iniquity.

Side 2:
At this my own heart quakes, and leaps from its place.
Listen, oh listen, to the blast of God's voice
and the sound that blares from God's mouth.
God hurls the lightning below the span of heaven,
it strikes to the very ends of the earth.

Side 1:
After it comes the roar of God's voice,
and peal of God's majestic thunder.
No doubt of it, but God reveals wonders,
and does great deeds that we cannot understand.

Second Reading

Francis the Ecologist (Reading from *First Life of St. Francis* by Thomas Celano, excerpt from Article 80 (adapted).)

Even for worms he had great affection because he had read what was said of the suffering Savior: 'I am a worm and not a man.' Moreover, he would pick them up along the road and put them in a safe place where they would not be trodden underfoot. We know that in winter, concerned about the bees lest they die of the cold, he would prepare honey and good wine for them! Their remarkable way of working stirred him to such praise of God that he would often spend a whole day in such prayer, lauding them and other creatures of God.

Reflection

The secular definition of ecology means the study of relationships between organisms, including humans, and their environment. Today, in Christian circles, the definition has been "baptized" to mean the practice of "good stewardship." Francis was a born Christian ecologist.

There are other examples in the life of Francis, besides the earthworms and bees, of how he displayed good stewardship of nature, of how he realized that animals have needs to be taken care of. For example he knew that a wolf was terrorizing the people of Gubbio, but only because the wolf was hungry. Francis arranged for the people to feed the wolf and harmony in the town was restored. Therefore, whether the story of the Wolf of Gubbio is true or fable, it is an example of how people recognized that Francis provided for the needs of animals. Francis also left the brothers explicit instructions on how to take care of vegetation. For example, when cutting firewood he told the brothers to take only branches, or at least leave the stump of the tree to resprout. Also, he instructed the brother gardener to not plant all the garden but to leave some natural vegetation as a border. In addition he taught the gardener to plant some flowers with the vegetables.

(Brief silent meditation.)

Response
Selections from Psalm 104 (*Alternate sides*)

Side 1:
Bless Yahweh, my soul.
Yahweh my God, how great you are!
Clothed in majesty and glory,
wrapped in a robe of light!

Side 2:
You stretch the heavens out like a tent,
you build your palace on the waters above;
using the clouds as your chariot,
you advance on the wings of the wind;
you use the winds as messengers and fiery flames as servants.

Side 1:
You set springs gushing in ravines,
running down between the mountains,
supplying water for wild animals,
attracting the thirsty wild donkeys;
near there the birds of the air make
their nests and sing among the branches.

Side 2:
You make fresh grass grow for cattle
and those plants made use of by humankind,
for them to get food from the soil: wine to make them cheerful,
oil to make them happy and bread to make them strong.

Side 1:
The trees of Yahweh get rain enough,
those cedars of Lebanon God planted;
here the little birds build their nest and,
on the highest branches, the stork has its home.
For the wild goats there are the mountains,
in the crags rock badgers hide.

Side 2:
You made the moon to tell the seasons,
the sun knows when to set: you bring darkness on,
night falls, all the forest animals come out: savage lions
roaring for their prey, claiming their food from God.

Side 1:
The sun rises, they retire,
going back to lie down in their lairs,
and people go out to work, and to labor until dusk.
Yahweh, what variety you have created,
arranged everything so wisely!
Earth is completely full of things you have made:

Side 2:
Among them vast expanse of ocean,
teeming with countless creatures, creatures large and small,
with the ships going to and fro and Leviathan
whom you made to amuse you.

Side 1:
All creatures depend on you to feed them throughout the year;
you provide the food they eat, with generous hand you satisfy their hunger.

Side 2:
You give breath, fresh life begins, you keep renewing the world.

Sides 1 & 2:
I mean to sing to Yahweh all my life,
I mean to play for my God as long as I live.
Bless Yahweh, my soul.

Third Reading

Creation called Francis to prayer (Readings from *The First Life of St. Francis* by Thomas Celano, excerpts from Articles 80 & 81 (adapted).)

For who could ever describe his great love whereby he was caught up in all things that belong to God? Who would be able to tell of the joy he felt as he contemplated in creatures the wisdom of the Creator, God's power and goodness? A marvelous and indescribable joy would often fill him when he beheld the sun and gazed at the moon, the stars and the whole sweep of the heavens. (1 Cel. 80) The beauty of the flowers brought him great delight of soul in their shape and color and sweet odor, and thus lifted his heart and soul to the One who is the Flower of Jesse. And when he came upon a field of flowers, he would preach to them as though they understood him and would invite them to praise God. He often did the same in fields of grain, in vineyards, in the woods, the while he called on all things, earth and fire, air and wind, to love and serve God! Truly, even then he had attained the freedom of the glory of the children of God. (1 Cel. 81)

Reflection

Francis believed that all the constituents of creation have intrinsic significance and value. They are not merely utilitarian, simply resources for human consumption. We are called to discover their beauty and dignity. We are to love, respect, understand and serve them. Thus creation is a pathway, or ladder, to God and can teach us about God.

(Brief silent meditation.)

Response

Canticle of the Sun (adapted)

All:
O most High, almighty God,
to you belong praise, glory, honor, and all blessing!

Praised be my God with all creatures;
and especially our brother the sun,
which brings us the day and the light;
fair is he, and shining with a very great splendor;
O God, he signifies you to us!

Praised be my God for our sister the moon,
and for the stars,
which God has set clear and lovely in heaven.
Praised be my God for our brother the wind,
and for air and cloud, calms and all weather,
by which you uphold in life all creatures.

Praised be my God for our sister water,
which is very serviceable to us,
and humble, and precious, and clean.

Praised by my God for brother fire,
through which you give us light in the darkness;
and he is bright, and pleasant,
and very mighty, and strong.

Praised be my God for our mother the Earth,
which sustains us and keeps us, and yields diverse fruits,
and flowers of many colors, and grass.

Praised be my God for all those who pardon
one another for God's love's sake,
and who endure weakness and tribulation;
blessed are they who peaceably shall endure,
for you, O most High, shall give them a crown!
Praised be my God for our sister, the death of the body,
from which no one escapes,
Woe to those who died in mortal sin!

Blessed are they who are found walking
by your most holy will,
for the second death shall have no power to do them harm.

Praise you, and bless you and give thanks to God,
and serve God with great humility.

(Invitation to share spontaneous prayers of praise and petition.)

The Prayer of Jesus

Closing Song
"Peace Prayer" *(By John B. Foley, SJ)*

(Adapted from a service developed by Don Rewers, OFM, for the Order of Friars Minors English Speaking Conference's Justice, Peace and the Integrity of Creation Council Meeting, October 1996.)

A Service of Repentance: Native American Day

For the environment you might want to use symbols of the elements—rocks, plants, a bowl of water, a feather, candles and/or Native American artwork or icons. In the center of these symbols place a bowl (or bowls) of ashes.

Song

"God of Day and God of Darkness," v.1 *(Text: Marty Haugen, Tune: BEACH SPRING, 87 87D; The Sacred Heart, 1844; Harmony: Marty Haugen, c. 1985 GIA.)*

Introduction

Leader:

We gather here today more than five hundred years after the coming of Europeans to this Western Hemisphere. We, the descendants of those first colonizers or of those who followed centuries later, have much to be grateful for in this land of plenty. But it is with great sadness that we must acknowledge the terrible evils inflicted by this coming on the peoples already present here.

We come to recognize and mourn the many injustices suffered by Native Americans at the hands of our ancestors, and even in this day, from government policies, societal racism and corporate greed.

We ask you, God of all Creation, to open our minds and hearts to see and realize, to deplore and try to make amends for the illegal seizure and dissipation of Indian resources without which there can be no cultural or economic survival for Native Americans.

Reading

Letter to the President of the United States by Chief Seattle, 1854 (excerpt)

Let us hear the words of a great Indian chief:

The great chief in Washington sends word that he wishes to buy our land. How can you buy or sell the sky? The warmth of the land? The idea is strange to us. Yet we do not own the freshness of the air or the sparkle of the water. How can you buy them from us? Every part of this earth is sacred to my people. Every shiny pine needle, every sandy shore every mist in the dark woods, every crane and humming insect is holy in the memory and experience of my people.

Litany of Forgiveness

(Some of this information is from *Our Brother's Keeper: The Indian In White America*, edited by Edgar S. Cahn, c. 1969.)

Response:

Forgive us, we pray. *(After every two stanzas. Bow at these words.)*

Reader 1:

A Washington State Indian child was expelled from a public school for objecting to her ancestors being called "dirty savages." She was then forced to attend the Bureau-run Fort Sill, Oklahoma boarding school because she was considered "uncontrollable." Hundreds of other problem children are routinely shipped thousands of miles from home, some from Alaska to Oklahoma. They see their parents once a year.

Reader 2:
A 16-year old took his life in the Ft. Hall, Idaho, County Jail, where he had been placed without a hearing and without his parents' knowledge, accused of drinking during school hours. Two other Indians, one 17 years old, had used the same pipe to hang themselves in the same cell in the previous 11 months. The suicide rate among Indian teenagers is three times the national rate (on some reservations, ten times the rate.)

All:
Forgive us, we pray.

Reader 1:
Over 10,000 traditional Navajos and Hopis are being relocated from their sacred land in Arizona to satisfy the mining companies' greed for the uranium and the trillion tons of coal under the land.

Reader 2:
Three hundred sixty-one treaties have been made between the U.S. government and the Indian nations. The same number have been broken or ignored in the name of progress.

All:
Forgive us, we pray.

Reader 1:
Nearly 200 Lakota Indians, including women and children trying to hide, were slaughtered by U.S. Cavalry at Wounded Knee.

Reader 2:
A "Trail of Tears" extended from the Southeastern states to Oklahoma when President Andrew Jackson forced the Cherokee Indians from their homes so the U.S. could take the gold believed to be there.

All:
Forgive us, we pray.

Reader 1:
In Brockton, Montana, children attend school where the windows are boarded up, and teachers are changed as many as five and six times a year.

Reader 2:
In Oka, near Montreal, Mohawks are struggling to keep their funeral grounds from becoming a golf course.

All:
Forgive us, we pray.

Reader 1:
Eight million dollars allotted by Congress for emergency shelters and halfway houses resulted in one shelter and no halfway houses.

Reader 2:
Five of every six people on the Pine Ridge, South Dakota reservation are jobless. Lack of job opportunities is a root cause of despair, alcoholism and suicide.

All:
Forgive us, we pray.

Reader 1:
Of the 550 million acres of land recognized as sovereign by the U.S., 50 million remain.

Reader 2:
Forty-three per cent of American Indians graduate from high school; 45% live in poverty.

All:
Forgive us, we pray.

Reader 1:
Indian tribes have been bombarded with slick proposals to turn their cherished land into dumps for other people's trash and toxic wastes.

Reader 2:
In 1954 Congress passed a termination policy to end all federal obligations and services to Indian tribes and liquidate tribal land holdings.

All:
Forgive us, we pray.

Reflection

(From the Latin American Council of Churches.) The Biblical message is sufficiently clear: wherever there is a human being who is hindered from living fully their humanity, there is a situation of sin.

Ceremony of Ashes

Leader:
(Spoken while holding a bowl of ashes.) As a sign of our repentance, of our sorrow for our sins, please come forward and mark each other with these ashes.

(While people are coming forward to mark each other with the ashes, sing v. 2 of "God of Day and God of Darkness." Continue instrumental until people are finished.)

Intercessions

Reader 1:
Please respond: Great Spirit, have mercy.

All:
Great Spirit, have mercy.

Reader 1:
For the Pima Indians of Arizona who suffer from the highest incidence of diabetes in the world... Great Spirit, have mercy.

Reader 2:
For the Omaha Indian Tribe who seek to recover 11,300 acres of highly valuable agricultural lands now occupied by politically powerful white land speculators...

Reader 1:
For the Inuits of the Northwest Territories whose food supplies are being poisoned by toxic wastes in the ocean...

Reader 2:
For the more than 40% of Indians who die without reaching their 45th birthday...

Reader 1:
For the many victims of violence who have no hope of redress because of the failures of the justice system...

All:
God of all, you have called each of us to live among our brothers and sisters in the world. May we be one with all whose daily experience of life is hardship, suffering and misery. Grant that we continue to keep them in our thoughts and prayers and to help them in their search for justice.

Song:
(Melody as in "God of Day and God of Darkness.")

God of North and South America, of the lands we call our home,
Others came here long before us, but were forced to fight or roam

For their years of bitter sorrow and their present agony, too,
Help us work with them for justice as God would have us do.

Reading:
(From *When Theology Listens to the Poor* by Leonardo Boff, English translation,
c. 1988, Harper & Row, Publishers.)

If people hope to have a better society, a new world, they shall have to do more than simply keep up a line of patter about living as brothers and sisters and building a world of communion. We are going to have to struggle. We are going to have to exert some effort if we hope to change society's distorted organization. This is the only way in which we shall take away the sin of the world. And the means will be political activity. The change will come from the bottom up. It is the little ones who are going to effectuate it. The great and mighty have no wish for change. In fact, they come right out and say, God willing, things will go on as they are. But the weak, the little ones, say, God willing, this is all going to change. This will come about, however, only if these same little ones exert pressure from below. It has been ever thus, all through the history of humanity.

(Silent reflection.)

Litany of Praise
(Stand)

Reader 1:
Please respond: We praise and glorify your name, Creator God.

ALL:
We praise and glorify your name, Creator God.

Reader 1:
For Blessed Kateri Tekawitha, who blossomed on the banks of the Mohawk and the St. Lawrence in her innocence and faith...

Reader 2:
For Juan Diego, whom the Blessed Mother used as her instrument to bless the Indian peoples of Mexico and all the Americas...

Reader 1:
For Roger Williams, who challenged the Puritans to treat the Indians fairly and to pay them for their land...

Reader 2:
For Chief Seattle, whose reverence for the earth and all of creation has inspired thousands...

Reader 1:
For the two French Holy Cross Sisters who taught the Indians in Pokagon, Michigan...

Reader 2:
For Isaac Joques and companions who gave their lives in evangelizing the Hurons and the Iroquois...

Reader 1:
For the countless Native Americans who shared their knowledge and skills with our ancestors for the good of all...

Reader 2:
For the League of the Iroquois whose Kaianerekowa (Great Law of Peace) guided the creation of the American Constitution...

Reader 1:
For Archbishop Weakland, who has founded in his diocese of Milwaukee the first Native American parish in the U.S...

Closing Prayer

"Traditional Native American (Ogibwa) Prayer" (From *American Indian Prayers and Poetry*, p. 13, edited by J. Ed Sharpe, 1985, Cherokee Publications, Cherokee, N.C.)

All:
O Great Spirit, whose voice I hear in the winds, and whose breath gives life to all the world, hear me! I am small and weak. I need your strength and wisdom.

Let me walk in beauty, and make my eyes ever behold the red and purple sunset.

Make my hands respect the things you have made and my ears sharp to hear your voice. Make me wise so that I may understand the things you have taught my people.

Let me learn the lessons you have hidden in every leaf and rock. I seek strength, not to be greater than my brother or sister, but to fight my greatest enemy–myself.

Make me always ready to come to you with clean hands and straight eyes. So when life fades, as the fading sunset, my spirit may come to you without shame.

Closing Song

"God of Day and God of Darkness," v.3

(Adapted from service planned by Sr. Patricia Cullen, CSC, and Sr. Catherine Francis Ford, CSC, for their congregation, Religious of the Holy Cross, on the occasion of the 500th anniversary of Columbus' Landing in America.)

A Service of Thanksgiving and Commitment for World Food Day

Preparing for the Service: This service was designed to be the culminating event of Bread for the World's fall campaign on domestic hunger, to be used for a Thanksgiving service. It is also an appropriate service for World Food Day.

You may want to order the bulletin inserts designed for this service since they include the "Affirmation and Commitment" form to be used during "The Time of Commitment." You may also wish to collect the completed forms and send them to Bread for the World's national office (1100 Wayne Ave., Suite 1000, Silver Spring, Maryland 20910.) Be sure to have pens or pencils available in the pews.

Much of the effectiveness of the service depends upon the testimony of the "witnesses," so you may want to select in advance the persons who will read the words of Jim, Cathy, Calvin, Carol, Arthur, Amos, Luke and the child Lisa. If possible, have them memorize their readings. If extemporaneous testimonies are given during "The Witness of the Church," request that each be limited to one or two minutes and end this section of the service with the "Carol" and "Arthur" readings. If children have undertaken a special project in the weeks prior to the service, include a brief presentation by them within this section.

If a sermon is given, request that it keep the subject and the mood of the service-using the Amos and/or Luke passages as texts. If you have a church or community choir, you may opt to include in place of the sermon a 15-minute segment from the new hunger oratorio Lazarus which can be ordered from Bread for the World.

Plan in advance how the offering will benefit hungry people in the community. If you plan to receive food items, you might invite worshippers to bring their gifts forward during the offertory. Following the service, you may also wish to set up a table for writing letters on pending domestic hunger legislation.

Opening Meditation

Leader:
During this autumn season, full of bountiful harvests and plentiful food, people of faith understand that God calls our nation not only to thanksgiving for these gifts, but to repentance and a new commitment. God calls us to repentance from a national mindset that resists public responsibility for hunger in our midst and a new commitment to address the needs of hungry people in our land. We know that hunger exists in this great land of plenty, and that it is growing. We also know that hunger need not exist anywhere in today's world, and certainly not in this country. And we know, beyond a shadow of any doubt, that the love of Christ calls us to do all we can to change the situation.

Therefore, let us take a few quiet moments to give thanks and to pray for our neighbors who will not eat enough this day–that they may be filled, and for our nation and those who shape its policies–that the elimination of hunger may truly become a national priority. And, let us pray for ourselves that we may be filled with such love for those who hunger that we commit ourselves to unaccustomed actions that will send a strong, determined signal to our national leaders to work for an end to hunger in our land of plenty.

(Time for silent reflection.)

A Psalm of Invocation

from Psalm 67 *(Read responsively.)*

Leader:
God, show kindness and bless us,

All:
And make your face to smile on us!

Leader:
For then the earth will acknowledge your ways,

All:
And all nations know your power to save.

Leader:
Let the nations praise you, O God,

All:
Let the nations praise you.

Leader:
Let the nations shout and sing for joy,

All:
Since you bring true justice to the world.

Leader:
The soil has given its harvest,

All:
God, our God, has blessed us.

Leader:
May God bless us, and let God be feared,

All:
To the very ends of the earth!

Opening Hymn

(Select a hymn of praise and thanksgiving.)

Prayer:
(Let the leader begin and close, with worshippers expressing aloud any prayers of thanksgiving, petition or supplication for forgiveness they may wish to offer; or the leader may pray the following prayer.)

Leader:
Most gracious God, who gives the fruits of the earth for the benefit of all your creatures, we give thanks to you for abundant harvests and plentiful food. We pray for those in our land who are denied these gifts, and seek your forgiveness for our complicity in their want. We thank you for our government, designed to be responsive to the will of the governed, and for the choices that are ours in this land of opportunity. We pray for those whose voices are not heard and for those who do not hear. Forgive us when our choices are selfish ones, and forgive us especially when we do not choose to raise our own voice against the pain of those among us who suffer needless want. Most of all, O God, we give you thanks for the revelation of your love in Jesus Christ, who came that everyone might have abundant life. Amen.

A Psalm of God's Love

From Psalm 103 *(Read responsively.)*

Leader:
Bless Yahweh, my soul!

All:
Bless God's holy name, all that is in me!

Leader:
Bless Yahweh, my soul;

All:
And remember all God's kindnesses:

Leader:
In forgiving all your offenses,

All:
In curing all your diseases,

Leader:
In redeeming your life from the pit,

All:
In crowning you with love and tenderness,

Leader:
In filling your years with prosperity,

All:
In renewing your youth like an eagle's.

Leader:
Yahweh, who does what is right,

All:
Is always on the side of the oppressed.

Leader:
Yahweh is tender and compassionate,

All:
Slow to anger and most loving.

Leader:
Yahweh never treats us wrongfully,

All:
Never punishes us as our sins deserve.

Leader:
As tenderly as a parent treats children,

All:
So Yahweh treats those who fear God.

Leader:
Yahweh knows what we are made of,

All:
Yahweh remembers we are dust,

Leader:
A human lasts no longer than grass,

All:
Lives no longer than a wild flower.

Leader:
Yet Yahweh's love for those who fear God,

All:
Lasts from all eternity and forever,

Leader:
Like God's goodness to their children's children,

All:
As long as they keep the covenant.

Leader:
Bless Yahweh, all angels,

All:
Heroes and Heroines attentive to God's Word.

Leader:
Bless Yahweh, all nations,

All:
Servants to perform God's will.

Leader:
Bless Yahweh, all creatures

All:
In every part of the world.

Leader:
Bless Yahweh, O my soul.

All:
All that is in me bless God's Holy Name.

The Witness From the World

Leader:
There are those in this great land of plenty who suffer today. One out of seven people in the United States mourn in a state of poverty and hunger. Let us now hear their testimony. As we hear these stories, may God's spirit lead us to action that will bring both immediate comfort and long lasting justice.

(The testimonies of Lisa, Jim, Cathy and Calvin follow; after each, the congregation responds by singing the refrain to "Balm in Gilead.")

Congregational Response:
"Balm in Gilead" *(Text: Jer. 8:22; Afro-American Spiritual, Tune: "Balm in Gilead," Irregular, Afro-American Spiritual, Acc. by Robert J. Batastini, c. 1987 GIA.)*

Lisa:
Things are a lot different since Daddy left. We used to keep a big bowl of fruit on the counter, and we could have some anytime we wanted. Now Mom hardly ever buys fruit. It costs too much. Mom's got a job now, but she doesn't make as much as Daddy did; so we have to sell our house. I don't know where we'll go when we move. It makes Mom feel bad to say "no" all the time; so I try not to ask for much.

Jim:
I was born and raised in the country. Ever since my wife and I got married, I hired out to Will Larsen. He farmed 1,500 acres, and there was plenty to do—or at least there used to be. You've heard stories about a farm crisis? Farm families losing everything? Well, it's true. Larsens held out longer than most, but they finally went under too. Farming's all I know. I've been all over town looking for something else, but when farming's bad, everything's bad.

Cathy:
I used to watch "Ozzie and Harriet," and I believed I'd live like that when I grew up. But I'm 38 now and scraping for everything I get. Aid for Dependent Children gives me some help, and I work as a cashier when I can, but I can't get a good paying job without an education. It worries me that the kids have to eat so much macaroni, but meat might as well be gold. I'm doing the best I can, but I can't give them what they need.

Calvin:
I know I'm dirty and I smell bad, but when you live in the street, where're you going to clean up? I'm cold and hungry. Anybody who thinks I want to live like this is crazy. I used to be able to get jobs, but never could get ahead. All I can do now is sell my blood. Nobody's going to hire me. I can't get a job unless I'm cleaned up and dressed good, but how am I going do that unless I've got a job? I can't figure any way I can win.

The Witness From the Word

Leader:
Let us now hear the testimony of the Scriptures.

Reading from Hebrew Scripture:
Amos 8:4-7

Congregational Response:
"Mine Eyes Have Seen the Glory," refrain (Attributed to William Steffe; Text: Julia Ward Howe.)

New Testament Reading:
Luke 16:19-31

Response:
"Amazing Grace," v. 1-2

(Text: sts. 1-4, John Newton; st. 5 ascr. to John Rees / Music: Virginia Harmony, 1831.)

The Witness from the Church

Leader:
Let us now hear the testimonies of concerned Christians.

(Let members of the congregation who have recently visited hungry persons in the community briefly share their experiences, followed by the readings of Carol and Arthur. Or only the readings may be used. After each person speaks, the congregation responds by singing the chorus to "And They'll Know We Are Christians.")

Congregational Response:
"And They'll Know We Are Christians", refrain (By Peter Scholtes, c. 1966, F.E.L. Publication, Ltd., assigned 1991 to the Lorenz Corporation.)

Carol:
As I shopped, a family made their way down the aisle ahead of me. They carefully studied each item. "Too much," the mother said as she replaced a $1.09 can of pineapple. "Maybe after you find work." The mother stood by the cashier; the father unloaded groceries—a loaf of white bread, a bag of beans, a box of oatmeal...Several times the mother asked for a subtotal. When it reached $9, she said, "That's all for this week." A head of lettuce, a dozen eggs, and three bananas remained in the cart. The little boy cried when he realized the bananas—his bananas—had to go back. I watched the scene with growing anguish. Hungry people were not just in Africa, they lived in my neighborhood too.

Arthur:
Hunger was a daily reality for many people in the parish where I served as pastor. Young people, old people, families and children were caught in a cruel cycle of poverty that perpetuated suffering and killed dreams. The area churches made an important contribution by way of food and emergency funds, but the relief was temporary. Could Christians make a lasting difference? "Yes," thought a handful of us who came together in 1974. We began writing, calling and visiting our members of Congress, asking them to support anti hunger legislation. Now more than 50,000 members of Bread for the World are working to make a lasting difference for hungry people.

Sermon or Choral Selections from Lazarus *(optional)*

The Time of Commitment

(A period of silence follows as the congregation prayerfully considers the "Affirmation and Commitment" printed on the bottom of the bulletin insert. Those who are so moved may sign the form and present it to God as a part of their offering. The congregation may also want to read aloud the Statement of Affirmation and Commitment.)

Statement of Affirmation and Commitment

I affirm as a Christian responding to the Gospel's call to feed hungry people that...every person in this country and around the world has a basic right to an adequate diet; individuals, churches, communities and the government must work to assure this basic right to food; I must use the resources available to me, including my gift of citizenship, to address the root causes of hunger as well as the immediate needs of hungry people.

Therefore, I will commit myself to praying regularly for hungry people, to contributing my time and/or my money to alleviate the plight of those who are hungry in my community, and to advocating for these people that together we might create a just society where no one lacks the basic necessities of life.

The Offertory
(The congregation remains in prayerful silence as an offering to assist hungry people in the community is received.)

Closing Hymn
(Select a hymn of dedication and commitment.)

The Benediction
Leader:
Go forth in peace, and be of good courage; hold fast to that which is good, rejoicing in the power of the Holy Spirit. And may the God who fills the hungry with good things fill us all with Christ-like love and with a consuming hunger for justice in our land and in our world. Amen.

(Adapted from Bread for the World's Service of Thanksgiving and Commitment.)

A Prayer Service In Support of United States Immigrants: International Immigrants Day

Opening Song
"Drink Living Water/Tomen Agua Viva" *(By Colleen Fulmer and Rufino Zaragoza, OFM, c. 1990, Colleen Fulmer and Rufino Zaragoza, OFM, OCP Publications.)*

Opening Reflection
From "An Alien's Prayer" by Edward Hays (From *Prayers for a Planetary Pilgrim,* Forest of Peace Publishing, 251 Muncie Rd., Leavenworth, KS 66048.)

I wear the mark of your disapproval
and your often unspoken words pierce straight to my soul.
"Why didn't you stay where you belong?"

I feel the icy stare that says,
"Keep your distance, you foreigner, with your different-colored skin and your strange-sounding speech, with your culture, food, religion and clothing that are inferior to my own."

I'm an immigrant, a wetback, an alien, an outsider operating a sweatshop sewing machine; cheap labor, unwanted or dirty jobs are mine for the taking; I'm one of the countless invisible ones who puts fresh vegetables on your plate or stitches the fashion dresses and shirts that you buy in your stylish stores.

As Moses of old once said,
"Remember you were once aliens in the land of Egypt."

Remember that your grandfathers and grandmothers were immigrants, unwanted, were exploited cheap labor, second-class citizens, uneducated and poor, used and abused, ignored or looked down upon for their foreign religion, speech and food.

(Silent reflection.)

Naming of Countries of Origin
Leader:
Realizing that our ancestors, our grandmothers and grandfathers, were immigrants, that they all came from a foreign land, please call out now your family's country of origin.

Sung Response:
"God, Mother of Exiles" (v. 1 & 2) *(Music by Colleen Fulmer / text of refrain taken from the New Colussus by Emma Lazarus, c. 1985, The Loretto Spirituality Network.)*

Guided Meditation on the Migration Experience (adapted)
(Excerpt from *Who Are My Sisters and Brothers? A Catholic Educational Guide for Understanding and Welcoming Immigrants and Refugees,* c. 1996, United States Catholic Conference, Inc.)

Reader 1:

The political situation has been increasingly tense in my country. Two different political parties have been competing for power for some time, and there has been a great deal of pressure on me and all the people to support one side or the other. Last year, elections finally took place. All adults were required to vote, so even though my family did not really support either side, I voted. While the party for whom I voted won the election, immediately afterward there were demonstrations in the streets of the capital. Within a few months, opponents of the new government had formed a movement which became increasingly violent. Fighting broke out all around my town.

Soon it was no longer safe for my children to go to school, and it was also dangerous for me. The armed groups had begun to ask for identification in the streets. I feared that they would accuse me of being a government supporter or would try to make me join them. I lost my job when the government shut down most business activity in my area. I began having difficulty feeding my children because everything was rationed, and there was no fresh food; water was available only sometimes.

Ultimately, I knew that I could not survive where I was living, but my country is very small, and the situation was similar everywhere. Foreign countries were not issuing visas now to people from my country, and it was not possible to get permission to leave. So my family and I left during the night, without permission and without visas. Each of us carried only a small bag of clothing and food.

Reader 2:

Deuteronomy 10: 18b-19

Sung Response:

"God, Mother of Exiles" *(refrain)*

Reader 3:

After two exhausting weeks of walking, mostly traveling by night to avoid detection and the heat, my family arrived at the country which borders your own. We were fortunate, as the government authorities gave us temporary permission to enter. But my spouse and I and our children decided to move to a different city (reader could insert name of own city here) because there are more job opportunities than in the small towns near the border.

Reader 4:

Leviticus 19:9-10

Sung Response:

"God, Mother of Exiles" *(refrain)*

Reader 1:

It has now been a year since my family has lived in our new home. Despite the fact that I had a high school education and a good middle income job in my home country, I have had difficulty finding work and am earning only the minimum wage. My spouse is now also working to help support the family; this is something that never would have happened in my own country, and it is difficult for me to accept.

My children are attending school in your new city, and they seem to be okay. They are learning English much more quickly than my spouse and me. Many times it is embarrassing when they can communicate better than me, and I sometimes need to ask them to translate something. I try to encourage my children to continue to speak our own native language at home with the family, but they want to use their English as much as possible. Sometimes it seems as if they want to forget as much as possible about the country from which we came. Even though I know they just want to "fit in" with their new friends, it hurts me and sometimes makes me angry.

I am proud of where I came from—of my country, my family, my work and my culture. Sometimes I wonder if my life will ever be like that again, or if these new changes are permanent. I feel fortunate that my family can now live in safety, but it is difficult to adjust. Life seems so fast-paced here, and lots of strange products, music and television are everywhere. There aren't very many members of my ethnic group in your city. Various times, at work or in a store or in other places, I have noticed people staring at me or laughing or becoming impatient with the way I talk.

I go to an adult English class when I can, but it is difficult because I often work nights and cannot attend. Some of the people at work speak a little of your language and they are trying to help me. But it's not just communication. More than anything, I often feel very lonely. No members of my extended family live in this country, and it has been almost impossible to maintain contact with them since we left home.

Reader 2:
Exodus 23:9

Sung Response:
"God, Mother of Exiles" *(refrain)*

Reader 3:
Several times since my family arrived, I have had to go to different government offices, including the immigration office, to continue to work on our case or to apply for certain documents. There are always lots of forms to fill out and it is very confusing; sometimes I am not even really sure what it is I am doing, and it seems as if our case will never be finalized. I have begun to hear things from neighbors and other people at work about the immigration laws changing in this country, and I fear how these might affect me and my family.

Antiphonal Prayer:
(Adapted from *Who Are My Sisters and Brothers? A Catholic Educational Guide for Understanding and Welcoming Immigrants and Refugees*, c. 1996, USCC.)

Side 1:
The days are coming, says our God, when I will gather you. The days are soon coming when I will bring you to a land that I will show you, a land of peace where justice reigns.

Side 2:
The days are coming when I will cleanse you of all that holds you in fear and terror, of all that blinds you to truth.

Side 1:
On that day, you will cry with those who mourn; you will laugh with those rejoicing. You will stand speechless as a newborn child, and sing in joy before a mountain stream, and all creation will give glory.

Side 2:
The days are soon coming. They are already here, when I will give you a new heart and you will know me. On that day, the grain you have stored will feed the hungry. The wealth you have saved will protect the poor, and all children will find safe haven.

All:
On that day, all people will come into the land that God will show them, a land of peace, where justice reigns and all God's children will find safe haven.

Sung Response:
"God, Mother of Exiles" (v. 3 and 4)

Closing Prayer

All:

God of mercy and compassion, You gift us with family, friends and homeland—true marks of our identity.

Keep us ever mindful of those who suffer because of dispossession, homelessness and exile, who, through no fault or choice of their own, are forced to be pilgrims and strangers while others occupy their lands.

Grant us, we pray, a far-reaching mercy and compassion, that we may open our hearts and homes more fully in welcome and care for the strangers and refugees in our midst.

Teach us Your ways of justice, peace and reconciliation. Grant us the strength and courage to face the systems, policies and structures of our day that divide the human family, and transform them with Your love. We ask this in Your name. Amen.

Closing Song

"We Remember" *(v. 1, 3, 4) (By Marty Haugen, c. 1980, GIA.)*

(Adapted from resources produced by the National Council of Catholic Bishops.)

Commemoration of the Santa Cruz Massacre in East Timor

This liturgy and action was held outside of the Indonesian Consulate in San Francisco, California. Your group may want to consider holding the commemoration outside the Indonesian Consulate in your own city. You will need red pieces of paper with the names of the victims of the massacre written on them, as well as two baskets in which to place them. You will also need several pieces of chalk for people to use to inscribe the names of these martyrs on the sidewalk outside of the Consulate.

Opening Reflection/Prayer

Leader:
Today we gather to commemorate the lives of the estimated 271 East Timorese who were martyred by the Indonesian military on November 12, 1991 during a peaceful demonstration at the Santa Cruz cemetery in Dili, the capital of East Timor. Let us pray, for them and for ourselves:

O Holy One, be with us as we remember the lives and deaths of your faithful servants in East Timor, martyrs for the faith, martyrs for the cause of your justice and peace. We reverence their lives and their struggle. Let the profundity and courage of their witness sink deeply into our hearts and souls that we might be inspired to stand in solidarity with them as they fight for liberation and self-determination, and the dignity with which you intended all of us to be treated. We ask this in your merciful name. Amen.

Opening Song:
"The Cry of the Poor" (By John B. Foley, SJ, c. 1978, 1991, John B. Foley, SJ, and New Dawn Music.)

Reading and Dramatic Re-enactment:
(From *East Timor: Genocide in Paradise*, by Matthew Jardine, Tucson, c. 1995, Odonian Press.)

As this selection is read have twenty or so people re-enact the massacre. Half of the group enters with a coffin, slowly as if in a funeral procession. A drum beats in rhythm with the procession. The rest of the group then enters as the Indonesian assassins. They plant themselves and open fire. Those attending the funeral die and fall, being caught by someone so they do not hit the ground. All of this happens in slow motion. The assassins then depart, leaving behind the dead and those who mourn. (Developed by a dance and drill troop at St. Ignatius College Preparatory in San Francisco, California.)

Reader 1:
On November 12, 1991, a crowd of mourners gathered at a local parish church in East Timor's capital, Dili. They'd come to attend a memorial mass for Sebastiao Gomes, a pro-independence activist who had been killed at the same church by Indonesian soldiers two weeks earlier.

Reader 2:
Such killings had become common occurrences since the indonesian invasion. But this particular day of mourning would have special significance–in large part because journalists from the U.S. and Great Britain were there to report it.

Reader 1:
When the mass ended, a procession began to the Santa Cruz Cemetery, about a mile away. Although Indonesian soldiers lined the streets, the mourners unfurled banners and shouted pro-independence slogans. This uncharacteristically open defiance of Indonesian authority caught the attention of those whose homes and places of work lined the procession route. Supporters joined in, and soon the crowd had swelled to thousands.

"There is no silence
deep enough
No blackout dark enough
No corruption thick enough
No heart hollow enough
No grave wide enough
to bury your story and
keep it from us."

Reader 2:
At the cemetery, some of the crowd went to the gravesite with Sebastiao's family. Others waited outside the walls. They were the first to notice that Indonesian army trucks had blocked the road back to town, and that a column of armed soldiers was slowly making its way toward the crowd.

Reader 1:
Eyewitness Allan Nairn of the New Yorker reports what happened next. Without warning, and without provocation, "soldiers raised their rifles, and took aim. Then, acting in unison, they opened fire...Men and women fell, shivering, in the street, rolling from the impact of the bullets. Some were backpedaling, and tripping, their hands held up. Others simply tried to turn and run. The soldiers jumped over fallen bodies and fired at the people still upright. They chased down young boys and girls and shot them in the back." When it was over, more than 250 people had been killed and hundreds more wounded. (The soldiers also badly beat Nairn and fellow U.S. journalist Amy Goodman.)

Reader 2:
Max Stahl, a British journalist whose video camera captured the horror, called it a "cold-blooded and premeditated massacre." Eyewitnesses told him that Indonesian soldiers killed many of the wounded at the military hospital in Dili; they "crushed the skulls of the wounded with large rocks, ran over them with trucks, stabbed them and administered–with doctors present–poisonous disinfecting chemicals as medicines." Stahl estimates that 50-200 of the wounded died in this way.

Reader 1:
We show you this not to scare you, but to educate you. These things are going on and the world is not paying attention, but we ask you to. (Written by a St. Ignatius high school student.)

(Silent pause.)

Reading:
(Compiled and adapted from articles written by Rev. John Chamberlin, Ben Terrall and Greg Khehans for California/Nevada *The United Methodist Review.*)

Reader 1:
Such indisputable evidence of Indonesian atrocities provided by this massacre thrust the plight of the long-suffering East Timorese people into the spotlight of international attention. They have endured years of brutal repression since Indonesia's invasion and occupation of their country in 1975. This illegal annexation of East Timor has never been recognized by the U. N., which has passed ten resolutions condemning the invasion and calling on Indonesia to withdraw its forces of occupation.

Reader 2:
East Timor is tiny, about the size of Maryland, and was therefore no match for the fourth most populous country in the world. The result of Indonesia's takeover of East Timor has been devastating. By the late 1980s, 200,000 people, one-third of the island's population, had been killed by Indonesian bullets or forced starvation, making this the worst mass slaughter in proportion to population since the Nazi reign of terror during World War II.

Reader 1:
Today this genocidal repression continues. The current military crackdown is reported to be the worst in fifteen years. Arbitrary arrests and torture are routine, as are extrajudicial executions and the systematic use of rape and forced sterilization by the Indonesian military. The United States has assumed an active role in this ongoing bloodshed. Our country supplied many of the weapons used in the invasion and continues to send military aid to Indonesia.

(Silent pause.)

Prayer of Repentance

All:
O God, forgive us. We pray for our country's complicity in such suffering. Forgive us for our own hardness of heart, for not hearing the cry of the East Timorese, the cry of the poor. Show us your mercy and help us to heed your call to work for justice. Amen.

Sung Response

"The Cry of the Poor" *(v.3-4)*

Inscribing of the Names

(The list of names is found in Appendix A in the back of this book.)

Leader:
Let us now remember those 271 East Timorese killed in the Santa Cruz massacre. Let us inscribe their names on our hearts and on the sidewalk underneath us.

(Have pieces of chalk available. Two people hold baskets containing red slips of paper with the names of those massacred written on them. Those gathered take a slip of paper from a basket then, using chalk, write the name they are given on the sidewalk. When they are finished, they return the piece of paper to one of the baskets. As this is taking place, another person reads the names of the 271 victims out loud.).

Recommitment to Stand in Solidarity with the People of East Timor

Reader 1:
Echoes of the aspirations of the Indonesian people and youth reach me through the prison bars in Cipinang, your yearnings for a new spirit...we the people of East Timor call on you to help put an end to the oppression of the people of East Timor. (Xanana Gusmao, imprisoned East Timorese resistance leader, Cipinang Prison, November 28, 1993.)

Reader 2:
We ask people of the world...not to forget that we are here, struggling for life everyday...Keep speaking; everyone must keep speaking about us. (Bishop Carlos Filipe Ximenes Belo, Co-Recipient of the 1996 Nobel Peace Prize.)

Leader:
We have heard the pleas of our brothers and sisters in East Timor. Let us now recommit ourselves to stand in solidarity with them in their struggle for freedom.

All:
There is no silence deep enough
No blackout dark enough
No corruption thick enough
No business deal big enough
No politician bent enough
No heart hollow enough
No grave wide enough to bury your story and keep it from us.
("Solidarity Message from Bono of U2 to the Good People of East Timor.")

We hear your story.
As people of faith, we pledge to:
demand an end to Indonesia's illegal military occupation of East Timor and the ever-deteriorating human rights situation;

join 1996 Nobel Peace Prize laureates Bishop Carlos Belo and Dr. Jose Ramos-Horta in calling for President Clinton and Congress to support a U.N.-supervised referendum on the future of East Timor; and urge the U.S. government to end all military aid to Indonesia.

We ask your help, loving God, in fulfilling this pledge. Amen.

Closing Song:
"Be Light for Our Eyes" *(By David Haas, c. 1985, GIA.)*

Action

Those who feel so moved are invited to carry the basket of names to those who work at the Indonesian Consulate. If people are turned away, some may wish to climb the fence surrounding the Consulate and occupy the grounds, or simply block the gates.

(Adapted from a prayer service and action organized by East Timor Religious Outreach, 1600 Clay St., San Francisco, CA 94109 415/474-6219.)

"Do Not Weep for Them, Imitate Them:" Commemorating the Deaths of the Six Jesuits and Their Co-workers in El Salvador

Place icons of the martyrs of Central America, candles, and bright Guatemalan cloth on and around the altar.

Opening Song
"Paz Y Libertad" *(By Jose Luis Orozco, c. 1983, Jose Luis Orozco.)*

Opening Prayer
Leader:
We gather to commemorate the anniversary of the assassination of the six Jesuits and their two women co-workers by the Salvadoran military and to remember the more than 75,000 Salvadorans who were killed in a civil war funded by our government.

O God, be with us as we remember these martyrs. Help us to imitate their lives of loving service, of selfless sacrifice, and to carry on their legacy by working for justice for all those in Central America who continue to suffer the effects of economic oppression, torture and death.

Reading
from Yom Kippur Service

Reader 1:
We cannot pray to You, Infinite One, to banish war for You have filled the world with paths of peace if only we would share them.

Reader 2:
We cannot pray to You to end starvation, for there is enough food for all, if only we would share it.

Reader 1:
We cannot merely pray for prejudice to cease, for we might see the good in all that lies before our eyes, if only we would use them.

Reader 2:
We cannot merely pray "root out despair," for the spark of hope already waits within the human heart, for us to fan it into a flame.

Reader 1:
We must not ask You, Eternal One, to take the task that You have given us. We cannot shirk, we cannot flee away, avoiding obligation forever.

Reader 2:
Therefore we pray, Adonai, for wisdom, for will, for courage to do and to become, not only to look on with helpless yearning as though we had no strength.

Reader 1:
For Your sake and for ours, speedily and soon, let it be: that our land may be safe, that our lives may be blessed.

Reader 2:
May our words be pleasing in Your sight; may our deeds be acceptable to You, Shechina, our Rock and our Redeemer.

"Forgive us for the times we have been complacent, for the times we have been silent in the face of this evil. In the spirit of our martyred sisters and brothers, move us, O God, to proclaim the truth."

Litany of the Martyrs

Sung Refrain:
"We Lift Up Their Lives'" *(By John Foley, SJ, c. 1989 John Foley, SJ.)*

Reader 1:
Ignacio Ellacuria, rector of the Central American University. Fr. Ellacuria was a philosopher, theologian, politician, educator, humanist, and most of all, a priest who consciously shed his blood for justice and peace in El Salvador.

Reader 2:
Padre Rutilio Grande vivía y trabajaba con los pobres de El Salvador en Aguilares y el 12 de Marzo de 1977 fue asasinado. Campesinos Manuel Solorzano y Nelson Rutilio Lemus fueron martirados a su lado. (Fr. Rutilio Grande lived and worked with the poor of El Salvador in Aguilares, and on March 12, 1977 he was assassinated. Campesinos Manuel Solorzano and Nelson Rutilio Lemus were martyred alongside him.)

Refrain

Reader 1:
Ignacio Martin-Baro ministered to the people of Jayaque. He always had candy for the children. While a foreign journalist would have to arrange an appointment well in advance to see Nacho, any campesino from Jayaque could walk right into his office at any time.

Reader 2:
Elba Ramos fue una persona muy sensible a las necesidades de los demás, capaz a reconocer cuando uno tenía algún problema y siempre lista simpatizar y ofrecer consejo. Su hija Celina recibó una beca para sus estudios. Fue catequista en Las Delicias. (Elba Ramos was a person sensitive to the needs of others, able to recognize when another had some problem and ready to sympathize and offer advice. Her daughter, Celina, received a scholarship for her studies. She had served as a catechist in Las Delicias).

Refrain

Reader 1:
Our beloved Monsignor Romero: the voice of the voiceless.

Reader 2:
Amando Lopez, Juan Ramon Moreno, y Joaquin Lopez y Lopez fueron parte del corazón que cambió la manera en que la UCA fue universidad por enfocar su trabajo y como afectaría a los pobres. (Amando Lopez, Juan Ramon Moreno, and Joaquin Lopez y Lopez were part of the core that changed the way the UCA was a university by focusing their work on how it would affect the poor.)

Refrain

Reader 1:
Herbert Anaya, president of the non-governmental Human Rights Commission, gunned down in broad daylight in front of his small children. And for those who witness and work for human rights in Central America.

Reader 2:
Dorothy, Ita, Jean, y Maura. Por su compromiso a los desplazados y refugiados de El Salvador fueron sacados de su carro, violados y matados. Diciembre 1980. (Dorothy, Ita, Jean, and Maura. Because of their commitment to the displaced and refugees of El Salvador they were dragged from their van, raped and then shot. December 1980.)

Refrain

Reader 1:
Isabel Lopez, 10 years old; Anabel Beatriz Lopez, 2; Jose Dolores, 10; Blanca Lidia Guardado, 1 1/2; victims of the bombing of the community Corral de Piedra (Community Ellacuria) and for the thousands and thousands of children slaughtered during 10 years of war.

Reader 2:
Segundo Montes pasó sus fines de semana con la comunidad de Quezaltepeque. Los niños allí acariciaron su barba roja y poner sus caras cerca. Les gustó tocar su cara–una cara con ojos brilliantes que llenaron con lágrimas cuando fue presentado con un regalo. (Segundo Montes spent his weekends with the community of Quezaltepeque. The children there caressed his red beard and put their faces close. They loved to touch his face–a face with brilliant eyes that filled with tears when he was given a gift.)

Refrain

Offering of Flowers

(By representatives of the refugee community in your city or members of your parish who are active in supporting your sister parish, the children in your community, etc. Place flowers at the foot of the altar or interspersed among the icons of the martyrs.)

Message from Your Sister City

(if you have one...)

If your community does not have a sister city, you might want to sing the following song after the Gospel reading.

Song:
"Digo 'Sí' Señor" *(By Donna Pena, c. 1987, GIA.)*

Reading

Matthew 25:31-46

Reading

From *The Companions of Jesus* by John Sobrino, c. 1990 Orbis Books.

So what really remains from the martyrdom of these six Jesuits? I believe and hope their spirit remains, that they rise again, like Archbishop Romero, in the Salvadoran people, that they continue to be a light in this dark tunnel, and hope in this country of endless misfortunes. All martyrs rise again in history, each in their own way. Archbishop Romero's is exceptional and unrepeatable, but Rutilio Grande is also present in many peasants; the North American sisters are still alive in Chalatenango and La Libertad; Octavio Ortiz in El Despertar; and the hundreds of martyred peasants in their communities.

The martyred Jesuits too will live on in the Salvadoran people. I would like it if the Salvadoran people remembered them as witnesses to the truth, so that they go on believing that the truth is possible in their country; that they remember them as witnesses to justice–structural justice–so that the Salvadoran people retain the courage to believe that it is possible to change the country. I hope they remember them as faithful witnesses to the God of life, so that the Salvadorans go on seeing God as their defender; that they remember them as Jesuits who tried to undergo a difficult conversion and paid the price for defending faith and justice.

They also leave us good news, a gospel. On this sinful and senseless earth it is possible to live like human beings and like Christians. We can share in that current of history that Paul calls life in the Spirit and life in love, in that current of honesty, hope, and commitment that is always being threatened with suffocation but that time and time again bursts forth from the depths like a true miracle of God. Joining this current of history, which is that of the poor, has its price, but it encourages us to go on living, working, and believing, it offers meaning and salvation.

This is what I believe these new martyrs bequeath us. With it we can go on walking through history, humbly, as the prophet Micah says, amid suffering and darkness, but with God.

Covenant Renewal Statement

Leader(s):
You created all of us to enjoy the fullness of life. You formed each of us in our mother's womb that we might know one another as sister and brother.

And so, O Loving One, we lift up our prayers to you. We pray that the people of El Salvador might enjoy this gift of life, that they might know you as the God of the Exodus who leads them from the slavery of systematic poverty and oppression to the liberation which all of God's children were created to enjoy. Free the oppressed, the tortured, the raped, and the disappeared from the heavy burden that our country has helped to place on them.

Forgive those of us gathered here for the times we have been complacent, for the times we have been silent in the face of this evil. In the spirit of our martyred sisters and brothers, move us, O God, to proclaim the truth.

And so, we renew our covenant with the people of Central America...

All:
We choose to stand in solidarity with the peoples of Central America, especially the people of El Salvador. We renew our commitment not to weep for the martyrs but to imitate their witness of self-sacrificing love and service of the poor. We are moved to reflect on the lives of these women and men because they have helped to deepen our faith in the God of Life. In the name of this God, we promise to promote justice by working to end the suffering of all of our sisters and brothers throughout the world. We commit ourselves, as well, to the love of our enemy–praying constantly for the conversion of those who torture and kill, both in our own country and in Central America. We rely on God in all of this, asking that we be sustained in this covenant into which we have entered.

Final Blessing

Leader:
Let us go forth now, renewed by our commitment to stand in solidarity with our sisters and brothers in Central America. Renewed by the faith of this gathered community. Renewed by God's love for us. Let us go forth in peace.

Closing Song
"Send Down the Fire" (By Marty Haugen, c. 1987, GIA.)

(Adapted from a service planned by a coalition of groups in the San Francisco Bay Area involved in sanctuary work.)

Tenebrae: Service for People Living with HIV and AIDS (World AIDS Day)

Lighting and "decoration" should be subdued—tones of deep red or purple. In the center of a comfortably large space there are nine lit candles. There may also be a candle by a stand or ambo where the readings will take place. The candles may be on a table, an altar or on the floor, ideally on different levels with only one at the highest level, but the number of candles is of greater importance than their arrangement. If feasible a copy of the National Catholic AIDS Network (NCAN) "Mother of God, Light in All Darkness" icon might also be displayed. Out of sight of the gathered group there should be a single lit taper and a number of heavy books or drums or something that can be used to make a great deal of "booming" noise. It is also important to have someone available to work lights near the end of the service.

Background

Tenebrae is Latin for "darkness." The Tenebrae service is a traditional monastic service of readings done on Good Friday. This adaptation weaves the traditional scripture readings with excerpts from letters written by those who have struggled with the loss of a loved one from AIDS. Any appropriate readings might be used. The format is flexible. After each reading, a candle is blown out until darkness is all that remains. At this point the monks would bang their prayer books on their chairs, symbolizing the destruction of earth when the light of life (Christ) was snuffed out. After a few moments of such noise, silence returns and a single light was brought forward—a reminder that the darkness did not then and does not now have the final say.

Welcome/Introduction

(Give a brief introduction/explanation of what is to come. Don't give away the noise at the end, except to those who have been selected in advance to help with it. Extinguish candles after each reading, sung responses, sources of readings (prophets, psalms, Quilt letters, icon, etc.). The letters that follow are all from *A Promise to Remember: The Names Project Book of Letters: Remembrances of love from the contributors to the Quilt,* ed. by Joe Brown, c. 1992, The Names Project. Published by Avon Books.)

Song

"In the Light" *(By Michael John Poirier, c. 1986, Michael John Poirier, Peartree Productions.)*

(Choose verses that seem appropriate each time the song is sung in response—no more than one or two each time.)

Prayer

(From *the back of the NCAN icon prayer card*, by Fr. William McNicols, SJ, and used with permission of the National Catholic AIDS Network.)

All:
Mother of God, Light in All Darkness,
shelter Him, our flame of hope, with your tender hands.
And in times of dread and nightmares,
let Him be our dream of comfort.
And in our times of physical pain and suffering,
let Him be our healer. And in our times of separation,
from God and one another, let Him be our communion.
Amen.

Song:
"Healer of My Soul" *(v. 1 & 2) (By John Michael Talbot, c. 1983 John Michael Talbot, Birdwing Music/Cherry Lane Music Publishing Co., Inc.)*

"Oh, God, I didn't think anyone would ever hold me again. His words made me realize the enormity of the isolation he had endured since his diagnosis."

Reading 1

Jeremiah 8:18-9:1

Reading 2

As a volunteer in the Buddy Program of the San Diego AIDS Project, I was assigned to Reino soon after I completed my volunteer training in July of 1985. Over the nearly 14 months that we had together, we grew very close...He listened to my joys and sorrows as much as I listened to his, and those times that we shared are among the most valued that I've ever had...I entered the relationship expecting to be the nurturer, the giver. But Reino was also a skilled giver. No matter how sick he was, he found the words to touch my heart...

Once when he was particularly ill, I lay down beside him on his bed and held his frail body close to mine until he stopped shivering. He said, "Oh, God, I didn't think anyone would ever hold me again." His words made me realize the enormity of the isolation he had endured since his diagnosis. I knew that if I tried to speak, I would cry. We did a lot more holding after that.

Reino's final weeks were spent in a hospital, gradually succumbing to pneumonia. During that period we spent many silent hours just holding hands, no longer needing to speak...I spent his final night with him, listening to the pattern of his labored breathing, and hoping each time that it faltered it would not begin again. At 6 a.m., though he was still in a coma, I took him into my arms and said, "I know that it is time for you to rest now. We'll miss you very much. We'll cry and grieve and support one another. But it's OK for you to go." In less than an hour he had made his transition.

I was deeply honored that Reino allowed me to be part of this most intimate experience of letting go. He was not an educated man, but he taught me much. He was materially poor, but he found something to give. Now that I, too, am a person with AIDS, I am more fully aware of how he has prepared me. I know that he will assist me in my transition...

Love in the struggle, Robert "Jess" Jessop

Song:
"In the Light"

Reading 3

Psalm 102:1-11

Reading 4

This quilt was made for Bernhard Lehmann. I loved him with all my heart and soul for 23 years, 6 months and 20 days. He was what I lived for. We had planned to die together because we wanted to die together as we had faced life together. But he could not wait for me and now I am lost without his love. I pray there is an afterlife so I can be with him again. I don't fear death anymore for I feel it will reunite me with Bernie. ...What I loved most about Bernie were his hands. He had big, masculine, rough, strong hands. And as strong and serious as Bernie could be, you could touch his heart in an instant.

John Floda, Lover and best friend of Bernie Lehmann

Song:
"In the Light"

Reading 5
Psalm 88:1-15

Reading 6
My Dearest Bob, There is not a word to describe how much I miss you, much more than I ever realized I would. I miss not being able to talk to you because you always understood and you always made everything seem better. I really, really miss your sense of humor, your ability to express something comical.

The jokes that you could tell and then your laugh-I can still hear it. How I so enjoyed that funny little poem you and only you could recite; how I had always wanted you to record it for me, or I was going to and somehow it was never done and I am so sorry I didn't...I miss doing things for you and trying to make you feel better, and I miss sitting on your bed and our talks just before you went to sleep, and I miss holding your hand so it would not shake. I just miss everything about you.

When you died, I wanted to die. I kissed and held you and I hope you heard me say, "I love you." I didn't believe it at first, and I felt so numb, and all I could think was "it's over, and I didn't want it to be this way." I came home and, even though there were family and friends here, the house seemed so empty and all I could think was, you would never be back here and you would not be here for me to take care of...

Bob, I am so lonely for you. Not a day goes by that I don't cry. So many, many things make me think of you. It seems like it gets worse instead of better...I am in the car driving somewhere, and all of a sudden the tears roll down my face. It's the same in the grocery store or in the mall. I hold your picture and can almost feel you...

I wish I could have prevented your illness-God knows I would have given my life for you. I wish I could "kiss it all better" like I used to do when you were a little boy and make it go away...I'm angry at myself that there was absolutely not one thing in this world that I could do to save your life. I can never describe the totally helpless feeling I suffered each day... I only ask that you save a place for me the day I will see you again. Help me make it through all the days and nights till then...I will see you again, my friend, my son.

Your loving mother, Ruth M. Eshmont

Song:
"In the Light"

Reading 7
Psalm 22:2-3, 13-16, 17b-18a

Reading 8
My friend Kevin died two days after his 29th birthday. He had been in the hospital for two weeks, with what I thought was only pneumonia. I never saw him during those two weeks. To this day I regret that. But over the phone, he kept telling me he'd be getting out soon. He did get out, but not in the way I had thought.

Two years have passed since then. Not a day goes by that I don't think "Kevin should be here." All the talks we had about what was to come of our lives in the days to come...It feels odd living out my ambitions, knowing Kevin's will only remain in the memories of those who knew him.

When I learned of the NAMES Project, I knew I had to make a panel for Kevin. While trying to think of what it was to be, I heard the song "Empty Chairs at Empty Tables," from the cast album of Les Miserables. I knew then that was to become his panel. It expressed my feelings about Kevin being gone.

In the play, a man returns to the local tavern, where days earlier, all his friends were gathered, toasting to good times, shared laughter, companionship and conversation. Now the man is alone in the tavern. All his friends have been killed in the revolution. Being in that same room, thinking of what had once been, and realizing that those friends are now all gone. They should still be there, but are not.

This is what I feel with Kevin. He should be here. Kevin's panel illustrates a place once filled with life and happiness when he was there. Although he no longer sits at the table, his presence is still felt. But it's not the same as his being here. Kevin should still be sitting at the table.

With love, Tom Lawson

Song:
"Healer of My Soul" *(reprise)*

Reading 9
From the traditional Good Friday Reproaches (found in the Sacramentary) (Use two readers for this one. When the time comes to extinguish the last candle, one of the readers can go to the center while the other stays at the ambo so that both candles (in the center/at the ambo) can be extinguished simultaneously.)

Reader 1:
My people, what have I done to you? How have I offended you? Answer me!

Reader 2:
I led you out of Egypt, from slavery to freedom, but you led me to a cross.

Reader 1:
My people, what have I done to you? How have I offended you? Answer me!

Reader 2:
I opened the sea before you, but you opened my side with a spear.

Reader 1:
My people, what have I done to you? How have I offended you? Answer me!

Reader 2:
I led you on your way in a pillar of cloud, but you led me to Pilate's court.

Reader 1:
My people, what have I done to you? How have I offended you? Answer me!

Reader 2:
I planted you as my fairest vine and gave you saving water from the rock, but you gave me gall and vinegar to drink.

Reader 1:
My people, what have I done to you? How have I offended you? Answer me!

Reader 2:
I fed you with manna in the wilderness and brought you to a land of plenty, but you struck me down and scourged me.

Reader 1:
My people, what have I done to you? How have I offended you? Answer me!

Reader 2:
I gave you a royal scepter, but you gave me a crown of thorns.

Reader 1:
My people, what have I done to you? How have I offended you? Answer me!

Reader 2:
I raised you to the height of majesty, but you raised me high on a cross.

Reader 1:
My people, what have I done to you? How have I offended you? Answer me!

(When the last candle is extinguished, tumult ensues. When the sound dies away, a single taper is brought forward and placed by the Mother of God, Light in All Darkness icon, or an unlit candle could have been waiting by the icon and the taper used simply to light it.)

Closing Prayer

All:
Jesus,
enfold us,
enflame us with your holy fire,
that it might burn bright in our hearts-to warm
us when we are cold and alone,
to comfort us when we are frightened and in pain,
to light the way before us when we are
weary and without hope.
O precious light in our darkness, burn bright in us,
that we might see your face more clearly
in the faces of those around us,
this night and every night. Amen.

Song:
"In the Light"

(This service, which was prepared by Kate McMichael, was originally held during Holy Week at Newman Hall/Holy Spirit parish in Berkeley, California, as part of a campus ministry Lenten program. This format was particularly focused on the experience of people living with AIDS.)

Truth that Sets Free:
A Prayer Service and Morality Play Honoring the Memories of Maura Clarke, Ita Ford, Jean Donovan and Dorothy Kazel

You may wish to share the parts of the liturgy designated "Leader" among several people in the community.

Processional and Opening Song

"Be Not Afraid" *(By Robert J. Dufford, SJ, c. 1975, Robert J. Dufford, SJ, and North American Liturgy Resources.)*

If the service includes the play, the actors might be part of the processional, walking solemnly down the center aisle with the other service leaders.

Introduction and Opening Prayer

Leader:

On December 2, 1980, four North American women, sisters in faith, were murdered by members of the Salvadoran security forces. Our nation was on one side of a terrible civil war. We trained and funded the people who killed these women; then U.S. government officials covered up the truth about who committed the crime. This was not new. We had supported and protected the military dictators that ruled that country for a generation and who were still in power in 1980. We were reminded of this terrible truth once again on November 16, 1989, when U.S.-trained Salvadoran soldiers murdered six Jesuit priests and two women at the Central America University in San Salvador. Again, officials of our government covered up the truth about the crime to protect high level military officers.

The truth that emerged from a shallow grave along a Salvadoran roadside in December 1980 presents us with a tremendous challenge and an opportunity. But for us to embrace that truth, we have to look at it, receive its word, let it come to live in our hearts, listen to its consequences for us as people of faith and as citizens of the United States. And that means we must be open to the possibility of being changed, altered, by that truth. But here is our hope. This is exactly what we are challenged to do by our faith–to listen to God's word, to receive it and become partners in the covenant of liberation, the covenant of the Exodus, when God led the people out of slavery to freedom. In truth, promises Jesus, lies our real freedom.

Let us pray: *(pause)*

God, our loving Creator, open our hearts to receive your truth this day. Challenge us in the truth of the witness of these four women, Maura, Ita, Dorothy, and Jean, of the eight martyrs of the Central America University, of all the martyrs of Central America who gave their lives that we might hear your word, look at our world as it is, and hold dear the truth that sets free.

We know that in our time this message is not welcome, and often hearing your word takes courage. It is a hard word when it tells us about the state of sin in our world. But it is the word of our hope and our freedom, the word of redemption. Give us then this courage to embrace the truth revealed in the life and death of your martyrs. This we ask in the name of the one who sets free. Amen.

Penitential Rite

Leader:
Let us bow our heads and pray for God's mercy on us and on our world. The response is: God, have mercy on us and on our world.

All:
God, have mercy on us and on our world.

Leader:
Loving God, for the hardness of our hearts, as we encounter the truth of injustice, social violence, poverty and the death of your martyrs for the cause of your truth that our hearts may be changed from hearts of stone to hearts of flesh, we pray to our God...

Creator God, for the fear and denial that shields our souls from the encounter with truth, especially when it means that we must change our lives, our preconceptions and assumptions, our understanding of our world and the place of the United States in that world-for the courage to open ourselves to truth and its consequences in our lives, we pray to our God...

Tender God, who cries out in the hearts of the persecuted and the suffering, for the times we close our hearts to our own liberation, when we refuse your loving offer of redemption, freedom and joy because we cherish security built on our own terms more than yours-that we might be healed from our fear, hear the cries of your people, and allow ourselves to be set free, we pray to our God...

All:
Loving and tender God, open our hearts to your word. May we become a people in whom your word has a place, and room to be and to grow within this world. Make us instruments of liberation and witnesses to truth. This we ask in the names of our four sisters who gave their lives for the truth that sets free. Amen.

First Reading
Isaiah 55:10-11

Psalm Response
Psalm 25 "To You, O Lord"
(Text: Psalm 25:4-5, 8-9, 12-14 / Para. by Marty Haugen, c. 1982, GIA; Refrain trans., c. 1969, ICEL / Tune: Marty Haugen, c. 1982, GIA.)

Second Reading
John 8:31-47 *(If the play is to be performed, bring down the lights for the reading of the Gospel. Have just one light at the pulpit for the lector. Before the reading begins, the actors quietly and in darkness take their places.)*

Morality Play or Homily
(Where the play will not be performed, a homily or shared reflection may follow the readings. Suggested theme: the meaning of truth that has emerged from the deaths of the women, and other revelations about the role the U.S. played in supporting and working with human rights abusers and oppressors in Central America. Emphasize the special responsibility of the faith community to own this truth, to understand its historic and systemic roots, and to work to create a different history built on truth, integrity and justice.)

(The play can be ordered by mail from the Religious Task Force on Central America, 1747 Connecticut Ave., NW, Washington DC 20009-1108, or by calling 202/529-0441. If it is performed, conclude with a period of silence in the darkness. The silence could end with music or sacred dance.)

Litany of the Martyrs of Central America

Leader:
We are invited to hear the truth of our world in the testimony of the martyrs of our time. Let us now pronounce their names, make a place for them in our hearts, and become bearers of their word, their truth, to our world. Please stand. Our response will be " Presente!"

Reader 1:
Archbishop Oscar Romero, prophet and martyr of El Salvador... All: Presente!

Reader 2:
The Indian martyrs of the massacre in Santiago Atitlan, Guatemala, killed by the military for defending their human rights, December 2, 1990: Salvador Sosof, Pedro Mendoza Pablo, Gaspar Coo Sicay, Juan Carlos Pablo Sosof, Pedro Mendoza Catu, Pedro Cristal Mendoza, Geronimo Sojuel Sisay, Juan Ajuchan Mesia, Felipe Quiju Culan, Salvador Damian Yaqui, Pedro Damian Vasquez, Nicolas Ajtujal Sosof, Manuel Chiquita Gonzalez... Presente!

Reader 1:
Central American priests and religious who gave their lives for their people, especially: Octavio Ortiz, Alfonso Navarro, Rafael Palacios, Rutilio Grande, Tomas Zavaleta, Silvia Maribel, of El Salvador... Presente!

Reader 2:
Victoria de la Roca, Hermogenes Lopez, Pedro Caal, Carlos Galvez, Augusto Ramirez Monasterio, of Guatemala... Presente!

Reader 1:
Missioners and religious of other nations of the world who gave their lives in the cause of God's people, especially Ivan Betancourt of Colombia; Conrado de la Cruz of the Philippines; Faustino Villanueva, Moises Cisneros, Jose Maria Gran Cuera of Spain; Walter Voordeckers of Belgium; Tulio Marcelo Maruzzo of Italy; Raoul Leger of Canada... Presente!

Reader 2:
Scientists and professionals who worked for the cause of truth and justice, especially Myrna Mack of Guatemala and Maurice Demierre of Switzerland... Presente!

Reader 1:
Hundreds of martyred catechists and Delegates of the Word, among whom we remember: Laura Lopez and Jose Alfonso Acevedo of El Salvador; Emiliano Perez Obando and Felipe and Mery Barreda of Nicaragua; Lucio Aguirre Monge of Honduras; Diego Quic Apuchan of Guatemala... Presente!

Reader 2:
Martyrs in the cause of human rights, especially: Marianella Garcia Villas, Maria Magdelena Enriquez, Herbert Ernesto Anaya of El Salvador... Presente!

Reader 1:
Rosario Godoy de Cuevas, Hector Gomez Calito, Maria Mejia, Sebastian Velasquez Mejia, Juan Perebal Xirum, Santos Toj Reynoso, of Guatemala... Presente!

Reader 2:
Miguel Angel Pavon of Honduras... Presente!

Reader 1:
Those martyred at the hands of militaries in massacres throughout Central America: in Olancho and the El Astillero cooperative in Honduras; at the Sumpul and Lempa rivers and in El Mozote in El Salvador; at Panzos, the Spanish Embassy, Aguacate in Guatemala... Presente!

Reader 2:
The martyrs of the Central America University in San Salvador: Elba Julio Ramos, Celina Maricet, Ignacio Ellacuria, Segundo Montes, Ignacio Martin-Baro, Joaquin Lopez y Lopez, Amando Lopez, Juan Ramon Moreno... Presente!

Reader 1:
Our North American sisters and brothers who gave their lives, taking on the same fate as the poor of Central America: Michael Cypher, Maureen Courtney, James Carney, Stanley Rother, James Miller, William Woods, Benjamin Linder... Presente!

Reader 2:
Maura Clarke, Ita Ford, Jean Donovan, Dorothy Kazel... Presente!

Offering and Breaking of Bread

(If your community has a sister relationship in Central America, a mission connection, or other type of direct relationship, this would be a good time to express that solidarity with a material offering as a symbol of a new model relationship based on truth and justice. This would also be a good time to bring to the altar Central American artwork, banners or other symbols of your work of solidarity through the years. The bread, wine, or other food is brought to the altar in baskets and pitchers, possibly in a sacred dance, led by incense bearers).

(Members of returned delegations, refugees in the community, returned missioners, etc., could lead in the breaking of bread as another sign of a redeemed relationship).

Leader:
Creator God, you have given us the fruits of this earth to be shared by all, to nurture lives of dignity among all your people. This is one of the most abused truths of our world. Redeemer God, may this community, this gathering, be the seed of truth incarnate, the truth of your word spoken to us when you gave your people manna in the desert, when you proclaimed the true fast of justice in Isaiah, when Jesus fed the people in the desert, when he broke bread and shared the cup of wine, saying, "This is my body; this is my blood," and told us to do the same in his memory, as a sign of our new covenant with you.

May this food and drink be the source of the courage and strength that we need to look at the truth of our world, to become people of truth, people nurtured by truth. May this food help us to open a place within our hearts where there is room for your word of truth and life. This we ask in the names of our four sisters and all the martyrs of Central America. Amen.

(The bread, wine, or other food is now shared among the congregation. Accompany the sharing with "Pan de Vida.")

Song:
"Pan de Vida" *(Text: John. 13:1-5; Galatians 3:28-29; by Bob Hurd and Pia Moriarty / Text and music: Bob Hurd, c. 1988, OCP.)*

Prayer of Commitment
(The congregation is invited to join hands.)

Leader:
Today we have reflected on the truth that sets free. Peering into our world through the lens of the lives and deaths of our four sisters and the other martyrs of Central America, we have found a world of injustice, an injustice built on lies. We have learned that those who killed the women, those who covered up that crime, continue to kill and deceive so that we may never know truth. We have heard the word of the "father of lies." We have seen the result of the slavery of the human heart.

But we have also glimpsed the truth that sets free. We have heard the names, listened to the truth, of some of God's most precious children, of those who did not refuse to listen to God's words, but embraced them with all the love of their human hearts.

In their names, and in the name of the one who sets free, we commit ourselves this day to be people of truth, and therefore, truly free people. Let us pray. (pause)

Our response will be: We commit ourselves to you, loving God, and to one another, to live lives of truth that will make us free.

All:
We commit ourselves to you, loving God, and to one another, to live lives of truth that will make us free.

Leader:
We commit ourselves this day to make the word of Jesus our home, believing that in this home we will learn the truth that will make us free.

All:
We commit ourselves to you.

Leader:
We commit ourselves this day to reject the slavery of sin, the voice of the Satan of lies that tries to deceive our world.

All:
We commit ourselves to you.

Leader:
We commit ourselves this day to reject the lies that murder your precious people, to reject the false spirit that seeks to kill those who tell the truth.

All:
We commit ourselves to you.

Leader:
We commit ourselves this day to defend the lives of those who show us the truth, to tell their stories, to be bearers of their truth, of God's truth, in our world.

All:
We commit ourselves to you.

Leader:
We commit ourselves this day to listen, to become in this way children of God, as Jesus pronounced, to hear the truth as Jesus and the martyrs heard it from God.

All:
We commit ourselves to you.

Leader:
We commit ourselves this day to support one another in this sacred project, becoming a community of truth and justice.

All:
We commit ourselves to you.

Leader:
And now, as a sign of this commitment and solidarity, let us offer to one another an embrace of peace.

(Allow several minutes for people to greet one another in peace, then begin the music of the closing song.).

Closing Song and Recessional

Song:
"Digo, 'Sí' Señor" *(By Donna Pena, c. 1987, GIA.)*

(If the play has been performed, have the 'actors' join the service leaders in leading a solemn recessional out of the church. Allow a reception time when the community can visit together with the actors, service leaders, and one another as part of the forging of community bonds.)

(Adapted from the Religious Task Force on Central America's prayer service, "Truth That Sets Free.")

"All my days I have walked in ways that circled about myself. All my days I have marched to tunes that others played. But now, God, I am here, to seek your way, to hear your call. Take from me, at this moment, all that distracts and destroys."

Advent Reconciliation Service

The setting should be simple. Place an Advent wreath on a table draped with blue and purple cloth.

Lighting of the Advent Wreath
(Light the appropriate number of candles.)

Opening Song
"Remember Your Love" *(v.1) (Text: Mike Balhoff / Tune: Darryl Ducote and Gary Daigle, c. 1978, Damean Music.)*

Opening Prayer
Leader:
Let us kneel in prayer
...that we may "walk in the way of God"
...that our prayer may be sincere
...that our hearts may sing a new song.

(Stay kneeling in silence for a few moments.)

First Reading
All my days, I have walked in ways that circled about myself. All my days, I have marched to tunes that others played. But now, God, I am here, to seek your way, to hear your call. Take from me, at this moment, all that distracts and destroys. Take from me the fear and anxiety and insecurity that destroys the touch of your gentle love. I am here to sing the song of your forgiveness. Show me the way to rejoice in your love. (Karen Mangini)

Sung Response
"Remember Your Love" *(v.2)*

Dramatic Reading
Adapted from Mark 10:17-22 and Matthew 5

Reader 1:
There was once a person who asked Jesus, "What must I do to inherit eternal life?" I, too, ask the question. I, too, need to know the answer. What must I do to find salvation, peace, fullness of life? What must I do? What changes must I make? How must my life be different so that it can be eternal? (pause) Answer me, Jesus, please!

Reader 2:
Love God with all your heart, with all your mind, with all your soul, all the days of your life.

Reader 3:
Commitment to follow God's laws without reserve; total and complete trust in God; absolute confidence in God's love for me; this is what I am called to do! That doesn't sound too easy.

Reader 1:
The Gospel story goes on. The person responded to Jesus: "I have kept these commandments. I have always kept these commandments. What else? Is there more I can do?"

Reader 2:
Love your neighbor, as yourself.

Reader 3:
Be concerned with other people, with their welfare, their struggles, their pain - their lives. All that I would ever want for myself I should want for others. It is that simple! It is that serious!

Reader 1:
There's more to the Gospel. The person questioning Jesus is willing to try. "Yes, yes, Jesus, and is there more?" Anything, anything more to do? Jesus led the crowd up a hill. Then he sat down and began to teach the people.

Reader 2:
Blessed are the poor, for heaven is theirs.

Reader 3:
Poverty means not having enough money, and it sometimes can mean not having enough compassion.

Am I ever impoverished by my lack of compassion toward those who are materially poor? Do I ignore our homeless sisters and brothers as I pass them on the street? Do I give of my time and talent to those in need?

(Pause)

Reader 1:
Blessed are the sorrowful, for they shall be glad.

Reader 2:
Sorrow is a part of life that I often do not have control over.

Reader 3:
How do I accept the unforeseen sorrows that come my way? Do I inflict sorrow and pain on others by my lack of compassion and concern? Do I get angry when things don't go my own way? Do I get even with those who have caused my unhappiness?

(Pause)

Reader 1:
Blessed are the meek, for they shall inherit the earth.

Reader 2:
Meek doesn't mean letting people walk all over you. It means being gentle, patient and loving towards others. It also means recognizing your total dependence on God for everything you have and are.

Reader 3:
Do I thank God regularly for the many gifts I have been given, for the many beautiful people sent my way? Am I patient and kind toward the people who are a part of my life—my family, my friends, my community members? Am I a friend that someone can count on? Do I welcome the stranger in our midst?

(Pause)

Reader 1:
Blessed are the righteous, for they shall be satisfied.

Reader 2:
Being righteous means you do not lord it over others. It means you don't spend a lot of time bragging and boasting. It means you are truthful and just in your treatment of others.

Reader 3:
Am I truthful with my colleagues at work, with my spouse and my children, with my community members? Am I prejudiced toward those who are different from me? Am I just in my treatment of others? Am I humble, or do I feel the need to always be right?

(Pause)

Reader 1:
Blessed are the merciful, for they shall have mercy shown them.

Reader 2:
Mercy is not pity. Mercy is when you reach out to those in need. It is feeling with them and for them.

Reader 3:
Do I feel with those who suffer persecution or rejection? Do I feel for those who have less than I do? Do I feel with those who go to bed hungry while I waste food? Do I reach out to others that I don't like very well?

(Pause)

Reader 1:
Blessed are the pure of heart, for they shall see God.

Reader 2:
Pure of heart is not so much what I do as why I do it. It's my intention that counts.

Reader 3:
Do I do things just for the approval of others or because I really believe what I'm doing is right? Do I judge others, or am I accepting of them even if I disagree? Do I try to force my own agenda on others, always wanting them to do things my way?

(Pause)

Reader 1:
Blessed are the peacemakers, for they shall be called God's children.

Reader 2:
A peacemaker is not someone who is passive, but someone who actively listens and loves, who works for peace in our world.

Reader 3:
Do I allow people to be free by accepting them and listening to them? Am I willing to speak out when that isn't the popular thing to do? Do I attempt to resolve conflict in a nonviolent manner? Am I actively engaged in actions that will help make our society more just and peaceful?

(Pause)

Reader 1:
If you want to walk in the way of God. If you want to really respond to God's call, If you want to experience life that can be eternal, then you must become forgiving, follow me and become Christ for others.

Sung Response:
"Remember Your Love" *(v.4)*

Rite of Reconciliation

(This can be an opportunity for private confession and/or community reconciliation. Both options can be offered. For the community reconciliation, have representatives of your community stand in front of the altar, available to offer a sign of the community's forgiveness. Instrumental music can be played as people express their sorrow for their sins in whatever manner they feel most comfortable.)

Communal Prayer of Contrition

All:

God, my Creator, Redeemer and Life-Giving Spirit, I am sorry for all the times I have chosen to behave in a way that is opposed to your love, goodness and understanding. I am sorry for the wrong things that I have done and for the right things that I have failed to do. I ask for your continued love and care for me. Help me to make the correct choices, those choices that reflect my love for you, my love and concern for all those who are a part of my life and all those who cry out for justice and peace in our world. Thank you for forgiving me. Help me to be as forgiving of others as you always are of me. Amen.

Closing Prayer

Leader:

The Reign of God is most truly realized when we can stand together and call God our Father and Mother and see one another as brothers and sisters, and so we join hands and pray, "Our Father and Mother, who are in heaven…"

Final Blessing

Leader:

May the God who created you bless you with joy. May the God who loves you fill you with compassion. May the God who calls you by name be your source of strength. May the God who forgives you completely set you free from all that holds you bound. And may God always bless you and grant you and our world everlasting peace.

All:

Amen.

Closing Song

"Come to Set Us Free" *(By Bernadette Farrell, c. 1982, Bernadette Farrell.) (Adapted from a service for school worship created by Karen Mangini, principal of St. Agnes School in Concord.)*

"Mary, model of courage
Be our guide.
Model of strength
Model of truth
Model of openness
Mary, mother of
the liberator
Pray for us."

Feast of Our Lady of Guadalupe

The atmosphere of the room should be festive: an image of Our Lady of Guadalupe; red, green and white cloth; Mexican blankets; flowers (especially roses). At the foot of the image there should be a large clay pot filled with sand flanked by one or two larger candles and a basket of individual vigil candles.

Welcome

(Introduce key prayer/song leaders, explain (briefly!) what is to come and/or the reason for the gathering to honor Our Lady of Guadalupe. Practice music if it seems appropriate, and housekeeping, if there is to be a meal to follow.)

Song:
 "Come Emmanuel" *(Adapted for the season from "Come, O Lamb of God," c. 1982, Margie Duffy.)*

Invocation:

The Gloria (Sing in English and Spanish or either one after the other or woven together. Adapted (and translated into Spanish) from the Litany of Mary of Nazareth, c. Pax Christi USA.)

All:
Glory to you, God our Creator:
Breathe into us new life, new meaning.
Glory to you, God our Savior:
Lead us in your way of peace and justice.
Glory to you, Healing Spirit:
Transform us to empower others.

Gloria a ti, Dios nuestro Creador:
Infunde un nuevo sentido a nuestras vidas.
Gloria a ti, Dios nuestro Salvador:
Guíanos por el camino de la paz y la justicia.
Gloria a ti, Espíritu Consolador:
Transfórmanos para enriquecer a los demás.

Prayer

(This prayer and the reading from Isaiah to follow are from the Liturgy of the Hours for the Feast of Our Lady of Guadalupe.)

God of power and mercy, You blessed the Americas at Tepeyac with the presence of the Virgin Mary of Guadalupe. May her prayers help all men and women to accept each other as brothers and sisters. Through your justice present in our hearts may your peace reign in the world. We ask this through the one whose coming is certain, whose day draws near: your Child and our brother, Jesus. Amen.

Reading/Responsory

(The one below or any appropriate response verse could be used, either spoken or sung with the "verses" read.)

All:
Tú vas conmigo, tú vas conmigo.
In the darkness I shall have no fear.
Tú vas conmigo.

How beautiful upon the mountains
are the feet of the one who brings glad tidings,
announcing peace, bearing good news,
announcing salvation, and saying to Zion,
"Your God reigns."

All:
Tú vas conmigo, tú vas conmigo.
In the darkness I shall have no fear.
Tu vas conmigo.
Break out together in song,
O ruins of Jerusalem!
For God comforts the people,
our God redeems Jerusalem.
God has bared a holy arm
in the sight of all the nations;
all the ends of the earth will behold
the salvation of our God.

All:
Tú vas conmigo, tú vas conmigo.
In the darkness I shall have no fear.
Tú vas conmigo.

Though the mountains leave their place
and the hills be shaken,
my love shall never leave you,
nor my covenant of peace be shaken,
says God, who has mercy on you.

All:
Tú vas conmigo, tú vas conmigo.
In the darkness I shall have no fear.
Tú vas conmigo.

O afflicted one, storm-battered and unconsoled,
I lay pavements in carnelians,
and your foundations in sapphires;
I will make your battlements of rubies,
your gates of garnets, and all your walls of precious stones.
All your sons and daughters will be taught by God
and great shall be the peace of your children.
In justice you shall be established,
far from the fear of oppression,
where destruction cannot come near you.

All:
Tú vas conmigo, tú vas conmigo.
In the darkness I shall have no fear.
Tú vas conmigo.

Reading

(Or storytelling.) (From the story of Juan Diego and Our Lady - this can be told by someone who is acquainted with the story or read (perhaps in edited form) from the reading for the day in the Liturgy of the Hours.)

Shared Reflection

What does this story mean to you, how does it touch your heart, your life, your experience...

Song

"Te Agradezco" *(This song, as far as I know, is unpublished and was shared with me by a Mexican friar who was working in the parish. Notation could not be found, so this can be read or any song of thanksgiving that seems appropriate can be sung.)*

Te Agradezco (I Thank You)
Hay momentos (There are moments)
en que las palabras no alcanzan (that words are not enough)
para decirte lo que siento, (to tell you what I feel)
Bendito Salvador. (Blessed Savior)

Yo te agradezco (I thank you)
por todo lo que has hecho, (for all that you have done)
por todo lo que haces, (for all that you do)
por todo lo que harás. (for all that you will do)

Prayers

(Offer prayers—open to anyone who wishes to pray aloud—then invite all who wish to light a candle and place it in the sand at the feet of the image of Our Lady of Guadalupe, as a sign of their prayer and of the light of hope that shines in the darkness, both in the image of Our Lady and in the coming of Jesus into the world. Begin the Magnificat in accompaniment to the movement with the candles if it is a sung version. Otherwise, wait until all are finished so that it may be said in unison. If it is to be spoken by all, make sure that it is in the program.)

Magnificat

(Spanish and/or English depending on the demographics and number of the group - one example of a sung Magnificat in English is John Michael Talbot's "Holy is His Name," c. 1980, Birdwing Music/Cherry Lane Music. Administered by EMI Christian Music Publishing. Available from OCP.)

Litany of Mary of Nazareth

(Adapted Pax Christi litany - English and Spanish.)

Mary, model of courage...	María, modelo de valor...
Be our guide.	Sé nuestra guía
Model of strength...	Modelo de fortaleza...
Model of truth...	Modelo de confianza...
Model of openness...	Modelo de apertura...
Mary, mother of the liberator...	María, madre del libertador...
Pray for us.	Ruega por nosotros
Mother of the homeless...	Madre de los desamparados...
Mother of the refugee...	Madre de los refugiados...
Mother of the condemned...	Madre de los condenados...
Mary, comforter of the afflicted...	María, confortadora del afilijido...
Lead us to life.	Guíanos a la vida
Seeker of sanctuary...	De los que buscan refugio...
First disciple...	Del primer discipulo...
Seeker of God's will...	De los que buscan hacer la voluntud de Dios...
Mary, woman of mercy...	María, mujer de misericordia...
Empower us.	Apodérate de nosotros
Woman of faith...	Mujer de fe...
Woman of wisdom and understanding...	Mujer de sabiduría y entendimiento...
Woman pregnant with hope...	Mujer llena de esperanza...
Mary, Mother of Peace,	María, Madre de Paz,
we entrust our lives to you and to your son.	les confíamos nuestras vidas a ti y a tu hijo.
May we too be pregnant with hope, trusting that the reign of your son will one day dawn and spill its radiance even in the darkest corners of our world.	Que estemos nosotros llenos de esperanza, esperando que el reino de tu hijo con resplandor radiante venga a nosotros y a todos los rincones oscuros del mundo.
Teach us to live in unity,	Enséñanos a vivir en unidad.
Shelter us from despair.	Protéjenos de la desesperación.
Inspire us to act justly,	Inspíranos que actuemos justamente,
to revere all that God has made.	que honremos todo lo que Dios ha hecho.
Root us ever more firmly in the peace of Jesus. Amen.	Arráiganos aún más firmemente en la paz de Jesús. Amén.

Blessing

May God bless us and keep us. May God's goodness shine upon us and be gracious to us. May God look upon us kindly and give us peace.

Song

"Las Apariciones Guadalupanas"
(This is a traditional song for the feast and can be found in Flor y Canto published by OCP. This or any other appropriate (i.e., festive) song might be used.)

(Developed by Kate McMichael for St. Boniface Catholic Community.)

Christmas Eve Evening Prayer

This is an intimate gathering. It is preferable that people are seated in a circle. Place one large lit candle in a prominent place–either in the middle of the group or at the "front" of the circle. The candle could be set on a small table covered with red cloth and surrounded by greenery. Place small candles to be lit later in a basket near the large candle.

Call to Worship

Leader:
Let our spirits rejoice in God our Savior, who has done great things for us, and for all people.

All:
God scatters the proud in the imagination of their hearts, and raises up those who humble themselves.

Leader:
God fills the hungry with good things and satisfies those who thirst for goodness.

All:
Glory be to God in the highest, and on earth, peace and goodwill to all. Amen.

First Reading

Isaiah 9:1-6

Song:
"Christ Will Be Your Light" *(By David Haas, c. 1995, GIA.)*

Second Reading

(In three parts - pause between each reader.) Luke 2:1-14, Matthew 2:1-2, 7-12

Third Reading

The Mood of Christmas by Howard Thurman, c. 1985, Friends United Press.

The work of Christmas begins:
When the song of the angels is stilled,
When the star in the sky is gone,
When the Kings and Princes are home,
When the shepherds are back with their flocks.

The work of Christmas begins:
To find the lost, To heal the broken,
To feed the hungry, To release the prisoner,
To rebuild the nations,
To bring peace among people,
To make music in the heart.

(Silent reflection.)

Prayer of Light

Leader:

God promised a Messiah, one who would bring all people out of darkness...for he is the light of the world. Because we know and believe that Jesus is the light we have courage and faith to light our candles and pray for the many people who are in darkness in our world this evening. Though a candle is a small thing, one candle can light another and another. Light is the power to dispel darkness–the darkness of violence, the darkness of poverty, the darkness of pain. Through the sharing of our prayers and our lives, let us birth this new light in our world.

(Leader takes a small candle and lights it from the large candle and then invites others to do likewise. Leader invites people to express any prayer and/or intentions they might have for this season as they light their candles.)

Closing Prayer

(Spoken while standing.)

Side 1:

We light a candle to separate light and darkness–to praise all the elements of earth, sea and sky that sustain life.

Side 2:

We light a candle to remember the past–those people and events that have paved the road we walk today.

Side 1:

We light a candle for the future–for the children–for what we do now is the gift for those who come after.

Side 2:

We light a candle to remember the women and men, named and unnamed, who throughout time have used their power and gifts to make the world a better place.

Side 1:

We light a candle for beauty and truth and celebration and those who bring music, color, poetry, stories and new vision to the world.

Side 2:

We light a candle for all people–women and men, old and young, of all races and countries, of all faiths and beliefs and those without beliefs–who must act together for peace.

All:

We light a candle of hope whose brightness is fueled by both anger and courage, the anger needed to face the violence and pain of this world, and the courage to go on believing and dreaming of a better world yet to be. Let there be light!

Closing Song

"Silent Night" *(Text: Stille Nacht, Heilige Nacht; Joseph Mohr / Trans. John F. Young / Tune: STILLE NACHT, 66 89 66; Franz X Gruber.)*

(Adapted from an evening prayer service planned by Patricia Bruno, OP, for her religious community.)

Looking Into the Faces of the Children: Feast of the Holy Innocents

This liturgy is planned as a witness at a local military site. You will need several wooden crosses, perhaps painted white, to plant in the ground there.

Introduction

Leader:
Today death is placed side by side with birth. And why such a day of sorrow within these days of Christmas? Perhaps if told at any other season this story of such cruelty might make our faith seem absurd. But we know that in the midst of such violence, the Light which darkness cannot overcome–the Prince of Peace–has come into our world. Throughout every generation there are Herods who begrudge each new generation its very existence. Today, we remember all holy innocents of every time and place. For Rachel has not ceased her weeping.

Implanting of Crosses

Leader:
Please come forward and plant a cross for all of the children–all of the holy innocents–who have died throughout our world as a result of violence: from the ravages of war, from torture, abuse and neglect, from repressive boycotts and greedy economic policies that lead to hunger and starvation, from our hardness of heart.

Song:
"Cry of Ramah" *(Sung as people plant the crosses.) (By Colleen Fulmer, c. 1985, Loretto Spirituality Network.)*

Readings on the Holy Innocents

Leader:
Why do you come to me and why do I come to you on this day?

Reader 1:
The Innocents of Bethlehem. - Matthew 2:13-18

Leader:
Why do you come to me and why do I come to you on this day?

Reader 2:
The Innocents of Today *(Adapted from A Prayer/Pledge of Responsibility for Children by Ina J. Hughes.)*

We pray and accept responsibility for children who put chocolate fingers everywhere,
who like to be tickled,
who stomp in puddles and ruin their new pants,
who sneak popsicles before supper,
who erase holes in math workbooks,
who can never find their shoes.

Reader 3:
And we pray and accept responsibility for those who stare at photographers from behind barbed wire, who can't bound down the street in a new pair of sneakers, who never "counted potatoes," who are born in places where we wouldn't be caught dead, who never go to the circus, who live in an X-rated world.

Reader 2:
We pray and accept responsibility for children who bring us sticky kisses and fistfuls of dandelions, who sleep with the dog and bury goldfish, who hug us in a hurry and forget their lunch money, who cover themselves with Band-Aids and sing off key, who squeeze toothpaste all over the sink, who slurp their soup.

Reader 3:
And we pray and accept responsibility for those who never get dessert, who have no safe blanket to drag behind them, who watch their parents watch them die, who can't find any bread to steal, who don't have any rooms to clean up, whose pictures aren't on anybody's dresser, whose monsters are real.

Reader 2:
We pray and accept responsibility for children who spend all their allowance before Tuesday, who throw tantrums in the grocery store and pick at their food, who like ghost stories, who shove dirty clothes under the bed, and never rinse out the tub, who get visits from the tooth fairy, who don't like to be kissed in front of the carpool, who squirm in church or temple and scream in the phone, whose tears we sometimes laugh at and whose smiles can make us cry.

Reader 3:
And we pray and accept responsibility for those whose nightmares come in the daytime, who will eat anything, who have never seen a dentist, who aren't spoiled by anybody, who go to bed hungry and cry themselves to sleep, who live and move, but have no being.

Reader 2:
We pray and accept responsibility for children who want to be carried and for those who must, For those we never give up on and for those who don't get a second chance, For those we smother...and for those who will grab the hand of anybody kind enough to offer it.
(Pause for silent reflection.)

Intercessions

Leader:
Please offer any prayers you have on this day. Response: Grant us Peace the world does not give!

Our Response

Leader:
Why do you come to me and why do I come to you on this day?

All:
We come to you because the world needs to be saved for the future generations who must return the earth to peace. We have come to you not just for the stoppage of nuclear proliferation, nuclear plants, nuclear bombs, nuclear waste, but to stop the proliferation of nuclear minds, of nuclear generals, of nuclear presidents, of nuclear scientists who spread human and nuclear waste over the world.

Leader:
Why do you come to me and why do I come to you on this day?

All:

We come to you because the world needs sanity now, needs men and women who will not work to produce nuclear weapons, who will give up their need for excess wealth and learn how to share the world's resources. We come to you because we need to turn our eyes to the beauty of this planet, to the bright green laughter of trees, to the beautiful human animals waiting to smile their unprostituted smiles.

We come to you to talk about our inexperience at living as human beings—through death marches and camps, through middle passages and slavery and thundering countries raining hungry faces.

Leader:

Why do you come to me and why do I come to you on this day?

All:

We are here to move against leaving our shadows implanted on the earth while our bodies disintegrate in nuclear lightning. We are here because our scientists must be stripped of their imperialist dreams. We are here between the voices of our ancestors and the noise of the planet, between the surprise of death and life.

Leader:

Why do you come to me and why do I come to you on this day?

All:

We are here to say to YOU: My body is full of veins like the bombs waiting to burst with blood. We must learn to suckle life not bombs and rhetoric rising up in red, white and blue patriotism. We are here. And our breaths must thunder across the land arousing new breaths. New life. New people, who will live in peace and honor.

Song:

"Chant of A Wide Terrain" *(By Carolyn McDade from the album "This Tough Spun Web," c. 1986, Carolyn McDade.)*

(Adapted from a prayer service prepared by Carol Gilbert, OP, and Ardeth Platte, OP, for prayer and public witness at the ELF Site in Republic, Michigan.)

Our Cry
for
Justice

A Vigil of Witness Against Capital Punishment: Signing the Declaration of Life

Set up a table with candles at the front where copies of the "Declaration of Life" and pens are placed for the signing that will take place at the end of the service.

Opening

Leader:
Jesus was a victim of the death penalty.

Reading:
Luke 23:32-34

A Prayer to Abolish the Death Penalty

by Helen Prejean, CSJ *(Prayer card available through Pax Christi USA.)*

Leader:
Let us pray

All:
God of Compassion,
You let your rain fall on the just and unjust.
Expand and deepen our hearts
so that we may love as You love,
even those among us
who have caused the greatest pain by taking life.
For there is in our land a great cry for vengeance
as we fill up death rows and kill the killers
in the name of justice, in the name of peace.
Jesus, our brother,
you suffered execution at the hands of the state
but you did not let hatred overcome you.
Help us reach out to victims of violence
so that our enduring love may help them heal.
Holy Spirit of God,
You strengthen us in the struggle for justice.
Help us to work tirelessly
for the abolition of state-sanctioned death
and to renew our society in its very heart
so that violence will be no more. Amen.

Song

"Singing For Our Lives" *(By Holly Near, c. 1979, Hereford Music.)*

Reading

(Statement by Marietta Jaeger, murder victim's mother.)

Believe me, there are no amounts of retaliatory acts that will compensate for the loss of my little girl or restore her to my arms. Even to say that the death of one malfunctioning person is going to be just retribution is an insult to her immeasurable worth to me.

Reading

(Message written on behalf of Salamat Masih, Pakistani boy sentenced to death for blasphemy.)

Thank you ever so much for your letter of December 22, 1994. Thanks to the sustained efforts of Amnesty International and a host of other organizations, I feel that my contact with the free world has not been severed. I have received thousands of cards, facilitation messages and well-wishing letters from all over the world. I was delighted to get the drawings from children. Please thank them all on my behalf. It is this immense love which has given me great hope for the future.

(Silent reflection.)

Sung Response

"Singing For Our Lives" *(refrain only)*

Reading

(Statement by Coretta Scott King.) As one whose husband and mother-in-law have both died the victims of murder assassination, I stand firmly and unequivocally opposed to the death penalty for those convicted of capital offenses. An evil deed is not redeemed by an evil deed of retaliation. Justice is never advanced in the taking of a human life. Morality is never upheld by legalized murder.

Reading

(Final statement by Ken Saro-Wiwa to the military court.) We all stand before history. I am a man of peace, of ideas. Appalled by the denigrating poverty of my people who live on a richly endowed land, distressed by their political marginalization and economic strangulation...I have devoted my intellectual and material resources and my very life to a cause in which I have total belief and from which I cannot be blackmailed or intimidated. I have no doubt at all about the ultimate success of my cause...Neither imprisonment nor death can stop our ultimate victory...

On trial also is the Nigerian nation, its present rulers and those who assist them. Any nation which can do to the weak and disadvantaged what the Nigerian nation has done to the Ogoni loses a claim to independence and to freedom from outside influence. I am not one of those who shy away from protesting injustice and oppression, arguing that they are expected in a military regime. The military do not act alone. They are supported by a gaggle of politicians, lawyers, judges, academics, and businesspersons, all of them hiding under the claim that they are only doing their duty, men and women too afraid to wash their pants of urine. We all stand on trial for by our actions we have denigrated our country and jeopardized the future of our children.

(Silent reflection.)

Sung Response

"Singing For Our Lives" *(refrain only)*

Reading

(Excerpt from *Statement on Capital Punishment,* c. 1980, United States Catholic Conference, Washington DC. Used with permission. All rights reserved.)

Abolition of the death penalty would promote values that are important to us as citizens and as Christians...It is a manifestation of our freedom as moral persons striving for a just society. It is also a challenge to us as a people to find ways of dealing with criminals that manifest intelligence and compassion rather than power and vengeance...We urge our brothers and sisters in Christ to remember the teaching of Jesus who called us to be reconciled with those who have injured us (Mt. 5:43-45) and pray for forgiveness for our

sins "as we forgive those who have sinned against us" (Mt. 6:12). We call on you to contemplate the crucified Christ who set us the supreme example of forgiveness and of the triumph of compassionate love.

(Silent reflection.)

Our Response

Song:
"Here I Am, Lord"
(Text and music by Daniel L. Schutte, c. 1981, Daniel L Schutte and New Dawn Music.)

Leader:
We have heard God's call in the dark of a night filled with hatred, fear and revenge. We have heard the cry of God's people—the plea of those on death row for mercy. We have heard the cry of the families of victims of senseless crimes for healing, for wholeness, for an end to the bloodshed. Let us now respond to these cries and to God's call to be instruments of healing and love, instruments of true justice. Let us respond in prayer and in deed.

Prayers of Petition

Leader:
Our response to the petitions will be: Oh God, Hear Our Prayer. God of Life and Compassion, we stand before You, members of a society needing Your healing. We are confident that You will hear the prayers of our hearts. And so we ask that Your compassion be poured out on our world...

All:
Oh God, Hear Our Prayer.

Reader 1:
God of Compassion, we pray for the victims of crime and their families. May they know Your healing presence that transforms pain and anger in ways never thought possible, we pray.

All:
Oh God, Hear Our Prayer.

Reader 2:
God of Compassion, we pray for the victims of capital punishment and their families. May they be comforted in Your love, we pray.

All:
Oh God, Hear Our Prayer.

Reader 1:
God of Compassion, we pray for those who participate in executions and in all executions done in our name. May they, and we, be open to the ways You minister grace and conversion in the least likely places, we pray.

All:
Oh God, Hear Our Prayer.

Reader 2:
God of Compassion, we pray for those caught in the web of violence of our time, a violence against one another from the womb to the tomb. May they come to know Your breath of life, we pray.

All:
Oh God, Hear Our Prayer.

Reader 1:
God of Compassion, we pray for those oppressed by structures and policies that perpetuate violence and injustices. May we be inspirited with the courage to speak and act nonviolently for justice, peace and social transformation, that Your Reign may come, we pray.

All:
Oh God, Hear Our Prayer.

Reader 2:
God of Compassion, we pray for each of us suffering the effects of estrangement and polarization. May we open our hearts to Your gifts of forgiveness, reconciliation and unconditional love, we pray.

All:
Oh God, Hear Our Prayer.

Signing of the Declaration of Life

Leader:
As a sign of our willingness not only to pray for an end to capital punishment, but to work for its abolition, as well. As a sign of our willingness to embody in our lives, to proclaim with our very bodies, the forgiveness of which Jesus spoke, I invite any of you who so desire to come forward now and sign the "Declaration of Life," a document which states that if we are murdered, we do not want the perpetrators of such a crime to receive the death penalty. We want the spiral of violence to end with us.

(As people come forward to sign the document, play "Here I Am, Lord" in the background.)

Closing Prayer

Leader:
And so we go forward now, knowing that the violence stops with us. Bless us, O Compassionate One, and give us strength for the journey. Fill us with that amazing grace which breaks down walls of hatred and fear and allows Your love and mercy to enter in, that the process of healing and reconciliation might begin. Amen.

Closing Song

"Amazing Grace" *(Text: by Henry Williams Baker / Music: traditional Irish melody.)*

(Adapted from a vigil organized by All Saints Church in Pasadena, California, on the eve of the scheduled execution of Thomas M. Thompson in the state of California, and in remembrance of the woman he murdered, Ginger Fleischli, and, also adapted from a prayer service from an unknown source.)

Declaration of Life

I, the undersigned, being of sound and disposing mind and memory, do hereby in the presence of witnesses make this Declaration of Life.

Background

1. I believe that the killing of one human being by another is morally wrong.
2. I am opposed to capital punishment on any grounds whatsoever.
3. I believe it is morally wrong for any state or other governmental entity to take the life of a human being by way of capital punishment for any reason.
4. I believe that capital punishment is not a deterrent to crime and serves only the purpose of revenge.

THEREFORE, I hereby declare that should I die as a result of a violent crime, I request that the person or persons found guilty of homicide for my killing not be subject to or put in jeopardy of the death penalty under any circumstances, no matter how heinous their crime or how much I may have suffered.

I believe it is morally wrong for my death to be the reason for the killing of another human being.

I request that the Prosecutor or District Attorney having the jurisdiction of the person or persons alleged to have committed my homicide not file or prosecute an action for capital punishment as a result of my homicide.

I request that this Declaration be made admissible in any trial of any person charged with my homicide and read and delivered to the jury.

I request the Court to allow this Declaration to be admissible as a statement of the victim at the sentencing of the person or persons charged and convicted of my homicide; and to pass sentence in accordance with my wishes.

I request that the Governor or other executive officer(s) grant pardon, clemency or take whatever action is necessary to stay and prohibit the carrying out of the execution of any person or persons found guilty of my homicide.

This Declaration is not meant to be, and should not be taken as, a statement that the person or persons who have committed my homicide should go unpunished.

I request that my family and friends take whatever actions are necessary to carry out the intent and purpose of this Declaration; and I further request them to take no action contrary to this Declaration.

During my life, I want to feel confident that under no circumstances whatsoever will my death result in the capital punishment of another human being.

I request that, should I die under the circumstances as set forth in this Declaration and the death penalty is requested, my family, friends and personal representative deliver copies of this Declaration as follows: to the Prosecutor or District Attorney having jurisdiction over the person or persons charged with my homicide; to the attorney representing the person or persons charged with my homicide; to the judge presiding over the case involving my homicide; for recording, to the Recorder of the County in which my homicide took place and to the Recorder of the county in which the person or persons charged with my homicide are to be tried; to all newspapers, radio and television stations of general circulation in the County in which my homicide took place and the County in which the person or persons charged with my homicide are to be tried; and to any other person, persons or entities my family, friends or personal representative deem appropriate in order to carry out my wishes as set forth herein.

I affirm under the pain and penalties of perjury that the above Declaration of Life is true.

_____   _____
        Declarant signature   **Witness signature**

_____   _____
      Declarant printed name   **Witness printed name**

State of_____   **County of**_____

Before me, a Notary Public in and for said County and State, personally appeared the Declarant and acknowledged the execution of the foregoing instrument

this _____ day of _____, _____.

Witness my hand and notarial seal_____ Notary Public

A Service of Hope: Prayer Service on the Occasion of an Execution

This service can be held outside of a prison on the eve of an execution or in a church. A container holds candles representing the victim(s) and the executed. During the prayer service two people will reverently light the candles. These burn throughout the service and at the end. The candles representing the victim(s) are extinguished during the litany. The one representing the person to be executed is not extinguished. Small candles need to be provided for people to light during the latter part of the vigil.

Welcome

(Informally welcome people, introducing presiders and musicians, invite, and set the tone for the service. If it is a small group, you may want to invite people to introduce themselves to one another.)

Opening Hymn

"God, Teach Us Peacemaking"
(Traditional Irish melody, Harm. by David Evans / Words by Jane Parker Huber / Music from the Revised Church Hymnary, 1927, c. 1980, Jane Parker Huber. Used by permission of Oxford University Press. Taken from A Singing Faith *by Jane Parker Huber, #64.)*

Call to Prayer

Leader 1:
(Invite the community to pray using the words below or other appropriate words.)

Let us pray.
Loving God, be with us tonight as we gather to pray for all those affected by violence.

We pray for *(name)*, a victim of violence in *(year)*.

We pray for healing for her/his family and friends. Comfort and heal all those whose loved ones have died through violence in the state of *(name your state)*.

We pray for *(name)*—who is scheduled to die a violent death tonight. We pray for his/her family and friends—for their comfort and consolation. We pray especially for all others on death row in this state and across the country.

Help our nation, the state of *(name your state)*, and each of us to turn from revenge to forgiveness and unconditional love. Bring an end to the death penalty in this country. Hear our prayer.

All:
Amen.

Prayer of Confession

Leader 2:
Please respond: *Forgive us our sin.*

All:
Forgive us our sin.

Leader 2:
We recognize that the death penalty is part of the violence in our society. Let us ask forgiveness for all forms of violence. We acknowledge the violence we perpetuate in our world: providing weapons; imposing crushing debt payments; withholding food from governments which we call "enemies."

All:

Forgive us our sin.

We acknowledge the violence within our country: allowing millions of children and elderly to live in hunger and without homes or shelter; depriving the sick of adequate health care; imprisoning and executing racial minorities in disproportionate numbers.

All:

Forgive us our sin.

We acknowledge the violence in our communities and homes: battering children and abusing women; discriminating against minorities; destroying our environment; building walls of anger and hatred.

All:

Forgive us our sin.

We invite you to name the acts of violence which lie heavy on your heart.

(After all have had a chance to respond, leader leads response.)

All:

Forgive us our sinfulness, O God. Heal us of the wounds that afflict us and our society. Empower us to erase the hatred and violence that continue to scourge people and creation. Empower those of us gathered here tonight to continue our efforts to work for an end to the death penalty.

(Invite the congregation to be seated.)

Lighting of Candles
(While the congregation observes a few minutes of silence, two people light the candles in the front of the church.)

First Reading
(If family or friends of the person to be executed are present, invite them to tell something about the person and/or if there are members of murder victims' families present, invite them to offer testimony, as well.)
(Silence.)

Second Reading
(Adapted from "Fear To Hope: Statement of Religious Leaders in Virginia on Public Safety and the Death Penalty.")

Our religious traditions impel us to be concerned about public safety and to evaluate the death penalty from a moral perspective.

We understand the fears of the general public regarding crime. We share these fears. Drug trafficking and murder are terrible scourges that cry out for effective remedies. We must encourage personal responsibility, basic moral values and a respect for human life. At the same time, we must call upon society as a whole to remedy the social circumstances that contribute to hopelessness, despair and a breakdown in respect for the value of human life. Crushing poverty and chronic unemployment breed violence.

Despite our fears, we are called to look with honesty, courage and moral conviction at how our state of (_____) is attempting to stem the tide of violence. We can understand how fear and frustration may tempt us to find simple solutions. We are convinced that the escalating imposition of the death penalty is a misguided attempt to improve public safety.

We believe that the death penalty is morally objectionable and pragmatically ineffective for several reasons:

1. The death penalty is not a deterrent to crime. Numerous national and international studies have failed to document any deterrence effect. Most nations have abandoned it long ago and all of these nations have lower violent crime rates than our own.

2. The application of the death penalty in our nation is clearly discriminatory. Again, numerous studies have documented this fact. If a suspect is poor or a member of a minority group, the death penalty is much more likely to be imposed.

3. The death penalty eliminates the possibility of rehabilitation and it is more costly to administer than life in prison. Fiscal responsibility alone calls us to reexamine the death penalty.

4. The death penalty does not allow for human error. There is always the horrible possibility that an innocent person will be executed...Our sad history is that innocent persons have been executed, at least 23 in this century.

5. The death penalty undermines respect for human life and breeds yet more violence. State sanctioned killing weakens respect for human life. As a society, our attempts to encourage a respect for human life will not be credible until we repudiate the death penalty.

(Silence.)

Sung Response
"God, Teach us Peacemaking" *(refrain only)*

Third Reading
Matthew 5:43-48 or 7:1-5

(Silence.)

Closing Ritual
(Leader 1 invites all to stand.)

Leader 1:
We live in a time of darkness. Many lives have been snuffed out senselessly. Tonight we remember the victims and those executed in *(name your state)* in retaliation for their deaths, since the restitution of the death penalty.

(Remind the congregation that after both the name of the victim and of the person who is going to be executed have been read to respond with "Hold them in your care, God." Leader 1 reads the name of the victim, and Leader 2 reads the name of the executed. One person extinguishes one of the candles as the name of the victim is read.)

(Silence after the reading of the names.)

Leader 2:
(Invite people to come forward and encircle the candles. As they come forward, they light their candles from the one left burning. People can remain in silence or offer prayers, reflections, songs. An appropriate song is "Swing Low Sweet Chariot." They are invited to continue holding vigil until the execution takes place.)

Closing Prayer

Leader 2:
But darkness has not triumphed. Death and suffering are not to triumph over life. Revenge and anger shall not triumph over forgiveness and love. We pray that God will bless us, and go before us in the flame of these candles which we carry in our hearts as reminders of our burning desire to be co-creators of peace and justice in our world.

(Adapted from a prayer service created by Dr. Kathleen Kenney and Sr. Marilyn Winter, OP, from the Office of Justice and Peace and the Office of Worship, Catholic Diocese of Richmond, Virginia, on the occasion of executions being held regularly in the State of Virginia.)

Prayer Vigil for Victims of Gun Violence

Call to Prayer

Leader:
By gathering for a brief prayer vigil, we will stand in solidarity with our brothers and sisters against those who destroy our city by destroying its citizens. Whenever someone is killed, we are all affected. Whenever the life of one member of our body is extinguished, we all suffer.

Opening Scripture

Romans 8:31-39

Psalm

Psalm 23 *(This psalm is read by all.)*

Prayers of the Gathered Community

Leader:
I invite you to now offer any prayers that are in your heart. *(After each prayer the leader closes with "God, in Your Mercy" to which the group responds "Hear Our Prayer.")*

The Prayer of Jesus

Hymn:
"We Shall Overcome"
"We Shall Overcome"
"We Shall Live in Peace" *(someday)*
"We Shall Live in Hope" *(today)*

Closing Scripture

Revelations 21:1-7 *(Before the scripture passage is read the leader gives the following explanation of the ritual which will take place during the reading.)*

Leader:
As we listen to the words of the one who saw the coming of a new heaven and a new earth, a new Jerusalem, a new *(name your city)*, let us anoint this spot which has been so desecrated-and reconsecrate it to God and to God's desire for healing and love, for justice and peace. Let us reconsecrate it as a sign of hope for our city and all of its citizens, and for our world.

(During the reading someone anoints the ground with oil.)

Closing Prayer

Leader:
May the God of Peace and Mercy and Infinite Love be with you.

All:
And also with you.

Leader:
Let us go forth now remembering in sorrow the death of (name of victim) and carrying his/her memory with us as we pledge ourselves anew to work for peace in our world, in his/her name and in the name of our God who desires Life for all.

All:
Amen. So be it.

(Adapted from a vigil held in memory of JaRyan Cummings, age 5, at the site of his murder. JaRyan was the 94th victim of a violent death in Indianapolis as of July 1997. The vigil was developed by the Sanctuary Church Movement in Indianapolis, Indiana, in response to the need to promote peace in the city and a safe haven for all its citizens. For more information, contact The Church Federation of Greater Indianapolis at 317/926-5371.)

Unite Us in Justice and Love:
A Call for an End to Racism

Musical Preparation
Since several of these songs might be unfamiliar to the congregation, you probably want to practice the music before you begin the service.

(Begin in silence.)

Gathering Words
All:
(Based on The World Peace Prayer)

Lead us from death to life, from falsehood to truth.
Lead us from despair to hope, from fear to trust.
Let peace fill our hearts, our World, our universe.
Let us dream together, pray together, work together,
To build one world of peace and justice for all.

Hymn
"The Love of God is Broad Like Beach and Meadow"
(Text: Anders Frostenson / Tune: Lars Ake Lundberg, Melody and Swedish: c. Verbum Forlag AB, Stockholm, Sweden. English Text: Fred Kaan, c. Hope Publishing Co., Carol Stream, IL (in U.S.).)

Readings and Responses
(One or several readers can do the readings.)

It is an old problem. From early times debates raged over who could be in the communities of faith and who could not. Today we remember the pain.

In the Israelite community some called others "the descendants of Ham and Cannan" and proclaimed in Genesis 9: "Cursed be Canaan; lowest of slaves shall he be to his brothers." Divisions began early in our history.

Sung Response:
"Kyrie" *(Written in four languages: Swahili, English, French and Spanish) by G.M. Kolisi: South Africa; Arrangement: Anders Nyberg, c. Ultryck, Box 3039, S-750 03 Uppsala, Sweden. U.S. rights, Walton Music, 170 N.E. 33rd St., Fort Lauderdale, FL, 33334, U.S.A. French, Joelle Gouel, c. 1991, WCC.)*

Some in the community of faith called for racial purity, as in Nehemiah 13: "In those days also I saw Jews who had married women of Ashdod, Ammon and Moab; and half of their children spoke the language of Ashdod, and they could not speak the language of Judah, but spoke the language of various peoples. And I contended with them and cursed them and beat some of them and pulled out their hair; and I made them take an oath in the name of God, saying: You shall not give your daughters to their sons, or take their daughters for your sons or for yourselves." Division began early in our history.

Sung Response:
"Kyrie"

Some argued as in Acts 17: "From one ancestor God made all nations to inhabit the whole earth, and allotted the times of their existence and the boundaries of the places where they would live." Our history is filled with the setting of boundaries, denying visas, proclaiming homelands, creating reservations and ghettos, dividing people. We are still creating division.

Sung Response:
"Kyrie"

We read in the letter of Paul to the Romans, Chapter 11, regarding Jews and the Gentiles, and whether the Gentiles could be accepted into the faith (verses 13-20):

Now I am speaking to you Gentiles. Inasmuch then as I am an apostle to the Gentiles, I glorify my ministry in order to make my own people jealous, and thus save some of them. For if their rejection is the reconciliation of the world, what will their acceptance be but life from the dead! If the part of the dough offered as first fruits is holy, then the whole batch is holy; and if the root is holy, then the branches also are holy. But if some of the branches were broken off, and you, a wild olive shoot, were grafted in their place to share the rich root of the olive tree, do not boast over the branches. If you do boast, remember that it is not you that supports the root, but the root that supports you. You will say, "Branches were broken off so that I might be grafted in." That is true. They were broken off because of their unbelief, but you stand only through faith. So do not become proud, but stand in awe.

Sung Response:
"Kyrie"

Prayer

Leader:
Before You, O God, we are ashamed, for we continue to bring division into the work of Your creation.

All:
Christ, have mercy on us.

Leader:
We continue to draw boundaries between Your children, whether of race or nation, culture or class. ALL: Christ, have mercy on us.

Leader:
We have ignored the beam in our own eye, seeing only the mote in our neighbor's eye.

All:
Christ, have mercy on us.

Leader:
Prevent us, O God, from accepting too easily our state of division; save us from regarding as normal that which is a sin against You and against humanity.

All:
Unite us in justice and in love.

Leader:
Deliver us from a spirit of narrowness, bitterness or prejudice, teaching us instead to recognize the gifts of other cultures and experiences.

All:
Unite us in justice and in love.

Leader:
By your power, O God, graft us together in a common tree of life, rooted in the love of Christ Jesus.

All:
We ask this in Christ's name. Amen.

Allelujah
Andantino, Romania *(no copyright)*

Gospel Reading
Mark 12:28-34

Allelujah
(Silence.)

Prayers of Intercession
Sung Response:
"Kyrie Eleison" in Aramaic *(By Metropolitan Mar Gregorios Yohanna Ibrahim: Syria, found in 1995 service prepared by the World Council of Churches, Geneva, Switzerland (no copyright).)*

Prayer of Jesus

Passing of the Peace

Benediction

Hymn
"Soki Toko" *(By Christiane Engetele: Zaire, found in 1995 service prepared by the World Council of Churches, Geneva, Switzerland (no copyright).)*

(Adapted from a worship service prepared for the World Council of Churches' Central Committee on September 16, 1995.)

own. We have our bodies and our spirits and the justice of our cause as our weapons...Those who are willing to sacrifice have very little difficulty with people. They know what they are all about. People can't help but want to be near them to help them and work with them. That's what love is all about. *(Cesar Chavez.)*

Response:
Porque la locura de Dios es más sabia que los humanos, y la flaqueza de Dios, más poderosa que los humanos. *(For God's folly is wiser than humans, and God's weakness more powerful than humans. 1 Cor. 1:25.)*

Leader:
Nonviolence is a very powerful weapon. Most people don't understand the power of nonviolence and tend to be amazed by the whole idea. Those who have been involved in bringing about change and see the difference between violence and nonviolence are firmly committed to a lifetime of nonviolence, not because it is easy or because it is cowardly, but because it is an effective and very powerful way. Nonviolence means people in action. *(Cesar Chavez.)*

Response:
Pero los que confían en Yavé renuevan las fuerzas, echan alas como de águila, corren sin cansarse y caminan sin fatigarse. *(They that hope in God will renew their strength, they will soar as with eagles' wings. They will run and not grow weary, walk and not grow faint. Is. 40:31.)*

Leader:
We can choose to use our lives for others to bring about a better and more just world for our children. People who make that choice will know hardship and sacrifice. But if you give yourself totally to the nonviolent struggle for peace and justice, you also find that people will give you their hearts and you will never go hungry and never be alone. And in giving yourself you will discover a whole new life full of meaning and love. *(Cesar Chavez.)*

Response:
Pedid, y se os dará; buscad, y hallaréis; llamad, y se os abrirá. *(Ask, and you will receive. Seek, and you will find. Knock, and it will be opened to you. Matthew 7:7.)*

Leader:
What do we want the church to do? We don't ask for more cathedrals. We don't ask for bigger churches or fine gifts. We ask for its presence with us, beside us, as Christ among us. We ask the church to sacrifice with the people for social change, for justice, and for love of brother and sister. We don't ask for words. We ask for deeds. We don't ask for paternalism. We ask for servanthood. *(Cesar Chavez)*

Response:
Amen.

Song
"Here I am, Lord" *(Text: Isaiah 6; Dan Schutte, Tune: Dan Schutte; Arr. by Michael Pope, SJ, John Weissrock, c. 1981, Daniel L. Schutte and North American Liturgy Resource.)*

Charge to Those Present
(From *Loaves and Fishes* by Dorothy Day (adapted) c. 1963, Harper & Row.)

Listen to the words of Dorothy Day: Young people say, "What good can one person do? What is the sense of our small effort?" They cannot see that we must lay one brick at a time, take one step at a time; we can be responsible only for the one action of the present moment. But we can beg for an increase of love in our hearts that will vitalize and transform all our individual actions, and know that God will take them and multiply them, as Jesus multiplied the loaves and fishes.

The greatest challenge of the day is how to bring about a revolution of the heart, a revolution which has to start with each one of us. When we begin to take the lowest place, to wash the feet of others, to love our brothers (and sisters) with that burning love, that passion, which led to the Cross, then we can truly say, "Now I have begun."

Leader:

Let us begin with action. *(Leader explains National Farm Worker Ministry's current actions requested by farm worker organizations around the country. Some actions can be done after the gathering, i.e. letter-writing. Other actions can be done after the participants return home, i.e. making phone calls.)*

Closing Prayer

(By His Eminence Roger Cardinal Mahoney (adapted).)

Leader:

Let us go forward now to stand in solidarity with farm workers, our sisters and brothers, throughout the country. Let us pray:

All:

God of goodness, you give us the land to provide us with food. Hear the prayers of Your people and give all who work on that land a full measure of human dignity and justice. May we bring the spirit of Christ to all our efforts, and may these efforts yield a rich harvest of justice, peace, and love. We ask this in the name of Jesus Christ. Amen.

(Adapted from materials developed by the National Farm Worker Ministry, 1337 W. Ohio St., Chicago, IL 60622, 312/829-6436.)

A Day of Prayer for Victims of Landmines

Materials for this day of prayer were one of the most popular items produced by Lutheran Peace Fellowship. In these materials LPF suggests possibly holding this service on Veterans Day or on the Feast of the Holy Innocents.

Litany of Repentance

Reader 1:
Every 20 minutes, somewhere in the world, someone is killed or maimed by an anti-personnel landmine.

(Silence)

Sung Response:
"Let Your Mercy Be on Us" *(refrain only)*
(Text: Psalm 33:1, 4-5, 12, 18-19, 20, 22; Para. by Marty Haugen; Refrain 1 trans. c. 1969, ICEL; Refrain 2 and verses c. 1987, GIA / Tune: Marty Haugen, c. 1987, GIA.)

Reader 2:
An average of 26,000 people are killed or injured worldwide by landmines each year.

Sung Response:
(Refrain)

Reader 1:
Ten million landmines are produced each year.

Sung Response:
(Refrain)

Reader 2:
Over 60 countries have landmine incidents each year. The nations most affected by landmines are Afghanistan, Angola, Cambodia, Eritrea, Ethiopia, Iraq, Kuwait, Mozambique, Somalia, Sudan and the former Yugoslavia.

Sung Response:
(Refrain)

Reader 1:
The major producers and exporters of landmines over the past 25 years are Belgium, Bulgaria, China, the former Czechoslovakia, France, Hungary, Italy, the former Soviet Union, the United Kingdom, the former Yugoslavia and the United States. In September 1997, the U.S. refused to sign a treaty, endorsed by nearly 100 other nations, which would ban anti-personnel landmines.

Sung Response:
(Refrain and v.4.)

First Reading

"A Landmine in the Garden: The Story of Janita Domingas"
(From Angola, Africa. By Jonathon Frerichs, Lutheran World Relief.)

Rebels fighting against the Angolan government captured Janita Domingas' village in 1992. "The soldiers chased us and we hid in the bush," she says. "We spent the night outside in

"Janita stepped on a landmine in her own field. Nine months pregnant at the time, she spent an entire day lying where she fell until a passerby took her back to Luena, where she gave birth to a stillborn child."

the rain. In the morning we walked to the town of Luena and found refuge in a school." But then Luena itself came under siege. For weeks there was "no food, no airplanes," she says, referring to the relief flights that bring in everything from corn from the United Nations to quilts from the Lutheran World Relief (LWR).

Janita became so hungry that she decided to walk back to her village to get food from the garden for her family. She could not have known that rebel soldiers had already mined the area, scattering lethal antipersonnel landmines in fields, roads and gardens.

Janita stepped on a landmine in her own field. "The explosion shattered my leg," she says. Nine months pregnant at the time, she spent an entire day lying where she fell until a passerby took her back to Luena, where she gave birth to a stillborn child.

"My husband loved me when I was whole," she says, as she tells how she was abandoned after the landmine explosion. "If we women are handicapped, no man wants us. We cannot carry things as women are expected to do in our culture," she explains, with a hint of ridicule in her voice. Her eyes glisten with tears.

Crutches are hard to find and also expensive. Artificial limbs or physical therapy barely exist. Who helps such Angolans? "Only Lutheran World Federation (LWF)," according to women like Janita. The LWF with considerable LWR support has been in Luena since 1988—the only aid agency to stay through the last eight years of war, siege and stalemate.

Prayer

"A Prayer from Bishop Desmond Tutu" (adapted)
(The following prayer was offered by Archbishop Desmond Tutu of South Africa as part of the International Campaign to Ban Landmines.)

Leader:
Let us pray:
How can I walk in Your way without feet?
I was collecting sticks for the fire when I lost my arms.
I was taking the goats to water when I lost my feet.
I have a head but my head does not understand why there are landmines in the grazing land or why there is a tripwire across the dusty road to the market.
My heart is filled with a long ache...
I did not protest when the soldiers planted fear into the earth
that smothers the old people and the anxious mothers and fills the young men with hate. God, we are all accomplices in the crime of war which is a lust for power at all costs.
The cost is too much for humanity to bear.
God, give us back our humanity, our ubuntu.
Teach us to serve You without arms. Amen.

Third Reading

Jeremiah 31:15-17

Intercessory Prayers

Leader:
Let us now lift up our prayers to our God.

Sung Response:
"O Lord, Hear My Prayer" *(Text: Psalm 102; Taize Community, 1982 / Tune: Jacques Berthier, c. 1982, Les Presses de Taize.)*

Reader:
O God, our refuge, we pray for lands that have been torn by war, and for people who long for a safe return home. Keep your children safe from the threat of landmines in their fields, roads, bridges, school yards and playgrounds. Bring healing and hope to those who have been maimed by war. We pray especially for Angola, for Mozambique, for Cambodia, for Bosnia, for Afghanistan. *(Invite people to name other countries.)*

Sung Response:
(Refrain)

Reader:
Bless the work of all those who risk their lives working for peace: removing landmines, ministering to refugees and assisting their repatriation, working for economic development in war-torn countries, and working for nonviolent solutions to conflict.

Sung Response:
(Refrain)

Reader:
Bless all of us gathered here. Make us instruments of justice and peace that war and hatred and fear might be no more, that Rachel's weeping and mourning might finally cease. Let us be the hope for the future of our world.

Sung Response:
(Refrain)

Closing Prayer

All:
by Pope John Paul II (adapted)
(From Ecumenical Services for Peace and Justice Advocates, Philippines.)

To the Creator of nature and of men and women, of truth and beauty, we pray:

Hear our voice, for it is the voice of the victims of all wars and violence among individuals and nations;

Hear our voice, for it is the voice of all children who suffer and will suffer when people put their faith in weapons of war;

Hear our voice when we beg you to instill into the hearts of all human beings the wisdom of peace, the strength of justice and the joy of solidarity;

Hear our voice, for we speak for the multitudes in every country and in every period of history who do not want war and are ready to walk the road of peace;

Hear our voice and grant insight and strength so that we may always respond to hatred with love, to injustice with total dedication to justice, to need with the sharing of self, to war...with PEACE. O God, hear our voice, and grant to the world your everlasting peace.

Final Blessing

Leader:
Go now and make peace, God's peace:
the peace that breaks through the limits of our vision,
breaks free from the chains of our fears,
breaks down the barriers

between God's children.
Go now, make God's peace and receive it:
God's peace that comes in the flesh.
Go now, receiving God's peace:
and God's shalom, which passes all understanding,
will guard your hearts and your minds in Christ Jesus. Amen.

Closing Song

"Let Peace Fill the Earth" *(Based on a prayer for peace written by Rabbi Nachman. Setting and music: Ray Makeever, c. 1985, Ray Makeever, 1550 Douglas, Dubuque, IA 52001.)*

(Adapted from "Day of Prayer for Landmines Victims" produced by Lutheran Peace Fellowship, 1710 11th Ave., Seattle, WA 98122, 206/720-0313. Additional materials from "Peace Worship Resources" packet available for $6.00 from LPF.)

A Liturgical Celebration from Africa: Christ Our Liberator

The following rite was developed out of a need to create liturgies that speak to Africans in their situation, liturgies that speak to their specific needs. The rite is a liturgical adaptation inspired by 'Guest Christology.'* It inculturates the person and message of Jesus Christ as the guest-liberator in the lives of African Christians. In this liturgy, Jesus Christ comes as an unpretentious guest, seeking time and space to dwell in the midst of the Africans who welcome him into their lives, where he is initiated, accepted and proclaimed the liberator, who shares 'the joy and hope, the grief and anguish of the people of our time, especially of those who are poor or afflicted in any way.' (Vatican II, Gaudiem et Spes., #1.)

This rite takes place in the family of God, that is, the Christian community. Family of God is a preferred African metaphor for 'church.' It evokes the memories of all the members of the family, including the living, the dead, the yet unborn, who are afflicted in any way and in need of liberation. In addition, it celebrates Christ as the Word who takes flesh and dwells in our midst (John 1:14) and frees us from the shackles of sin, oppression and injustice.

This liturgy has been adapted for use by people of any culture or race who seek to stand in solidarity with our African sisters and brothers.

The Rite
(As members of the community gather to welcome Christ, the presider welcomes everyone.)

Song
"Jesu Tawa Pano / Jesus, We Are Here" *(Text: Zimbabwean; Patrick Matsikenyiri / Tune: Patrick Matsikenyiri, c. 1990, Patrick Matsikenyiri in Gather Comprehensive, #705.)*

Introduction and Invocation
Presider:
Today, we gather as one family to receive Christ our Liberator. He comes to us, seeking to become the one who liberates all of us, especially the peoples of Africa, from the bondage of sin, oppression, division and injustice. To welcome him as a community, let us acknowledge in our midst the presence of our ancestors, all our parents, relatives and friends who have gone before us and who are with us today to receive the freedom of Christ our Liberator.

(The presider names some departed members of the community. After each name all respond "Present!" The presider then invites those gathered to add other names of those who have died.)

*See E. B. Udohop, Guest Christology (Frankfurt am Main: Verlag Peter Lang, 1988); E. Orobator, "The Quest for an African Christ: An Essay on Contemporary African Christology," in *Hekima Review*, #11, Sept. 1994, pp. 75-99.

The Word
Reader 1:
Christ our Liberator says: "Listen! I am standing and knocking at your door. If you hear my voice and open the door, I will come in and we will eat together." (Rev. 3:20)

All:
We know God our Creator, the Supreme Being who sends rain to water the land and makes fruitful the labor of our hands; we acknowledge our ancestors who protect us, but who are you Jesus Christ, for us?

Reader 1:
(Luke 19:1-10 or 10:38-42)

All:
We rejoice and are glad. We welcome Christ as the Liberator of all people, to grow as one of us, to learn from us and to be a source of blessing, freedom and fullness of life for our community and for the peoples of Africa.

(A symbol of welcome is offered. Depending on the place, this symbol is something that is customarily reserved for guests such as kola-nut, a bowl of water, chai (tea), etc.)

Presider:
(Takes the symbol of welcome and prays:) Christ our Liberator, we offer you *(the symbol: kola-nut, etc.),* sign of friendship, solidarity and welcome from our family. Accept it and make our community your home.

All:
Accept this symbol of ourselves and dwell in our community as one of us!

Song
"Jesus, Come to Us" *(By David Haas, c. 1987, OCP.)*

The Trials of the Word
Presider:
Christ, our Liberator, as a member of our family, you share our joys and our sorrows. You share the joys and sorrows of our African sisters and brothers. We present them before you. Share with us our life and destiny and the life and destiny of the peoples of Africa.

Reader 2:
Christ our Liberator, your sons and daughters of Africa are fruitful in birth and are blessed with strong and faithful brothers and sisters...

All:
Let us rejoice with our sisters and brothers!

Reader 3:
Their land is well watered and the yield of their harvest is bountiful...

All:
Let us rejoice with our sisters and brothers!

Reader 2:
Their land is plagued by sickness and diseases of all kinds: malaria, AIDS, meningitis...

All:
Christ, free them!

Reader 3:
They are burdened by unemployment and unfair economic structural adjustment programs...

All:
Christ, free them!

Reader 2:
They are oppressed by countless forms of injustice. They are saddled with the burden of corrupt leaders and are denied their human rights and civil liberties...

All:
Christ, free them!

Reader 3:
Their hopes and aspirations are assailed by many setbacks, like tribalism, ethnic hatred, division and violence.

All:
Christ, free them!

(A moment of silence.)

Presider:
Christ shares in the joys and in the sorrows of the peoples of Africa. Christ feels their pains and mourns with them. He is in solidarity with them and He speaks to them in their oppression. We, too, seek to stand in solidarity with the peoples of Africa in their suffering.

Reader 4:
(Reads Luke 4:18-19 or Matthew 11:28-30.)

All:
Christ our Liberator, we offer you the joys and the sorrows of the peoples of Africa; give rest and peace to their troubled hearts and may peace and justice reign in their community, our community, and in our world. Amen!

Presider:
Christ, our Liberator takes upon himself all of our world's pains, sorrows, disappointments, cares and worries by dying for us, as one of our family. He is sent to us by God, our Creator and Sustainer, to give us life in abundance and to proclaim to us the freedom of God's children.

All:
May His death on the cross become the source of liberation for all people, especially the peoples of Africa.

Resurrection and Proclamation of Christ as the Risen Savior and Liberator

Presider:
Sons and daughters, Christ, our brother and kin, has died to free all people from all forms of oppression and injustice. God, the Creator and the Sustainer of the life of our community, has raised Jesus from the dead. Let us rejoice and be glad.

All:
We rejoice and are glad!

Presider:
Jesus Christ our brother is risen from the dead.

All:
We rejoice and are glad!

Presider:
He is the Liberator of our community and of the community of the peoples of Africa.

All:
We rejoice and are glad!

Presider:
He is the master-builder of our global community.

All:
We rejoice and are glad!

Presider:
Jesus Christ is the life-giver of our global community.

All:
We rejoice and are glad!

Presider:
Jesus Christ empowers us to overcome all the structures of oppression and injustice in our world.

All:
We rejoice and are glad!

Presider:
Jesus Christ is fully one of us; He is present in our efforts to heal the world, in our efforts to heal the wounds of the peoples of Africa.

All:
We rejoice and are glad!

Sending Forth

Presider:
Jesus Christ has come as our Liberator; we have welcomed Him as one of our family. He now dwells among us. He has taken our joys, pains and sorrows, and the joys, pains and sorrows of our African sisters and brothers, upon Himself. He has liberated all of us from that which holds us captive and oppressed. We rejoice in His presence and are glad.

All:
We proclaim Him as the God of our life, the giver of new life to our human family.

Presider:
Empowered by the presence of Jesus Christ our Liberator, let us go forth as bearers of the seeds of this new life.

All:
Amen! We agree! Let it be so!

Closing Song

"Freedom is Coming" *(Text: South African / Tune: South African, c. 1984, Ultryck.)*

(Adapted from a rite created by A. Emmanuel Orobator, SJ.)

Mass for Haiti:
A Liturgy of Conversion

(Adaptable as a prayer service)

Gathering Song
"Voices that Challenge" *(By David Haas, c. 1990, GIA.)*

Greeting
Penitential Rite Presider:
For the times we have remained silent...

All:
Jesus have mercy.

Presider:
For the times we turned away because we could not bear to look...

All:
Christ have mercy.

Presider:
For the times we failed to acknowledge the Love that makes us family...

All:
Jesus have mercy.

Opening Prayer Presider:
God of the powerless, we come together to join our brothers and sisters in Haiti, to be with them as your children, to accept their struggles as our struggles. Like Simon, we offer ourselves to help carry the cross. We come together to acknowledge that their blood is our blood as we embrace the awareness that we are them. We ask this through Jesus Christ, liberator of the poor. Amen.

First Reading
Jeremiah 30:18-22

Responsorial
Psalm 15: "Create in Me an Upright Spirit"
(By Keith Paulson-Thorp, c. 1997, Keith Paulson-Thorp, written especially for this service, available through Pax Christi Palm Beach, Sandra Barron at 561/575-1795.)

Gospel Reading
Matthew 25:31-46

Presentation of the Gifts
(Instrumental music.)

Liturgy of the Eucharist

Communion Song
"Now We Remain" *(By David Haas, c. 1983, GIA.)*

Communion Meditation
"Sacre Coeur" by Nancy McDonald (From *Come with Me to Haiti*, c. Pax Christi USA.)

The church is locked but it doesn't matter
The Mass has moved back to the street
where it first began
Somehow we had forgotten that crucifixion
always happens in the open on a dung heap
But our memory was jogged, once more
by the work of human hands
Here in the chimeric heat of midday
Here in the uncompromising sun
clothed in our proud raiment of sweat and grime
we place our flowers on the true altar
the broken pavement stones outside the church
On this place marked fast with human blood,
the bodies of Antoine Izmery and
Guy Malary and four thousand others names and unnamed
have lain unattended
gathered flies and maggots in the coagulating blood.
And in this seemingly groundless, vacant dying
have given birth, have offered life again
have bled into the soil and soul of this nation
and consecrated air and muck alike
and if the muck then not us as well
for are we not made from dust and spit
In the violence of such testimony,
we join our hands and beg forgiveness
for all we've done and failed to do.
This dying is the work of liturgy.
This dreadful life is the infinite act of hope.
In this presence all else becomes gibberish
and we stand amazed that we can hold the mystery
in our hands

Holy Holy Holy All is Holy

The air, the flowers
the stench of sewage in the street
They embraced it all–they loved and touched it
and dying gave it back to us, redeemed
And in the presence of this chosen crucifixion
this play out of optimistic death
can we continue to deny: This is our body
must we not cry out:
This is our blood

The church is locked. Does it matter?
We know for certain
He is not in the tomb.

Closing Prayer

(Written by the Peace and Justice Commission, Diocese of Lansing, Michigan.)

All:
Loving God, Emmanuel,
God who is with us,
with all of our hearts, we pray

We pray for those who are oppressed and violated:
May their tortures and unjust imprisonment come to an end.
May the people have the necessities of life
May all who are in exile be allowed to return safely to their homeland.

We also pray for the perpetrators of this violence. While we abhor what they are doing to the people, we love them knowing that they too are our brothers and sisters. It is with your grace and love that their hearts and actions will be changed.

And we pray for all those whose hands and hearts reach out with love and peace. We pray for their safety and their continuing efforts to bring your nonviolent love to the Haitians and all those in war torn countries.

In the spirit of Jean-Bertrand Aristide, we say...
"Alone we are weak;
together we are strong;
united we are Lavalas."*

(*Lavalas is a gentle flowing spring that persists in eroding away evil, a nonviolent force that cannot be turned away. The nonviolent movement which swept Jean-Bertrand Aristide into power as president of Haiti called itself "Lavalas.")

Presider:
Let us go forth as the embodiment of Lavalas, as the embodiment of the Resurrection.

All:
Amen!

Sending Forth

"The Harvest of Justice" *(By David Haas, c. 1985, GIA.)*

(Adapted from a Mass planned by Pax Christi Palm Beach.)

"How long,
O loving God,
will we continue
to kill in
Your name?"

A Service of Prayer for Peace in the Middle East

You may want to choose three presiders from the three religious traditions represented in the Middle East: Jewish, Muslim and Christian.

Hymn

"God of Abraham" *(By Bernadette Farrell, c. 1990, Bernadette Farrell. Published by OCP.)(Add verses: Lead us to justice, lead us to peace, lead us to love, lead us to truth, etc. End with "lead us to freedom.")*

Interfaith Opening Prayer

(Adapted by the Interfaith Witness for Peace in the Middle East from "A Service of Prayer for Peace in the Middle East," by the U. S. Interreligious Committee for Peace in the Middle East.)

Leader 1:
Let us pray for peace in the Middle East:

All:
O God of Peace and Justice: We beseech You to bless those entrusted with charting peace for the Middle East and its people. Grant them the patience, understanding, vision and courage needed for this formidable challenge. Entrust them with full awareness of their great task and of the fearful consequences should peace elude their efforts.

Help these Muslim, Jewish and Christian peacemakers to transcend the strictures of their histories, and their experiences of pain and oppression. Infuse in them your spirit so they may understand that ultimately, no one people will prosper until peace with justice is secured for all peoples of the Middle East.

At the same time, sustain us as we draw upon the moving power of your Spirit to calm waters churning with generations of conflict.

Guide us as we give shape to a new vision in which all the peoples of our one Creator will find reconciliation and wholeness.

Strengthen our resolve to act in support of our nations' leaders to forge in the Middle East a full and lasting peace for both the children of Israel and the Palestinian people.

Enable us to bring about a Peace in Jerusalem as a light to all of the nations and peoples of the world.

To this we say: Salaam, Shalom, Peace. Amen.

Penitential Rite

(Adapted from Prayers for Peace in the Middle East, prepared by a Christian, a Jew and Muslim, from the U. S. Interreligious Committee for Peace in the Middle East.)

Leader 1:
Let us ask our God for forgiveness for the times we have not been people of peace, for the times we have not furthered the establishment of peace in the Middle East.

Leader 2:
Eternal God, shepherd of every hope, refuge of every bewildered heart, and fountain of forgiveness, receive our prayer of peace in the Middle East.

All:
Save us from weak resignation to violence. Teach us that restraint is the highest expression of power, that thoughtfulness and tenderness are marks of the strong.

Leader 3:
Help us to love our enemies, not by countenancing their sins, but by remembering our own. And may we never for a moment forget that we are all fed by the same food, hurt by the same weapons, and yearn for our children and their future.

All:
O God, as Muslims, Jews and Christians, we acknowledge that You have made of one blood all the nations of the earth. You love all of us as if all were but one, and care for each as if You had nothing else for which to care.

Leader 2:
Remembering such love, may we not weary in our efforts to fashion out of our failures today some great good for all people tomorrow. And not unto us, O God, not unto us, but unto Your name be the glory. To this we say:

All:
Salaam, Shalom, Peace. Amen.

Reading
From the Jewish Tradition, Micah 4:1-4

Spoken Response:
(The following spoken responses are all adapted from Prayers for Peace in the Middle East.)

All:
O God, who makes peace and harmony
in the heavenly spheres,
help Your bewildered humanity understand
the futility of war, and hatred and violence.
Help us to overcome the rationalizations
that ultimately end in justification of actions
which inevitably lead to bloodshed and suffering.
As hundreds of thousands of human beings
look at their brothers and sisters
over the barrels of guns, cannons and missiles,
help us to hear Your voice
which counsels compassion,
patience and rational discourse.

How long, O loving God,
will we continue to kill in Your name?

Reading
From the Christian tradition, Matthew 5:1-12

Spoken Response
All:
Help us to understand
that the search for peace and well-being
is not weakness nor lack of conviction
but rather the only way to insure continued life
on this planet upon which
You have placed us.

O God, cherisher and sustainer of all beings,
sovereign One over all your creation,

in your boundless mercy and care,
teach us wisdom and compassion to face
this threat of suffering, discord and death.
Teach us, our most holy creator,
to love mercy and justice,
as You love mercy and justice.

How long, O loving God,
will we continue to kill in Your name?
How long will we refuse to register
the unalterable fact that all human creatures
on this earth are brothers and sisters.

Reading
From the Islamic tradition verses from The Holy Quran (adapted)

Say ye:
"We Believe in God, and the revelation given to us and to Abraham, Ismail, Isaac and Jacob and the Tribes, and that given to Moses and Jesus, and that given to all Prophets from their God: we make no differences between one and another of them: and we bow to God in Islam." *(Sura II, v. 136.)*

If the enemy incline towards peace, do thou (also) incline towards peace, and trust in God: for God is the One that heareth and knoweth (all things). *(Sura VIII, v. 61.)*

And the servants of the Most Gracious are those who walk on the earth in humility, and when the ignorant address them, they say, "Peace!" *(Sura XXV, v. 63.)*

O Humankind! We created you from a single (pair) of a male and a female, and made you into nations and tribes, that ye know each other (not that ye may despise each other). Verily the most honored of you in the sight of God is (the one who is) the most righteous of you. And God has full knowledge and is well acquainted (with all things). *(Sura XLIX, v. 13.)*

Spoken Response
All:
How long, O loving God, will we continue to kill in Your name?

O God, guide us to your ways,
the ways of righteousness and peace.
Grant us peace, O God of peace.
Help us to do your will in our lives,
in our relations and in our affairs.
Forgive us all your creatures in Your mercy
and save us from our own evil.
Yours alone is all praise,
all dominion and all power
forever and ever. Amen.

Shared Greeting of Shalom/Salaam/Peace
(Leader 3 introduces.)

Blessings
Jewish/Christian/Muslim *(The prayer leaders can either use one of these blessings or speak spontaneously at this time.)*

Christian:
May God bless you and keep you.
May God walk with you and protect you.
May God's face turn to you and grant you a long life in peace and justice.

Jewish:
(Same prayer in Hebrew.)

Yivarechecha adonai v'yishmarech. Ya'air adonai panav aylechaa v'yichunecha. Yi'sa adonai panav aylecha v'yasaim l'cha shalom.

Muslim:
O Allah, You are peacc.
Through You flows peace.
May all Your creation in this world live forever and ever
in peace and happiness. Amen.

Hymn

"Let There Be Peace on Earth"
(By Sy Miller and Jill Jackson, c. 1955, assigned to Jan-Lee Music, c. renewed 1983.)

(Adapted from an interfaith prayer service prepared by the U.S. Interreligious Committee for Peace in the Middle East, Greene & Westview, 3rd Floor, Philadelphia, Pennsylvania 19119, (215) 438-4142.)

A Call for Jubilee: Release Those in Debt!

You will need candles for everyone in the group to light during the Commitment to Solidarity part of the service.

Call to Worship

Leader:
Let us find stillness, a time to gather our thoughts, to connect our spirits and bodies, to reach within ourselves, to connect with those that gather here in this community of love and witness, and with those throughout the world to share our strength and our wisdom.

Will you please join hands with the persons next to you, and pray with me our call to worship:

All:
Generous, Loving and Living God, who shared the gift of life with us,
we pray to be released from the captivity of our wants;
we seek healing from the blindness of wealth and power;
and freedom from the prisons of unjust relationships;
we pray for new vision to see the suffering of the world's people;
new ears to hear the cries of the poor; we pray that we may find the wisdom
and courage to end the imprisonment of debt for all the world. Amen.

Opening Song

"Open My Eyes" *(By Jesse Manibusan, c. 1988, OCP.)*

Reading

Leviticus 25:9-10

Trumpet Call

(A trumpet is sounded.)

Good News for the Poor

Scripture Reading:
Luke 4:16-20

Contemporary Reading:
In the Philippines, the government's proclamations of turning the country into a newly industrialized economy by the year 2000 only means doom for tribal minorities. Indeed, in the last three years, "progress and modernization for much of the nation have resulted in impoverishment and social segregation for indigenous peoples."

"The pineapple is more important than the people," says one woman worker for a transnational fruit processor. There are days when work is for 12 hours or 3.8 hours (because four hours would entitle them to a full days wages) and days when while preparing for work they suddenly hear over the radio that they are to stay home. The workers' schedule depends on the supply of pineapples; they never know how long they are to work from one day to the next.

Let us proclaim Good News to the poor!

All:
Let us proclaim good news for the poor!

Sung Response
"Open My Eyes" *(v.1)*

Liberty for Captives
Scripture Reading:
Isaiah 58:6-10

Contemporary Reading:
In Zambia, currency devaluations and other economic measures taken under the country's mandated economic adjustment program caused the price of a loaf of bread to increase from 12 kwacha in 1990 to 350 kwacha in 1993. Layoffs required by this program caused more than 72,000 people to lose their jobs.

A few years ago Evelina Phiri had a pretty nice life. Her husband had a Zambian government driver's job, and her seven children had access to a public health clinic and primary education. As a result of the economic "adjustment," Mr. Phiri lost his job and user fees were instituted at the clinic and school. The changes caused Evelina's family to pull their four girls out of school. She can no longer afford health care for her daughters.

Evelina now works in a stone quarry, breaking and bagging rocks in return for food and rations. Let us set the captives free!

All:
Let us set the captives free!

Sung Response
"Open My Eyes" (v. 2)

Sight For the Blind
Scripture Reading:
Isaiah 42:16-22

Contemporary Reading:
In 1978 the richest 10 percent of the population enjoyed 37 percent of Chile's national income, while the poorest 50 percent of the population had 20 percent of that income. By 1988, after economic adjustments, the top 10 percent had 47 percent of the income and the poorest 50 percent only 17 percent.

In Peru, certain industries prefer to employ women because they work for lower wages and tolerate more exploitative conditions than men. In the fish canneries of Chimbote, on the northern coast of Peru, over half of the workers are women. Julia, one of the workers there, says she began to work at the factory because her husband's pay was not sufficient to support their five children in school. Julia adds salt and hot sauce by hand to the open packages of fish. When she gets home she sticks her hands in cold water for several hours to stop the pain. The first few days she says she wanted to scream in pain. They won't even let her leave the machine to go to the bathroom.

Let us open the eyes of the blind!

All:
Let us open the eyes of the blind!

Sung Response
"Open My Eyes Lord" *(v. 1)*

Release for Prisoners

Scripture Reading:
Amos 8:4-8 and 9:13-15

Contemporary Reading:
In 1990, after years of economic adjustment, poverty afflicted 32.5 percent of people in Latin America, a significant increase from the 27.5 percent living below the poverty line 10 years earlier. The number of people living in extreme poverty increased between 1980 and 1990 from 62 million to 93 million people.

Despite projections for continued economic growth, the U.N.'s Economic Commission for Latin America projects that the number of poor people in the region may double to 192 million out of a total 440 million by the year 2000. By 1990 minimum wages in Latin America were 20 percent lower than 10 years earlier and the poorest 20 percent of the population had witnessed a one-fifth fall in their share of national income.

In the cool of the morning the young woman, she will not say her name, leaves her shanty on the denuded hillside with hundreds of others moving towards the "free zone" near San Marcos. Under the passive gaze of guards armed with automatic rifles, the women stop to chat, then stroll through the gates topped with razor wire to their dollar-a-day jobs in the textile sweat shops.

Let us release all prisoners!

All:
Let us release all prisoners!

Sung Response
"Open My Eyes Lord" *(all verses)*

Year of God's Favor

Scripture Reading:
Isaiah 6:6-8

Contemporary Reading:
"Declaration for Change on the Fiftieth Anniversary of the World Bank and IMF"

Sustainable, equitable development will be achieved only though a redistribution of power and resources from the rich to the poor. This will require a transformation of the international economic system. As international institutions whose policies shape economic systems and affect the lives of billions throughout the world, the World Bank, International Monetary Fund and their member governments must work in support of global, social, political and economic justice by taking the following steps:

1) Replace Structural Adjustment Programs with policies and projects which meet the needs of the poor and promote sustainable, participatory and equitable development.

2) Cancel or substantially reduce multilateral debt, especially of the poorest countries, and increase support for the reduction of commercial and bilateral debt.

3) Democratize the World Bank and the IMF and make them accountable to the people affected by their policies and projects. This requires democratic voting allocations, increased transparency, access to information and participation at every stage of projects, programs and policies.

Let us announce a Year of God's Favor!

All:
Let us announce a Year of God's Favor!

Call to Jubilee: Commitment to Solidarity

Leader:

As a sign of your commitment to this call for jubilee, to announce a year of God's favor, please come forward and light a candle of hope that will banish the night of violence and injustice.

(Leader lights their candle and then passes the light around. All hold their candles as they read the statement of commitment).

All:

Here we are God, send us. We affirm this declaration for change and pledge to work for the forgiveness of debts and the end of structural adjustment programs. We stand in solidarity with our sisters and brothers throughout the world who suffer so much because of such unjust economic policies. Help us, O God, to proclaim good news to these people, your poor, to proclaim liberty for all captives, sight for the blind and release for prisoners everywhere. We declare this to be a Jubilee year: a year of God's favor. We proclaim ourselves to be a Jubilee people.

Closing Song

"This Little Light of Mine"
(Text: Afro-American Spiritual / Tune: Afro-American spiritual; Arr. by James Moore, Jr., c. 1987, GIA.)

(Adapted from Call to Jubilee service developed by the Religious Working Group on the World Bank and the IMF on the occasion of the executive board meetings of the World Bank and the IMF which are held two out of every three years in Washington D.C. Over the last few years the Religious Working Group has held major interfaith services each October.)

Closing the School of Assassins: A Prayer Service in the Spirit of St. Francis

The leader roles can be divided up among several people.

Introduction

Leader:

St. Francis of Assisi was a man of peace. Choosing God as his Father and Mother and Jesus as his brother enabled him to see all men and women as his brothers and sisters. He strove to live in harmony with all of creation. Thomas of Celano says of Francis: "In all his preaching before he proposed the Word of God to those gathered about, he first prayed for peace for them, saying, 'God give you peace.' He always most devoutly announced peace to all he met...For this reason many who hated peace and had hated salvation embraced peace, through the cooperation of God with all their hearts, and were made children of peace and seekers after eternal salvation."

We remember also the martyrs of Central America who embraced peace and brought truth into the darkness of repression, injustice, and war. They showed by their example how to search for the truth in our reality. Let us become bearers of truth and makers of peace as we keep their light and their passion for peace alive in our world.

Song

"Prayer of St. Francis" *(By Sebastian Temple, c. 1967, OCP.)*

Reading:

"Francis and the Taming of the Wolf" (Cf. OMNIBUS, pp. 1348-1351, or the story as told by Murray Bodo in *Journey and the Dream*.)

Prayer

Leader:

Gracious God, creator of all the universe, deep within each of our hearts dwell both the wolf and the lamb. Empower us to perceive the way of peace and harmony, and grant to our own hearts and the hearts of all our brothers and sisters the ability to live in peace. We ask this in Jesus' name. Amen.

Readings

(Adapted from the *Witness for Peace* newsletter, Spring 1994.)

Soldiers at the School of Assassins are trained in Low Intensity Conflict, a cynical... strategy for maintaining U.S. military influence south of our borders, without using (or losing) large numbers of U.S. troops. Instead, soldiers from Latin America and the Caribbean are trained in 'dirty little war' techniques by U.S. personnel.

(From *The Presbyterian Peace Fellowship* newsletter.)

Each year, nearly 2,000 soldiers from Latin America and the Caribbean train at the School of the Americas (SOA) at U.S. taxpayers' expense. Students and instructors receive an allowance of $25,000 per person, in addition to their regular salaries. According to the U.S. Congress, school operating expenses are $5.8 million a year, not counting the salaries for the 129–person staff or the recently completed $30 million renovation of the SOA complex. School of the Americas troops receive weekly trips to Disney World, Atlanta Braves games, and other perks—all at U.S. taxpayers' expense. According to a Fort Benning officer, "Their time here shows them the good life"—not democracy. They go home thinking that if their army stays in power, they can experience the same perks at home that they experienced here.

Antiphonal Response
Isaiah 11:1-9

Side 1:
A shoot springs from the stock of Jesse, a scion thrusts from his roots: on him the spirit of Yahweh rests, a spirit of wisdom and insight, a spirit of counsel and power, a spirit of knowledge and of the fear of Yahweh. (The fear of Yahweh is his breath.)

Side 2:
He does not judge by appearances, he gives no verdict on hearsay, but judges the wretched with integrity, and with equity gives a verdict for the poor of the land. His word is a rod that strikes the ruthless, his sentences bring death to the wicked.

Side 1:
Integrity is the loincloth around his waist, faithfulness the belt about his hips.

Side 2:
The wolf lives with the lamb, the panther lies down with the kid, the calf and lion cub feed together with a little child to lead them. The cow and the bear make friends, their young lie down together. The lion eats straw like the ox. The infant plays over the cobra's hole; into the viper's lair the young child puts a hand.

All:
They will neither harm nor destroy my holy mountain, for the country is filled with the knowledge of Yahweh as the waters swell the sea.

Reading
Excerpt from *Theology of Christian Solidarity* by Jon Sobrino and Juan Hernandez Pico, c. 1985, Orbis Books.

For the past few years
one of the words heard most often in Central America,
and throughout the world, regarding Central America,
has been "solidarity:"
solidarity with El Salvador,
solidarity with Nicaragua,
solidarity with Guatemala,
solidarity with Central America.

Solidarity is another name for the kind of love
that moves feet, hands, hearts, material goods,
assistance, and sacrifice toward the pain, danger,
misfortune, disaster, repression,
or death
of other persons or a whole people.
The aim is to share with them
and help them rise up, become free,
claim justice, rebuild.

In the pain, misfortune, oppression,
and death
of the people,
God is silent.

God is silent on the cross,
in the crucified.
And the silence is God's word,
God's cry.

In solidarity God speaks the language of love.
God makes a statement, utters a self-revelation,
and takes up a presence in solidarity.

God is love,
God stands in solidarity,
God is solidarity.
Where there is solidarity, there is God...

God speaks where there is solidarity with Central America.
And God calls for solidarity with Central America,
with its people, with the suffering poor.

Penitential Litany

Leader:
United in the memory of all those who have suffered and died because of the School of the Americas, let us acknowledge the times we have not stood in solidarity with our sisters and brothers from Central America. Let us acknowledge our guilt and our sorrow. Please respond, "Have mercy on us, O God."

All:
Have mercy on us, O God.

Leader:
For the times we fear to stand up for what we believe... Have mercy on us, O God.
For neglecting to challenge those who exert power unjustly...
For choosing to sit back and let others do the works of justice and peace-making...
For neglecting our call to be a voice that challenges the structures of government when they are oppressive...
For resisting the call to suffer persecution for the sake of justice...
For the times we go about our busy days, forgetting our brothers and sisters whose only struggle is to survive that day...
For the guilt that is ours in the assassination of thousands of the innocent poor...

Closing Prayer

Leader:
We have gathered to remember those who have struggled for justice and died for peace and truth. We are challenged, as they were, by the words from Isaiah, to bring the calf, the lion and the yearling together, to allow the cow and the bear to eat together, to support and affirm one another as we speak out in truth, stretch ourselves in love, and take on the responsibility to grapple with what it means when Isaiah says, "They will neither harm nor destroy on all my holy mountain."

That we still gather all across the United States and in Central America to remember these martyrs says something about the power of the truth that they bear with their witness. They challenge us to understand how they lived, why they died, who killed them, and who was responsible. These martyrs are a light for us and we remember them in love and gratitude.

In the name of all of these martyrs, let us say:

All:
Presente!

Closing Song

"Now is the Time"
(By Francisco Herrara, c. 1990, Francisco Herrara, 415/643-9362.)

Now is the time for us
To raise our voice
Hasn't it been enough
that's been destroyed.

Now is the time for us
To use our hands
So we can spread the truth
Throughout the land.

(Adapted from a liturgy from an unknown source.)

Singing for our Lives: Prayer Service in Solidarity with Lesbian and Gay People

This liturgy has been created to give the participants an opportunity to express their solidarity with lesbian women, gay men, and other members of the sexual minority community who are misunderstood and discriminated against in our heterosexist society. The liturgy can be held on or near the last Sunday in June, which is designated in many places as Gay Pride Day in commemoration of the Stonewall Riots in New York City in 1969, an event which is widely acknowledged as marking the beginning of the modern gay and lesbian civil rights movement.

This liturgy can be celebrated almost anyplace. The space might be decorated with a rainbow flag, with some plants or flowers, and with candles if the liturgy is to be held in the evening.

Welcome/Introduction
(Keeping in mind the particular audience and the occasion, a leader may welcome the group and make some remarks as to why they have been invited to gather for prayer at this time.)

Opening Song
"Singing For Our Lives" *(By Holly Near, c. 1979, Hereford Music.) This simple song was written by folk singer Holly Near at the time of the jury verdict in the trial of Dan White, convicted of the murders of Mayor George Moscone and Supervisor Harvey Milk in San Francisco. Many in the gay community felt that the verdict and punishment in White's case was more lenient than it otherwise would have been had one of his victims not been a leader in the gay community. The announcement of the verdict elicited a violent response in San Francisco, and Near wrote this song to give folks who were justifiably angry another way of responding to the event.*

Opening Prayer

Leader 1:
We thank you, God,
source of all life and holiness,
for creating this planet we call home
and for blessing it with life in such abundance and diversity.
You have created humans of many colors
and have blessed them with the wisdom and intelligence
to give birth to many cultures.

Leader 2:
You have created humans with sexualities,
and have blessed them with unique perspectives
on what it means to be women and men
called to be in relationship to you and to one another.
Yet, in our sinful, broken human condition,
many of us are threatened by those who are different from ourselves.

Leader 1:
Open our minds, loving God,
that we come to understand those who are different from ourselves
as your gift to us,
inviting us to an ever greater appreciation of that marvelous diversity
which finds its source in you.

Leader 2:
Open our hearts
that we might be moved to act with courage
against ignorance and injustice;
that we might be moved to stand in solidarity
with the lesbian and gay members
of the human family to which you have given birth.
We make this prayer in the name of Jesus, your child and our brother,
who always stood with those on the margins of society. Amen.

(Four suggested readings follow. They have been chosen to highlight different aspects of the struggles of gay and lesbian persons and their families, the social justice challenges which the situation of lesbian and gay persons presents to church and to society, and the joy and peace which flows from coming to a sense of self-acceptance as a lesbian woman or a gay man. All of the excerpts below were written by women and men who are people of faith, people who have risked much in order to come out as lesbian or gay themselves or who have taken significant risks in order to be in solidarity with gay and lesbian people. Feel free to edit the readings according to the needs of the particular occasion, or to substitute other readings which may seem more appropriate. Silence, instrumental music, or other hymns might be used between each reading.)

First Reading

"The Struggle of Parents of Gay and Lesbian Children"
(By Robert Nugent, SDS, from "Gay Sons and Lesbian Daughters" in *Building Bridges: Gay and Lesbian Reality and the Catholic Church*, by Jeannine Gramick, SSND, and Robert Nugent, SDS, c. 1992, Twenty-Third Publications, Mystic, CT.)

I knew why they came to my apartment for counseling, but it took them a long time to say it. They were a Catholic couple in their mid-40s, parents of two children, both Catholic college graduates, both professionals in a small suburban area. Their younger child, a boy, was still in high school and their daughter was a sophomore in a small Midwestern college. They had just returned from a Christmas meeting with their daughter in Chicago. She took them out to dinner to a nice restaurant, and she had a drink or two before dinner. Then she told them. The mother became physically ill and had to leave the table.

They both shifted nervously on the couch, their eyes down, as they came closer to telling me. Finally, the father, filling up with tears as he spoke, said softly, guiltily, "Our daughter is a homosexual." The mother was crying, too. So we sat quietly for a few moments. Then we began to talk about how they felt about what they now knew, what it really meant to them and to the family, and how they were going to cope with it.

It was not an unusual session for me. Since the early seventies I had been through similar scenes with countless parents. The couple was fortunate. They had someone to talk to about the situation.

They could ask some basic questions, and I promised them some good reading materials. I might see them again, or I might not. Sometimes all such people need is a start on the road to discovery and eventual acceptance.

There are many parents who will not or cannot bring themselves to tell someone about a homosexual son or daughter. Whether they suspect it, or have discovered it accidentally, or the child has shared it with them, their confusion and pain finds no healing ministry. Their questions go unanswered. Their fears go unallayed. "What will the pastor think of us as parents?" "What will the rest of the family think when they find out?"

Sung Response

"Singing For Our Lives"

Second Reading

"Homophobia and Lesbian Women"
(By Jeannine Gramick, SSND, from "Lesbian Women and the Church" in *Building Bridges: Gay and Lesbian Reality and the Catholic Church* by Jeannine Gramick, SSND, and Robert Nugent, SDS, c. 1992, Twenty-Third Publications, Mystic, CT.)

From lesbian women I learned much about society's homophobia and negative judgments about homosexuality. Societal attitudes toward lesbianism are marked by widespread, almost universal, intolerance. I learned that homophobia can be extreme, it can be subtle, and it can be very personal.

If women (generally) have felt marginalized, ignored or unempowered in societal and ecclesial milieus, lesbian women, relegated to the lowest rung of the power-elite ladder, feel the oppression in multiple measure. One of the largest minorities, lesbian women across the globe number upwards of 140 million, more than nine times the number of world Jews. Lesbian women are often subjected to unjust and outright discrimination, mental abuse, and even physical violence.

Lesbian women have been sentenced to many years of hard labor in Pakistan and the (former) Soviet Union and forced into mental institutions in China. An Argentinian woman's social position is jeopardized by a public disclosure of lesbianism. In Iran, lesbian and gay people have been persecuted. Almost everywhere lesbian women, if open about their orientation, fear for their lives and their livelihood. Necessary secrecy and enforced invisibility rob lesbian women of their human, God-given dignity. They are forced to maintain a heterosexual charade...

From lesbian women I learned that homophobia can be subtly as well as blatantly mani-fested. Discrimination in employment, for example, can be motivated by homophobia but masked in the guise of happenstance. I have met a number of lesbian women who said that their positions at work were eliminated when their employers learned of their lesbianism, although this reason was never mentioned...

From lesbian women I also learned that homophobia can be rooted in personal fears and anxieties about one's sexuality. More and more we are beginning to realize that same-sex erotic feelings, even though not predominant in most individuals, are quite natural. But unless we make friends with our own homosexual passions, we will be imprisoned by them. Repressed feelings, which we consider unacceptable, invariably erupt in unhealthy ways, destructive of self or others.

Sharing

(Depending upon the size and nature of the group of participants in this liturgy, the leaders may choose to include a time of sharing. People might be asked to share very briefly with the group something about the way in which their lives have been touched by the struggle of gay and lesbian people in our society.)

A Litany

Solidarity With Gay and Lesbian People
(This litany is meant to be led by one speaker with the congregation responding with the refrain: "We will stand in solidarity with lesbian and gay people." Members of the congregation might be given candles which could be lit before the litany as a sign of the participant's commitment to solidarity with gay and lesbian people.)

Reader:
Because gay and lesbian people are discriminated against in housing and employment...

All:
We will stand in solidarity with lesbian and gay people.

Reader:
Because how lesbian and gay people act is often perceived to be more important than who they are...

All:
We will stand in solidarity with lesbian and gay people.

Because harassment and violence against gay and lesbian people is often blamed on the victim rather than on ecclesial and societal complicity in homophobia...

All:
We will stand...

Because the self-affirmation of who they are as lesbian and gay people is often erroneously interpreted as an effort to "recruit" others...

All:
We will stand...

Because the suitability of gay and lesbian people to be parents to their children or role models to other young people is so often questioned...

All:
We will stand...

Because lesbian and gay people are so constantly forced, in our homophobic society, to question their worth as human beings...

All:
We will stand...

Because lesbian and gay history is virtually absent from literature...

All:
We will stand...

Because homophobia is so often sanctioned by our state and federal courts and endorsed by ecclesiastical officials...

All:
We will stand...

Third Reading

"Coming Out" by Carter Heyward (From *Touching Our Strength: The Erotic as Power and the Love of God*, c. 1989, Harper and Row, San Francisco.)

Coming out is a relational process associated with lesbians' and gay men's public affirmation of ourselves in relation to one another. Coming out of the closet in which our relational lives are kept hidden from public view and, usually, condemnation, we move into a shared power.... This power is sacred because it is shared. It is transforming because it is creative. And our power is liberating because it moves the struggle for justice. By this power, in this power, and with this power, we find ourselves-in-relation, breaking out of the isolation imposed by silence and invisibility.

Coming out, we well may be drawn into our power in right relation.

I suspect that nothing is more heartbreaking to God than the denial of our power to recognize, call forth, and celebrate right relation among ourselves. Locked within ourselves, holding secrets and denial, we embody not merely the fear of our relational possibilities; we also embody the rejection of the sacred ground of our being, which is none other than our power to connect.

The fear of mutuality is the fear of our intrinsic interrelatedness, the fact that literally I am nobody without you. Our we-ness created my I-ness and yours as well. And we fear this creation, this calling forth of ourselves, in this particular social location in the late twentieth century. Our fear of mutuality is embedded in such structures of advanced patriarchal capitalism as marriage, sexual "identity," family, education, business, medicine, religion and psychotherapy. This fear is so deeply structured into our social organization and psyches that we have learned not only to accept as normal but also to affirm it as a good sign of a healthy self, separate and independent...

Coming out of the chilly delusion that personhood is autonomous, breaking free of the notion that self-possession should be our personal and professional goal, we come into our power to call forth the YES that connects us... Coming out, we invite each other through the veils of fear set between us for generations.

Sung Response
"Singing For Our Lives"

Fourth Reading
"The Mystery of Being Gay" by Malcom Boyd
(From *Take Off The Masks*, Garden City, NY: Doubleday and Company, 1978.)

The mystery of being gay puzzles and astonishes me. Why are there gays? What does it mean to be the Jew, the black, the gay, someone who must suffer in a particular way within the "normal majority" culture? What, if any, unique mission or vocation is involved in this? One is compelled to ask such questions when one is different and belongs to such a sharply defined minority.

Gay used to stand for pretense and patterned choreography, playing prescribed roles and wearing masks. "Make it gay" was the watchword. It meant "put on the ritz," "keep the act going," "don't let down your guard," "keep on smiling"- especially to conceal your sadness.

But there has been a change. Gay now means a new honesty. Where it used to signify a mask, now it is a call to take off the masks. Its definition has shifted from form to content, sheer style to reality.

So, gay has something of universal meaning to say to everybody. Take off the masks of repressed anger, self-pity, sexual deceit, hypocrisy, social exploitation, and spiritual arrogance. Let communication be an event that involves people, not a charade of puppets. Be yourself. Relate to other selves without inhibition and pretense. Help others to be themselves, too.

The journey toward self-honesty includes the study of one's myths. Everybody has them. So do you and I. Since we invariably create many of our personal myths, it should not be extraordinarily difficult for us to perceive them honestly.

Also, most of us have painstakingly constructed our own masks, the ones we wear and change ritualistically as we move from one situation to another, this relationship to that. To take off the masks is to stop the ritual for its own sake, and let life replace it.

What happens to a person whose mask has been shed? Speaking for myself, I feel better than ever before. I am incredibly energized. I acknowledge the mystery of my creation, and my own mission within it. The reality of my self, as a person created in God's image, is openly shared for the first time. I am grateful that I did not go to the grave without sharing it happily. My closet door is unhinged. Light and air are flooding into that claustrophobic dungeon cell in which I spent more than fifty years of my life.

Beyond all expectation, I have discovered release and freedom, joy and love. Isn't the purpose of our lives to develop and evolve with every breath we take, in every second we live? I have been able to risk everything, and this at an age when many people begin to settle in for their end.

With great zest I celebrate life. I have countless friends. I am filled with joy and gratitude. I love. I am evolving as a person. How could I possibly ask for anything more?

I have learned that a mask is a lie, that it obscures deep truths, that it gets in the way of life. The time has come to take off the masks.

Closing Prayer

An adaptation of the Prayer of Jesus (From *A New Zealand Prayer Book*, c. 1989, William Collins Publishers Ltd., Auckland, New Zealand.)

All:
Eternal Spirit,
Earth-Maker, Pain-bearer, Life-giver,
Source of all that is and that shall be,
Father and Mother of us all, Loving God,
in whom is heaven:

The hallowing of your name echos through the universe!
The way of your justice be followed by the peoples of the world!
Your heavenly will be done by all created beings!
Your commonwealth of peace and freedom sustain our hope and come on Earth!

With the bread we need for today, feed us.
In the hurts we absorb from one another, forgive us.
In times of temptation and test, strengthen us.
From trials too great to endure, spare us.
From the grip of all that is evil, free us.
For you reign in the glory of the power that is love, now and forever. Amen.

Closing Song
"We Are Called" *(By David Haas, c. 1988, GIA.)*

(Developed specifically for this book by David Gentry-Akin, a theologian, writer and teacher who lives in the San Francisco Bay Area.)

Resurrection Vigil: Ministry Rooted in Baptism

Background

The resurrection vigil has been a part of the church's public prayer since the 4th century, first attested to in Jerusalem. It was originally a watch on Saturday night before Sunday, which always commemorated the resurrection. The liturgy is specifically a commemorative of the women who brought spices to the tomb early on the first Easter morning and were the first to see the risen Christ.

The baptismal memorial was used to connect the resurrection of Christ to the individual Christian's resurrection - that stress should remain and be augmented only by the fact that all calls to ministry are rooted in baptism.

The vigiling format of reading-response-prayer was the most common prayer format in the early church.

At the front of the group should be placed the Paschal candle, or a large white candle , a pitcher of water and a large bowl.

Candle Lighting

(Invite someone to light the Paschal candle.)

Opening Prayer

Presider:
In the beginning was the word and the word was God—a light that shines in the darkness, a light that darkness could not overpower and so we pray: Be here among us, bring us to life.

All:
Bring us to life.

Presider:
Light in the midst of us...*Bring us to life.*
Flame of our life, God in the midst of us...*Bring us to life.*
Be our Bread, be in our blood...*Bring us to life.*
Do not turn away, do not let us die...*Bring us to life.*
Soul of our heart and light of our light...*Bring us to life.*
On this night, be our God...*Bring us to life.*
O God, come back and restore us to honor...*Bring us to life.*
O God, come back and give us peace...*Bring us to life.*

Opening Song

"Psalm 27" *(c. 1984, ICEL)*

Reading

Jeremiah 1:4-10

Reflection

by Mary Ruth Quinn (adapted)

These are times to witness to the greatness of God and the inscrutable wisdom of the Spirit. This is not a time to falter but to walk forward in prayerful discernment. Speaking truth to power, being that power that God fully created us to be. We are already consecrated people.

Before our birth, before our baptism, before whatever the future ordains for us. We are anointed prophets. We must not capitulate to fear... Did God wait for the world to be ready before calling and sending the prophet Jeremiah and Jesus? Our mandate from God is to continue the work of Christ Jesus and history shows that is never easy. The words we hear today are hard on our ears - to pluck up, to destroy, to overthrow. Easier are the words to plant, and to build. Yet every prophet knows plucking up is as important as building. Conversion of the human heart and transformation of human structures need and require both.

How can we remember and be guided in our common purpose? Let's recall the place where Jesus consecrated and knew us - the womb. In traditional Judaism and Christianity the womb was considered unclean and impure and yet God called that "holy ground." The place of our consecration. In this place of our womb, we as women, experience the paschal mystery every month. In the shedding of that womb there is a dying and a rising to new life. There is a bleeding, there is a pain and a new openness to new hope, to new life, to new possibilities. The shedding of our wombs reminds us of the shedding of women's tears everywhere. In that womb is the place where blood and water commingle in a consecration...

In God's womb, we are created holy and compassionate people. We read in scripture that the Hebrew word "rahim" speaks of God's compassion. God's very womb is moved in compassion for us. And like God, we too are moved in compassion toward one another. To live with compassion, to act with passion and with justice. In our womb, we create the embodied chalice of new possibilities. There is one woman who believed in new possibilities and in her consecration and because of her and because of you we are all gathered here in prayer. Hallowed be your name and your journeys and each of your sacred stories of consecrated life.

Psalm Prayer

Presider:
Let us pray.

God our sustainer, You have called your people out into the wilderness to travel your unknown ways. Make us strong - able to leave behind false security and comfort and give us new hope in our calling, that the desert may bloom like a rose and your promises be fulfilled in us. We ask this through Christ, our brother and our friend. Amen.

Reading:
1 Corinthians 12:4-11

Song

"Veni Sancte Spiritus" *(Text: Come Holy Spirit; verses drawn from Pentecost Sequence; Taize Community, 1978 / Tune: Jacques Berthier, c. 1979, Les Presses de Taize.)*

Psalm Prayer

Presider:
Let us pray.

O Covenant God, you call us to the risk of commitment even from the place of despair. As Ruth and Naomi loved and held onto one another abandoning the ways of the past, so may we also not be divided but travel together into that strange land where you will lead us. We ask this through Jesus the Christ. Amen.

Reading

Luke 18:1-8

Psalm Prayer

Presider:
Let us pray.

O God, the power of the powerless, you have chosen as your witnesses those whose voices are not heard. Grant that as women first announced the resurrection though they were not believed, grant that we too have the courage to persist in proclaiming your word. In the name of Jesus Christ. Amen.

Gospel Acclamation

"Easter Alleluia"
(Text: Marty Haugen; Tune: O FILLII ET FILIAE; 10 10 10 with alleluias; adapted by Marty Haugen, c. 1986, GIA.)

Gospel

Mark 16:1-7

Reflection

"Who will Roll Away the Stone?" by Cindy Pile

Who will roll away the stone for us from the door of the tomb?

Like the women who approached the place of death and finality early that morning, carrying with them not only spices but a deep sense of anguish and betrayal, we gather with our experience of our pain and our anguish. We come to ask: "Who will roll away the stone, who will take away the obstacles that keep our gifts and our call to ministry in the church from being fully recognized?"

The answer comes to us in the words we just heard proclaimed. The stone was rolled back. The early morning sun was already streaming in, permeating the darkness and dankness of the cave. He is risen. He is not here. God had removed the stone and in many senses, God has already removed our stone.

As we gather here today, women and men together, and pray that the gifts of leadership which women have to offer the church be fully recognized and confirmed, we experience Christ present among us. As women continue to dance and to pray, to theologize and to minister we experience the rolled back stone and the risen Christ. Jesus is present in the women who continue to be faithful to the call of the Gospel despite the suppression of their voices and experience.

What then is left to do, but to spread this wondrous, incredible news? Go, tell our sisters and brothers, tell our bishops, tell the whole of humanity that he is risen. He is alive and this is where you will find him. The risen Christ has appeared just as he promised and you will recognize him in us - in the women who like Jesus have wounds in their hearts and yet have faith in their souls. He can be found in the women who have known the agony of the crucified one and yet continue to proclaim him as risen.

Baptismal Memorial

Blessing of the Water

Presider:

And now we'll bless this water in remembrance of our baptism.
(The presider pours water into the bowl.)

Loving God,
Creator of the heavens and earth
You have made the water a beautiful gift to us.
Through it You refresh us and sustain our lives.
You cleanse us and support all growing things.
Your Son promised to give us living water,
and gave us the gift of the Spirit flowing through us.
Into the waters of baptism we were plunged into the death of Jesus
and raised to new life in You.
(The presider invites those gathered to extend their hands over the water.)

All:

By this water we remember our baptism. Out of this water we rise with new life, forgiven of
sin and one in Christ. Members of Christ's holy body.

Presider:

Bless this water and make it a source of life, of refreshment, of cleanliness and joy to all.
Bless all gathered here, bless us in our work and in our lives. As ministers in the church,
as people of God. We ask this through Jesus the Christ. Amen. I now invite you to come
forward and bless yourselves and one another with this holy and life-giving water.

*(As people start to come forward begin singing "There is One Lord" by Owen Alstott, c. 1984,
OCP (replace the word Lord with Love), and then to read the Litany of Holy Women as the song
continues to be sung.)*

Litany of Holy Women

Noah's wife
on an ark for 40 days and nights with all those animals.

Sarah, Heart of the Covenant, Mother of Nations
who conceived laughter in her old age.

Rebekah, Woman of Ingenuity
achieving her own purposes in a patriarchal world.

Rachel, who waited seven years and seven days
waited for love, waited for life.

Mother and sister of Moses and Pharaoh's daughter
whose courage allowed Moses to live and accomplish the Exodus.

Hannah,
Witness to the power of prayer and consequences of faith.

Wise woman of Tekoa
whom men in authority consulted for the wisdom of her words.

Woman of womanly wisdom
Wiser than the wisdom
of Solomon whose mother's love saved her child from
the stinging slice of the sword.

Huldah, Prophet of Israel
whose judgment shaped the canon that contains God's holy word.
Mary, Mother of Jesus, the Christ
a woman one of us.

Elizabeth
who proved that one is never too old
to have their dreams come true.

Anna, Prophet at prayer in the temple when Jesus was presented to God
who from that moment began proclaiming Jesus and salvation to all.

Mary, mother of Joseph and James
who joined Jesus in ministry.

Salome, who followed Jesus and shared in his ministry.

Mary and Martha of Bethany
all friends with whom he felt at home and shared his ministry.

Generous widow, praised by Jesus because she gave all she had.

Prophetic woman, who discerned the truth and proclaimed
Jesus Messiah by anointing his head with oil.

Priscilla, known also as Prisca,
church leader and teacher in a team ministry with her husband.

Chloe, prominent in the Corinthian Church.

Four women prophets - daughters of Philip
who preached prophetically.

Women of Corinth who prayed and prophesied in Church
whom Paul enjoined to keep silent.

Rhoda, maid at the house of Mary
mother of John Mark who, in her joy at seeing Peter,
left him standing at the gate.

Claudia, in ministry in the Church.

All those women of the early Church
who were truly pioneers, prophets, preachers, pastoral leaders,
following in the footsteps of Jesus.
Lucy, who according to tradition witnessed to her faith by giving generously to the poor,
and who during an early Christian persecution
was denounced by the man to whom she was betrothed.
She was martyred in the year 303.

Monica, mother of Augustine
who beseeched God for his conversion until her prayer was heard
who was influential in the life of her son and the Church because of her piety.

Paula, scholarly friend of Jerome, respected Doctor of the Church
whose circle of learning for women in Rome remains virtually unknown.

Bridget, patron saint of Ireland
who founded a monastic center of learning
in the fifth century, influential in politics and Church affairs.

Hildegard of Bingen
12th century mystic, one of the great minds of medieval Europe,
abbess, scientist, scholar, composer, visionary, poet.

Closing Prayer

Presider:
Let us now pray for God's blessing.

Loving God, we have gathered here as people of faith, seeking your wisdom and guidance,
patience and power. Help us to continue to grow in the knowledge and love of your son
Jesus Christ that we might live and work and celebrate truly as one body. We ask this
through Jesus Christ. Amen.

Closing Song

"Freedom is Coming" *(Text: South African, Tune: South African, c., 1994, Utryck.)*

(This prayer service and public witness with adaptations was organized by Women's
Ministry Dialogue on the occasion of the National Catholic Conference of Bishops'
meeting at Santa Clara University, Santa Clara, California in June 1990.)

Prayer Vigil for Disarmament

When people arrive, pass out candles for the lighting ritual.

Call To Repentance

Reader:

Poor countries now spend $185 billion yearly on arms and soldiers - more than double the development aid they receive from all sources. Because the United States has become the largest exporter of weapons to the world we pray, Christ have mercy.

All:

Christ have mercy.

Reader:

We could provide clean water, prevent soil erosion and eliminate illiteracy worldwide while reversing ozone depletion and stopping global warming with only 25 percent of the world's total annual military expenditures. For our misappropriation of the wealth you have given us we pray, Christ have mercy.

All:

Christ have mercy.

Reader:

Archbishop May tells us, "When a weapons manufacturer says we must build weapons because we need jobs, it is troubling indeed...unemployment is not an excuse to make war or things of war." For the times when we have made jobs hostage to the proliferation of weapons we pray, Christ have mercy.

All:

Christ have mercy.

Scripture Reading

Jeremiah 5:23-28, 13:15-16

(Silent reflection.)

Lighting of the Candles

Leader:

In the midst of the darkness of such violence, we look for the light. As a sign of our faith, our hope, in this light - the Light who has already come into the world, the Light that the darkness can never overcome - let us light these candles which we now hold.

(Leader lights their candle and then lights the candle of the next person and so on...)

Song

"Prayer for Peace" *(By David Haas, c. 1987, GIA.)*

Reading

Words of Martin Luther King Jr.

Reader 1:
These are revolutionary times. All over the globe people are revolting against old systems of exploitation and oppression, and out of the wombs of a frail world, new systems of justice and equality are being born. The shirtless and barefoot people of the land are rising up as never before. "The people who sat in darkness have seen a great light." We in the West must support these revolutions...Our only hope today lies in our ability to recapture the revolutionary spirit and go out into a sometimes hostile world declaring eternal hostility to poverty, racism and militarism.

All:
Make us a light to the world.

Reader 2:
I refuse to accept the view that humankind is so tragically bound to the starless midnight of racism that the bright daybreak of peace and kinship can never become a reality...I believe that even amid today's mortar bursts and whining bullets, there is still hope for a brighter tomorrow. I believe that wounded justice lying prostrate on the blood-flowing streets of our nations can be lifted from the dust of shame to reign supreme among the children of humankind.

All:
Make us a light to the world.

Reader 3:
Christians of the United States, I must say to you what was written to the Roman Christians years ago, "Be not conformed to this world: but be transformed by the renewing of your mind." You have a dual citizenry. Your highest loyalty is to God, and not to the mores or the folkways, the state or the nation or any human-made institution. If any earthly institution or custom conflicts with God's will, it is your Christian duty to oppose it.

All:
Make us a light to the world.

Reader 4:
Expediency asks the question, "Is it politic?" and vanity comes along and asks the question, "Is it popular?" And there comes a time when one must take a position that is neither safe nor politic nor popular, but one must do it because conscience tells them it is right. And this is where I believe we must go, as ministers of the Gospel.

All:
Make us a light to the world.

Reader 5:
So often the contemporary church is ineffectual and weak, with an uncertain voice. So often it is an arch defender of the status quo...If today's church does not recapture the sacrificial spirit of the early church it will lose its authenticity, forfeit the loyalty of millions and be dismissed as an irrelevant social club with no meaning for the twentieth century.

All:
Make us a light to the world.

Reader 6:
A nation that continues year after year to spend more money on military defense than on programs of social uplift is approaching spiritual death...Our scientific power has outrun our spiritual power. We have guided missiles and misguided people.

All:
Make us a light to the world.

Reader 7:
Dear God, we thank you for the gift of Martin Luther King, Jr. His public witness to peace with justice is an example of what it means to be Christian disciples. Grant us the same light that led Martin to the mountaintop to see the promised land.

All:
Amen.

Prayers of the Faithful

Leader:
Our God stands ready to give us what we need to be a light to the nations and so we respond...

All:
God be our light.

Leader:
That our government, business and community leaders might work together to provide our defense workers in the United States with meaningful work that protects the environment and serves the human needs of the poor at home and around the world, we pray...

All:
God be our light.

That we might have the courage to raise our voices and actively work to end the evils of racism, poverty and militarism, we pray...

All:
God be our light.

Please add your own intentions...*(God be our light).*

Our Mother and Father, who art in heaven...

Closing Song
"World Peace Prayer" *(By Marty Haugen, c. 1985, GIA.)*

(Adapted from a prayer vigil planned by Tricia Sullivan for an Air Force arms bazaar held in Washington DC.)

We Stand in Solidarity: Prayer for Those Going to Prison for Reasons of Conscience

This service can be held several days before someone goes to jail, or it can be held outside of the jail itself immediately before the person begins serving their sentence.

Call to Prayer

Leader:

We gather together today/this evening to pray for *(name)* who will begin serving her/his prison sentence in a few days/hours because s/he took part in an action at *(describe reasons for action)*. We ask that God bless *(name)* with an abundance of strength and courage and with the awareness that we as a community stand in solidarity with her/him. We come together, as well, to remember all prisoners of conscience throughout the world.

Reading

(From *Peace Behind Bars* by John Dear, S.J., Sheed & Ward, 1995 p. 230.)

Matthew 25 insists that Christ is present among those in prison. Our jails and prisons are packed with the poor and the marginalized, especially with African-Americans and Latinos. Since Scripture maintains that God takes the side of the oppressed and is determined to liberate them, I knew that God was in our midst.

I liked to compare ourselves with Shadrach, Meshach and Abednego, in the fiery furnace for refusing to worship the emperor's idols. While the flames burned around us, we remained unburned, and a fourth person like a Son of God stood in our midst. We realized that Christ presented himself to us in the suffering prisoners around us.

Going to jail on behalf of disarmament and peace offers a living solidarity with the poor that is not available in any other way. I found myself without any possessions and without the freedom to do as I please. I tasted for a few months the bitter poverty, powerlessness and helplessness which is the daily lot for most of humanity. For someone with a vow of poverty, it was nothing less than a revelation. Christ among the poor is teaching me a new lesson.

(Silent reflection.)

Readings

(Take turns reading these passages aloud, with a brief pause between each one.)

There may be times when we are powerless to prevent injustice, but there must never be a time when we fail to protest. (By Elie Wiesel, *Peacemaking Day By Day II*, p.68, c. Pax Christi USA.)

There is nothing wrong with a traffic law which says you have to stop for a red light. But when a fire is raging, the fire truck goes right through the red light...Or, when a person is bleeding to death, the ambulance goes through those red lights at top speed...Disinherited people all over the world are bleeding to death from deep social and economic wounds. They need brigades of ambulance drivers who will have to ignore the red lights of the present system until the emergency is solved...Massive civil disobedience is a strategy for social change which is at least as forceful as an ambulance with its sirens on full. (By Martin Luther King, Jr., *Peacemaking Day By Day II*, p.50.)

Everywhere one turns, in jail or out, with prisoners, with movement people, with militant clergy persons, dove politicians, well-meaning bureaucrats of all denominations and hues, the big question is, "What will it (the action) cost me?" Rarely is the question turned around to become, "What will it cost me if I don't act?" (By Philip Berrigan in *Peacemaking Day By Day II*, p.52.)

When nothing seems to help, I go look at a stonecutter hammering away at a rock perhaps a hundred times without as much as a crack showing in it. Yet at the hundredth and first blow it will split in two, and I know it was not that blow that did it but all that had gone before. *(By Jacob Riis.)*

The soul of our country needs to be awakened...When the leaders act contrary to conscience, we must act contrary to the leaders. (By Veterans Fast for Life, *Peacemaking Day By Day II*, p.43.)

What I want to bring out is how a pebble cast into a pond causes ripples that spread in all directions. Each one of our thoughts, words and deeds is like that. (By Dorothy Day, *Peacemaking Day By Day II*, p.24.)

Resistance and nonviolence are not in themselves good. There is another element in our struggle that then makes our resistance and nonviolence truly meaningful. That element is reconciliation. The tactics of nonviolence without the spirit of nonviolence may become a new kind of violence. (By Rev. Martin Luther King, Jr., *Peacemaking Day By Day II*, p.132.)

Jesus promised those who would follow his leadings only three things; that they should be absurdly happy, entirely fearless, and always in trouble. (By Marty Babcock, *Peacemaking Day By Day II*, p.120.)

If civil disobedience is enacted in a prayerful spirit of nonviolent love, it takes on the nature of a sacrament. When civil disobedience is engaged in a prayerful spirit of nonviolent love as a sacrament, God is present. In that presence, God's love transforms the hearts and moves the minds of all those involved, setting forth a peaceful tide of love that converts people, beginning with those committing the civil disobedience, and transforms the violent structures of injustice into nonviolent channels of justice. *(By John Dear, SJ.)*

Shared Prayers
(All are invited to share their prayers for the person going to prison.)

Closing Prayer
"Imprisonment After Civil Disobedience" *(By Tom Cordaro (adapted) c. Pax Christi USA.)*

All:
Saving Jesus, who suffered the humiliation of imprisonment, come to our sister/brother (name) now in her/his hour of need. Free his/her heart from fear and anguish as s/he contemplates her/his imprisonment. Do not abandon her/him to the darkness of the pit. Do not cut her/him off from family and this community of faith. Be his/her light in the darkness of the prison cell, and help her/him to see your light in the eyes of those who share imprisonment with her/him.

Give her/him the courage to be vulnerable to all s/he meets so that, in her/his weakness, your loving power might be known. Give her/him the virtues of patience and long-suffering that s/he might be light to all who live in darkness. May s/he be sustained by the prayers of those who love her/him. And may her/his imprisonment be a living witness to your faith which calls us not to count the cost. Amen.

Blessing

Leader:
Please extend your hands over (name) as we pray together:

All:
May God bless you and keep you.
May the light of God's face shine upon you.
May God be gracious to you.
May God look upon you kindly.
May God fill you with peace. Amen.

Closing Song

"We Are Called" *(By David Haas, c. 1988, GIA.)*

(Adapted from a prayer service developed by Nancy Small and Michelle Balek, OSF, before Ray La Port, a volunteer with Pax Christi USA, served time in prison for an action he had participated in at the School of the Americas.)

Table of Many Breads

Many types of bread will be used in this ritual. You might want to ask community members to, when possible, bake some of the bread themselves, or to be responsible for bringing one loaf. You will want to present such a variety of breads in an array of baskets and plates. You might also want to prepare the area where the bread will be placed with colorful fabric, candles, etc. You will need two leaders and two readers for this service.

Opening Song

"Song of the Body of Christ" *(v. 1-3)*
(Text: David Haas / Music: traditional Hawaiian melody, c. 1989, GIA.)

Opening Prayer

Leader 1:
We give you thanks God of Abundant Life,
for bread and friendship and hope.
With these gifts of Your grace we are nourished.
With these signs of Your presence we are able to be faithful.
Continue then to nourish us, inspire us and call us.
That we might help make Your reign more of a reality in our day. Amen.

Reading

Exodus 16:4, 13a-18

Introduction to the Rite

Leader 2:
No matter what culture, what part of the world, seed, grain, wheat, rice cakes, tortillas or rye bread, bread symbolizes our lives of struggle and promise. Throughout the world, in different lands, and in our own country, the struggle for life, for dignity, for bread, still continues. But within the struggle lives a voice - a cry of hope, a whisper of promise, a plea for wholeness. For though we have many grains, there is only one loaf so that we might be joined together.

These breads we have brought this evening are symbols of our bondedness, brought forth from seed to loaf in a birthing process. Seeds nourished by Mother Earth and "lifed" into growth...then harvested and crushed into flour. Flour yeasted, then kneaded by loving hands, shaped and baked with care.

Presentation of Breads

(Various people bring forth each type of bread as two people read the "Blessing of Many Breads: A Taste of Justice" by Diann L. Neu from *Women-Church Sourcebook*, c. 1993, WATER, The Women's Alliance for Theology, Ethics and Ritual, 8035 13th St., Silver Spring, MD 20910, 301/589-2509.)

Reader 1:
We bring rye bread to the table today. It is the staple bread of the laboring class in much of Eastern Europe. Let it represent for us all women and men who work for justice. Let it symbolize all who are unemployed and seeking jobs. Let it remind us of women and men who are discriminated against in wages and work.

Reader 2:
We bring rice cakes to the table. Rice in antiquity was in many places very rare and treasured. Thus, it was kept for medicinal uses. Let these rice cakes represent women and men who are ill, especially those living with AIDS. Let these cakes remind us of the healing that is needed because of the rejection and pain that church, family and society has caused.

Reader 1:

We bring sourdough bread to the table. It has as its leavening agent a small amount of dough kept from the last batch. Let us hold in mind our mothers and fathers, our grandparents and all of our ancestors, those whose life blood we have in our veins.

Reader 2:

We bring unleavened bread calling to mind refugees and those in exile. Let this matzoh, so important in Passover meals, remind us of our Jewish brothers and sisters. Let it represent all those peoples around the world who are in refugee camps.

Reader 1:

We bring cornbread to the table. This cornbread represents our African American sisters and brothers who are oppressed by racism, sexism and unjust structures. Let this remind us of people of all races and cultures who have been enslaved by injustice.

Reader 2:

We bring tortillas to the table. Tortillas remind us most immediately of our brothers and sisters of Central America. Let these tortillas symbolize all of the Latino peoples who have suffered in war, those who are bereaved, and those immigrants in this country who live in fear of deportation. Let these tortillas remind us of our peacemakers who struggle for peace and justice even at the cost of their own lives.

Reader 1:

We bring shortbread (gingerbread) to the table. Shortbread (gingerbread) brings to mind children. Let it signify little girls and boys and those especially concerned for children. Let it symbolize mothers and fathers, teachers and midwives. Those who care for children. Those who are role models for the next generation.

Reader 2:

We bring saltines to this table. It represents the elderly, the "salty ones." Those who have endured. Those who have learned wisdom, those who are fragile.

Reader 1:

We bring pita bread to the table. It is a symbol of Middle Eastern people, and speaks of the capacity of all those people with space within to hold others in hospitality despite the suffering endured because of our country's greed. Those who are a steady, secure, quiet presence in the midst of a harsh and barren land.

Blessing of Breads

Leader 1:

As Christians, bread not only speaks of our oneness as sisters and brothers, but also touches into the mystery of the reign of God among us. In the Bible, bread often signifies food, nourishment and more. We eat bread in anticipation of the coming of God's reign, that messianic banquet to which all are invited.

Jesus says, "I am the Bread of Life. I am the living bread that comes down from heaven. Whoever eats this bread shall never die." When the disciples ate with Jesus, they realized that he was alive. Their eyes were opened in the breaking of the bread. Let us approach the bread before us that our eyes might be opened and we might recognize Jesus, the Crucified and Risen One, and one another, in the breaking of the bread.

Leader 2:

This bread is a reminder that anyone who comes to this table and eats of this bread believes in a new world. We believe in a world where bread is for everyone, a world where one day poor people will eat their fill and rich people will share what they have. Everyone who shares in this bread shares in a covenant with the brokenhearted and with all those who are

185

yearning for justice. For this bread evokes a hunger in us that will never be satisfied until we taste the reign of God in all its fullness.

Let us approach this table, then, in confidence, in anticipation of the coming of God's reign. I invite you to extend your hands in blessing over this bread.

All:

We ask you, Loving God, to bless us and to bless all hands and hearts that have yeasted us. Bless our memories of our ancestors who have brought us to this place. And bless this bread which will make us holy as we wait and work for the fulfillment of your promise.

(Invite people to come forward and take a piece of one or two types of bread that spoke to them, to return to their seats and then to share the bread with the person next to them as they explain why they chose that particular bread.)

Leader 1:

Let us now stand, join hands, and ask God to provide us with the bread that we need each day to continue our journey as seekers of justice and peace.

The Prayer of Jesus

Kiss of Peace and Dismissal

Leader 2:

God has nourished us through this bread, through the Word, and through this community gathered here this evening. Let us go in peace-and let us share a sign of that peace with one another.

Closing Song

"One Bread, One Body"
(By John Foley, SJ, c. 1978, John Foley, SJ and North American Liturgy Resources.)

(Adapted from a ritual used by Patricia Bruno, OP, and Jude Siciliano, OP, for a parish retreat.)

Interfaith Fast for Justice for Homeless People

You will need one loaf, or several loaves, of bread, depending on the size of the congregation, to be brought forward and blessed as part of the service.

Opening Song

"The Circle's Larger" *(v.1) (By Colleen Fulmer, c. 1990, Loretto Spirituality Network.)*

Opening Prayer

Leader 1:

We gather today to open a fast for justice for our homeless sisters and brothers. We gather to speak out on their behalf because if we don't speak, then who will? If we don't speak out now, then when? And if we don't speak out here, in this city, in this country, then where will we speak? So let us speak out loudly and clearly. Let us open our circle wider to include all who seek a home.

Calls to Compassion and Justice from Various Faith Traditions

The Buddhist Faith:
(From The Metta Sutta.)

This is what should be accomplished by the one who is wise, who seeks the good and has obtained peace:

Let one be strenuous, upright and sincere, without pride, easily contented and joyous.
Let one not be submerged by the things of the world.
Let one not take upon one's self the burden of riches.
Let one's senses be controlled.
Let one be wise but not puffed up, and let one not desire great possessions,
even for one's family. Let one do nothing that is mean or that the wise would reprove.
May all beings be happy.
May they be joyous and live in safety.

All living beings, whether weak or strong, in high or middle or low realms of existence, small or great, visible or invisible, near or far, born or to be born, may all beings be happy.

Let no one deceive another. Nor despise any being in any state; let none by anger or hatred wish harm to another.

Even as a mother at the risk of her life watches over and protects her only child, so with a boundless mind should one cherish all living things, suffusing love over the entire world, above, below, and all around, without limit; so let one cultivate an infinite good will toward the whole world.

Standing or walking, sitting or lying down, during all one's waking hours, let one cherish the thought that this way of living is the best in the world.

Christian Faith:
John 13:34-35

"We seek to mend the brokenness caused by poverty; we seek to heal the brokenness of our own hardended hearts; we seek an end to the cruel persecution of the poor."

Muslim Faith:
(Adapted from The Holy Quran.)

O you who believe! Stand firmly for justice, bearers of witness for God, even though it be against yourselves or your parents or near relatives. Whether someone is rich or poor, God's claim takes precedence over (the claims of) either of them. So do not follow your own desires lest you swerve from justice; and if you lapse or fall away (from truth), then verily, God is aware of what you do. *(Quran, Sura Nisa: v. 135.)*

O you who believe! For the sake of God, stand up to uphold justice and let not ill will towards any people impel you to deviate from justice. Act justly. This indeed is akin to piety. Be mindful of God; for assuredly, God knoweth all that you do. *(Quran, Sura Maldah: v.8.)*

Jewish Faith:
Isaiah 58: 6-11

(Silent reflection.)

Leader 2:
Please spend a few moments in silence to reflect on your own sources of inspiration: from your faith tradition, from other prophetic people, and to consider how you personally may be called to offer a moral response to the cry of the poor.

(Allow time for silent reflection.)

A Communal Response to the Call

Reader 1:
The kind of fasting I want is this: Remove the chains of oppression and the yoke of injustice, and let the oppressed go free.

All:
The soul of this nation hungers for justice.

Reader 2:
Share your food with the hungry and open your homes to the homeless poor.

All:
The soul of this nation hungers for compassion.

Reader 1:
Millions of people go homeless each night in cities and towns throughout our country.

All:
The soul of this nation hungers for housing.

Reader 2:
Homeless people are being criminalized - arrested for sitting on sidewalks, for begging for money, for sleeping on park benches.

All:
The soul of this nation hungers for mercy.

Reader 1:
Homeless people are reviled as outcasts, rejected as untouchables, driven out of our cities and out of our hearts.

All:
The soul of this nation hungers for forgiveness and tolerance.

Reader 2:
We seek to mend the brokenness caused by poverty; we seek to heal the brokenness of our own hardened hearts; we seek an end to the cruel persecution of the poor.

All:
The soul of this nation hungers for a heart of compassion, not a heart of stone.

Reader 1:
We pray that this fast brings good news for the poor, justice for the oppressed and freedom for the captive. We fast for the day when the meek inherit the earth and the reign of God comes in its fullness.

All:
The soul of this nation hungers for deliverance from our fear, our greed; from our sinfulness.

Our Personal Response
Our Vow to Fast

Leader 1:
Is this not the kind of fasting I desire: to remove the chains of the oppressed and the yoke of injustice, to let the oppressed go free, to share your food with the hungry and open your homes to the homeless? Anyone who is so moved to undertake a fast such as this today, to make a personal vow to fast - for a few hours, a few days, or for the entire time - please make that commitment now either silently within your own heart or spoken aloud before this community.

(Allow time for people to declare their intention to fast.)

Blessing of Fasters

Leader 2:
Please place your hands on the people next to you. Loving God, be with us as we embark on this fast which You so desire. Bless us today as we open our fast, bless us as it becomes more challenging, more difficult to fulfill the vow which we have made before You and this assembly. O Steadfast One, pour out Your strength upon us, make us single-hearted, dedicated, faithful servants in our pursuit of Your justice and Your peace in our world.

Blessing of the Bread
(Members of the community bring forth one loaf of bread which Leader 1 holds up high and invites those gathered to extend their hands over the bread.)

Leader 1:
O Holy One, bless this bread, symbol of Your faithfulness to us, symbol of Your desire to give us all that we need on our journey. Bless this bread, symbol of Your will to satisfy the hunger of those who cry out for food and to shelter those who plead for a home. Bless this bread, symbol of our faithfulness to You and to Your call to stand in solidarity with our homeless sisters and brothers.

(People come forward to break off a piece of the bread. The two leaders can hold the one loaf, or several loaves, depending on the size of the congregation and people can break off pieces. Or the leaders can pass the bread to the first person who breaks off a piece and then passes the loaf to the next person and so on. It is important that people actually break off a piece of bread, rather than have a piece simply handed to them. All return to their seats with the piece of bread. In the background, play the song "There is A Feast" by Colleen Fulmer, c. 1985, Loretto Spirituality Network.)

Sharing of Bread

All:

With this bread, I open my fast. With this bread, I open my fast. With this bread, I open my fast. The soul of this nation hungers and thirsts for justice!

(All eat the bread.)

Sharing a Sign of Peace

Closing Song

"There is A Feast" *(By Colleen Fulmer, c. 1985, Loretto Spirituality Network.)*

(Adapted from the opening service for A Fast for Justice which Religious Witness with Homeless People, an interfaith coalition based in San Francisco, organized in 1995.)

We are a Kaleidoscope of Educators: Called to Reflect the Light of Christ

Place a large candle in a central place in the room - near the altar if you are in a chapel or on a table if you are in a smaller room. Have small candles on hand for people to light later on. Also have ready a slide show that depicts various aspects of the life of your school: students and teachers in class, students at sporting, service and social events, the community at prayer, staff members in their offices, etc.

Call to Prayer

Leader:

Good and Gracious God, we come before You today, in the presence of this community, to reaffirm our commitment to Your work. We are Jesus Christ in the world today. We are called to be a light to all nations. With the guidance and support of Your spirit, we bring Your word to all the people in our school communities. Let us not forget You are always with us. Let our lights burn forever with Your love. We ask this through Jesus Christ, the light of lights, our brother and friend. Amen.

All:

Loving God, every good thing comes from You. Fill us with Your light and Your love and enable us to be a grateful people. By Your constant care, protect the good You have given us. Help us, in turn, to share that good with others.

Lighting of Candle

(Invite someone to light the large candle.)

Song

"Be Light for Our Eyes"
(Text: David Haas / Tune: David Haas and Marty Haugen, c. 1985, GIA.)

First Reading

Isaiah 58:10-11a

Sung Response

"I Have Loved You" *(By Michael Joncas, c. 1979, New Dawn Music.)*

Second Reading

(Excerpt from *To Teach As Jesus Did*, # 13, 23, 28, c. 1973, United States Catholic Conference, Washington DC. Used with permission. All rights reserved.)

Education is one of the most important ways by which the Church fulfills its commitment to the dignity of the person and the building of community...Community is at the heart of Christian education not simply as a concept to be taught but as a reality to be lived. Through education (children) must be moved to build community in all areas of life; they can do this best if they have learned the meaning of community by experiencing it. Formed by this experience, they are better able to build community in their families, their places of work, their neighborhoods, their nation, their world...The experience of Christian community leads naturally to service. Christ gives His people different gifts not only for themselves but for others. Each must serve the other for the good of all.

"The experience of Christian community leads naturally to service."

Alleluia

Gospel
Matthew 5: 14-16

Sung Response with Slides
"City of God"
(Text: Dan Schutte / Tune: Dan Schutte; Acc. by John Weissrock, c. 1981, Daniel L Schutte and North American Liturgy Resources.)

(Begin to show the slide show with instrumental accompaniment, then invite the congregation to join in singing.)

Lighting of Individual Candles
(The leader lights his or her candle from the large candle and then proclaims, "You are called to be the light of Christ!" The congregation responds, "Thanks be to God!" As the light is passed on, each person again says, "You are called to be the light of Christ!" while the person whose candle is being lit responds, "Thanks be to God!")

Litany of Re-Commitment
Leader:
Please respond "I do!" after each statement.

Do you believe in God, the Creator, maker of heaven and earth, the source of our being? I do!
Do you believe in Jesus Christ, God's Son, the light of life, the light of all lights? I do!
Do you believe in the Spirit whose presence is felt in our enthusiasm and in our work? I do!
Do you commit yourself to bringing the word of God to God's children on earth? I do!
Do you promise to care for others in the way of Jesus Christ? I do!
Do you promise to witness to the gospel even in the face of harassment, frustration and apathy? I do!
Do you promise to remain open to the surprises of the Spirit? I do!
Do you commit yourself to the support of your school community? I do!

Leader:
As a seal of our commitment, let us join in praying the prayer of our Christian community, the prayer that Jesus taught us.

The Prayer of Jesus
Final Blessing
Side 1:
Loving and Gracious God, We ask You to bless each of us called to be administrators, teachers and staff in the special ministry of leading, teaching and serving in our Catholic schools.

Side 2:
We pray for each of our students and bring them before You with their unique personalities and all their gifts, challenges and needs.

Side 1:
We remember the parents and guardians of the many children entrusted to our care and ask You to sustain them with Your strength in the joys and burdens of their vocation.

Side 2:
We bring to mind our pastors and church leaders with whom we are called to collaborate that they may receive Your Spirit of Wisdom as they work with us in the great mission of education.

Side 1:
We ask blessings of peace on all our past students our youngest graduates seeking meaning in their future, our oldest alumni bearing the burden of age, and our students who now enjoy eternal glory.

Side 2:
We reverence our predecessors, and ask blessings in full measure for the principals, teachers, and staff members, who labored tirelessly to establish and maintain our schools.

Side 1:
We give thanks for our benefactors, whose gifts of time, talent and treasure create possibilities and assure opportunities for our schools to succeed beyond our hopes and dreams.

All:
We ask You, God of all Wisdom, to send Your Holy Spirit to be our constant companion in all our efforts - the greatest to the least -to form community and to teach as Jesus did. We make this prayer in the name of Jesus Christ, our Brother and our Teacher. Amen.

Closing Song

"City of God" *(v. 1, 4)*

(Adapted from a liturgy planned by Karen Mangini.)

Children's Advent Liturgy

Light one out of the four candles in the Advent wreath. Have another unlit candle placed in the middle of the wreath. Through readings and ritual, involve as many students as possible in the liturgy.

Time to Listen

Reader 1:
A reading from the prophet Isaiah: The people who walked in darkness have seen a great light; upon those who dwelt in the land of gloom a light has shone.

Reader 2:
They lived in the land of shadows, but now a light is shining on them. You have given them great joy, God, You have made them happy.

Response

Reader 1:
Jesus Christ is with us in our homes as we live, work, and play with our families. However, we often ignore this presence of Christ in our homes. We aggravate our parents, who are already burdened with work and stress. We resist doing our share of family chores. We make our brothers and sisters unhappy. We choose to live in the darkness.

(The first candle is blown out.)

Leader:
Let us pause and think about the ways we have sinned at home.

(Pause for one minute then re-light the first candle. Ask participants to repeat the following refrain after you: Come, Jesus, burn brightly during the hours I spend at home with my family.)

All:
Come, Jesus, burn brightly during the hours I spend at home with my family.

(The second candle is lit.)

Reader 2:
Jesus Christ is with us at school and during all after-school activities. He is in our class-rooms, hallways, and lunchrooms. However, we tend to ignore this presence of Christ in the way we behave. We live, study, work, and play as though Jesus Christ makes no difference in our school life. We choose to live in the darkness.

(The candle is blown out.)

Leader:
Let us pause and think about the ways we have sinned during school hours.

(Pause for one minute and then re-light the second candle, saying: Come, Jesus, burn brightly during my school hours.)

All:
Come, Jesus, burn brightly during my school hours.

(The third candle is lit).

Reader 3:
Jesus Christ is with us in our parish as we come together to pray, worship, and grow in faith. However, we often ignore this presence of Christ, not listening to the word of Scripture when it is read and preached. We sometimes refuse to go to church or complain loudly about going. We do not pray. We refuse to give our time to parish youth activities. We do not want to hear about our Gospel responsibility to feed the hungry and serve the poor. We choose to live in the darkness.

(The third candle is blown out.)

Leader:
Let us pause and evaluate the way we spend our time at the parish, especially at liturgy.

(Pause for one minute and then re-light the third candle, saying: Come, Jesus, burn brightly while I pray, worship, and search for a better relationship with you.)

All:
Come, Jesus, burn brightly while I pray, worship, and search for a better relationship with you.

(The fourth candle is lit.)

Reader 4:
Jesus Christ is with us whenever we spend time with our friends. We often ignore this presence of Christ in the things we do and the way we talk. We pick and choose our friends on the basis of popularity. We gossip. We use people. We act as though Jesus Christ makes no difference to us and our friends. We choose to live in the darkness.

(The fourth candle is blown out.)

Leader:
Let us pause and think about the ways we sin when we are with our friends.

(Pause for one minute and then re-light the fourth candle, saying: Come, Jesus, burn brightly while I am with my friends.)

All:
Come, Jesus, burn brightly while I am with my friends.

(The fifth candle is lit.)

Reader 5:
Jesus Christ is with us when we meet people who are different from us - when we pass by a homeless person on the street, when we try to talk to someone who speaks a different language from us, when we visit an elderly relative in a nursing home. We often ignore this presence of Christ in these people because perhaps they frighten us or perhaps we do not know how to help them or what to say to them. And so we ignore them. We run away from them. We make fun of them. We choose to live in the darkness.

(The fifth candle is blown out.)

Leader:
Let us pause and think about how we treat people who are different from us.

(Pause for one minute and then re-light the fifth candle, saying: Come, Jesus, burn brightly when I meet someone in need.)

All:
Come, Jesus, burn brightly when I meet someone in need.

Act of Reconciliation

Give each participant five blank Christmas cards. Invite them to write a Christmas message to five people, one from home, one from school, one from the parish and one from their peer group, with whom they need to be reconciled, and to someone in need. For example: At home, it could be a parent or sibling; at school, a teacher or classmate; in the parish, the priest or youth minister; among friends, anyone they have hurt or been hurt by; among those in need, someone in a nursing home, a homeless shelter or an AIDS hospice.

The children can go to individual confession at this time and work on their cards before or after confession. If they don't finish them during this time, encourage them to finish them at home that night. Invite the children to take the cards home with them as a reminder of their need for reconciliation, and when they feel able to do so, to actually give the cards to the persons involved.

Closing Prayer

Leader:
Come, Jesus, be with us at home and be with us at school. Teach us to acknowledge Your presence when we gather in our parish to pray and worship. Most of all, teach us to be aware of Your presence among our friends and among those who are strangers to us. You are our best and most faithful friend. Show us how to return Your love. We ask You these things in the name of the Creator, Redeemer and Sanctifier.

All:
Amen.

(Adapted from an Advent prayer service prepared by Karen Mangini for the children in her school.)

Children's Lenten Service

You will want to place a Bible on a table at the front of the room. One of the teachers can take it down for a student to do the reading and then return it to the table. You will also need pieces of paper and pencils for the children to write down something they can do during Lent to help their love to grow.

Song

"Grow Strong" *(By Jack Miffleton, c. 1979, World Library Publications, Inc.)*

Opening Prayer

Leader:
We grow in many ways - in our bodies, our minds, our hearts, and in our spirits. During this season of Lent let us thank God for all of the gifts we have been given by trying to grow ever closer to God, that we might become more like God in everything we do and say.

Reading

Colossians 3:12-17

This is a reading from St. Paul to his friends, the Colossians:

Because you have been chosen by God, be kind to others, be humble and patient too. Bear with one another; if someone hurts you, forgive them just as God would forgive you. Above all, love one another, for if you have love, you have everything. Be peacemakers and let peace be in your hearts. Be thankful. Let the word of Jesus dwell in your hearts. Live God's word. Sing joyfully to God from your hearts. Whatever you do, in words or in deeds, do it in the name of Jesus and wherever you go always give thanks to God. This is the word of God.

All:
Thanks be to God.

(Return Bible to table.)

Prayer

Leader:
Gentle and loving God, we thank You for all the good things You constantly bless our lives with. We thank You for our parents who love us so much, even though sometimes it may not feel that way. We thank You for our brothers and sisters who care about us. We thank You for our families who take care of us and for good friends who mean so much to us. We thank You for everything You have given us, even when life seems pretty tough. Please be with us always. Help us to appreciate all that You have given us and to remember to treat all Your gifts with tender love and gentle care. This we ask through Jesus Christ Your son. Amen.

Leader:
God, help us to grow in your love.

Girls:
God, there are many ways to grow.

Boys:
Help us to grow in your love.

"Help us to grow in our care for others. Make us thoughtful. Help us to be cheerful givers."

Girls:
Help us to grow in our care for others.

Boys:
Make us thoughtful.

Girls:
Help us to be cheerful givers.

Boys:
Help us to put others first.

All:
Jesus, you grew in wisdom and age and grace before God and other people.
Help us to do the same.

Offering

(A period of silence and quiet reflection with music. The children are to write down something they can do during Lent to help their love to grow. Then they bring up what they have written and place it on the table next to the Bible.)

Penitential Rite

Leader:
Our response will be:
May God bless us with all goodness.

All:
May God bless us with all goodness.

Reader 1:
For the times I was selfish and demanded my own way. We ask You to forgive us loving God...

All:
May God bless us with all goodness.

Reader 2:
For the times I disobeyed my parents or teachers. We ask You to forgive us loving God...

All:
May God bless us with all goodness.

Reader 1:
For the times I hurt others by putting them down and making fun of them. We ask You to forgive us loving God...

All:
May God bless us with all goodness.

Reader 2:
For the times I did not allow other children to play because I do not like them.
We ask You to forgive us loving God...

All:
May God bless us with all goodness.

Reader 1:

For the times I cheated in schoolwork or in games. We ask You to forgive us loving God...

All:

May God bless us with all goodness.

Reader 2:

For the times I told lies to keep out of trouble. We ask You to forgive us loving God...

All:

May God bless us with all goodness.

Reader 1:

For the times I took things that belonged to others. We ask You to forgive us loving God...

All:

May God bless us with all goodness.

Reader 2:

For the times I hit or pushed others because I was angry. We ask You to forgive us loving God...

All:

May God bless us with all goodness.

Reader 1:

For the times I refused to forgive someone for hurting me. We ask You to forgive us loving God... May God bless us with all goodness.

Reader 2:

For the times I have been lazy and my parents or teachers had to ask me over and over again to do something. We ask You to forgive us loving God...

All:

May God bless us with all goodness.

Reader 1:

For the times I have walked by someone in need and not stopped to help. We ask You to forgive us loving God...

All:

May God bless us with all goodness.

All:

We are very sorry, dear God, for all the times we have offended You because You are always so good and we should love You better than we have. We are especially sorry for having hurt You by treating others badly. We know that You love each of us and want us to become more like You by loving each other. Please help us to do this now and for the rest of our lives. Amen.

Closing Song

"Grow Strong"

(Adapted from a Lenten prayer service created by Karen Mangini.)

House Blessing and Liturgy

You will need several bowls of water and possibly branches/palm leaves for the blessing of the rooms, as well as bread and wine for the Liturgy of the Eucharist.

Entrance Song

"Gather Us In" *(By Marty Haugen, c. 1982, GIA.)*

Welcome/Introductions

Leader 1:
Peace be with this house and all who live and visit here.

All:
And also with you.

Leader 2:
The Word became flesh and made its dwelling place among us. It is Christ who enlightens our hearts and homes with his love - Christ, risen from the dead, who is our source of hope, joy and comfort. May all who enter this home find Christ's light and love.

Gloria

House Blessing

Blessing of the Rooms and Those Present

Blessing of the Water and Sprinkling
Leader 1:
Let this water call to mind our baptism in Christ, who by his death and resurrection has redeemed us.

(Sprinkles people with the water.)

Blessing of the Places

(People move from room to room as each space is blessed. Have on hand several bowls of water and branches or palm leaves (or hands!) so not only the leaders, but everyone gathered can help bless at least some of the rooms.)

Leader 2:
(At the Entrance) Jesus, as you entered Jericho, you went and stayed in the home of Zacchaeus, a tax collector and a wealthy man. Though your followers complained that you would stay at a sinner's house, you were welcomed there joyfully. You told him "Today, salvation has come to this house...for the Son has come to seek out and save what was lost." We pray that you will accompany each person who enters this house and fill us with your love.

Leader 1:
(Living Rooms/Areas) Jesus, you were born of Mary and became flesh. With Mary and Joseph, you formed the Holy Family. The three wise men represented us in presenting their gifts to you in praise and adoration; grant that those living here may find the treasure of your Spirit within themselves and within us. Remain in our home, that we may know you as our guest and honor you as our foundation.

Leader 2:
(Dining Room/Kitchen) Jesus, you dined with sinners and outcasts, fed the hungry crowds with what seemed like mere scraps, and shared food with your friends at Passover. Then, it was in the breaking of the bread that they recognized you again after your resurrection. May your love burn in our hearts here as we, through the power of your Spirit, make miracles happen. Though they be small, let us recognize your presence in them.

Leader 1:

(Bedrooms) Jesus, you said that you had no place to rest your head, but in the spirit of poverty accepted the hospitality of your friends. Your call has come to many in their dreams and you have raised many from the dead as they lay in their beds. Grant, Jesus, that those who are in need may find a place of rest and hospitality here, that your Word may bring us healing and new life as we place our weary heads in your lap.

Leader 2:

(Bathrooms) Jesus, as we wash our bodies, may we remember how we have been washed and made new through our baptism. Wash away our pain and sorrow. Grant that we will come to know you in the waters.

Leader 1:

(Entire House and Yard) Jesus, you told us: "When you give a lunch or dinner, do not ask your friends who may repay you. Instead, invite those who cannot repay you - the poor, the crippled, the blind, the lame. May this house and its surroundings be open to those whom you invite and may we be repaid with your love.

Leader 2:

May Christ Jesus dwell here with us, keep us from all harm, and make us one in mind and heart, now and forever. May almighty God bless us all, the Creator, Savior and Sanctifying Spirit. Amen.

Liturgy of the Word

First Reading:
Matthew 13:31-32

Celtic Alleluia
(c. 1985, Fintan O'Carroll and Christopher Walker, OCP.)

Second Reading:
(Adapted from *Hind's Feet on High Places* by Hannah Hurnard, c. 1975, Tyndale Publishers Inc., Living Books Edition.)

Narrator:
The Shepherd said to Much-Afraid:

Shepherd:
There is still one thing more, the most important thing of all. No one is allowed to dwell in the Kin-dom of Love, unless they have the flower of Love already blooming in their hearts. Has love been planted in your heart, Much-Afraid?

Narrator:
As the Shepherd said this he looked at her very steadily and she realized that his eyes were searching into the very depths of her heart and knew all that was there far better than she did herself... (After a long pause she answered:)

Much-Afraid:
I see the longing to be loved and admired growing in my heart, Shepherd, but I don't think I see the kind of Love that you are talking about, at least nothing like the love which I see in you.

Shepherd:
Then will you let me plant the seed of true Love there now? It will take you some time to develop hind's feet and to climb to the High Places, and if I put the seed in your heart now it will be ready to bloom by the time you get there.

Narrator:
The Shepherd put his hand in his bosom, drew something forth, and laid it in the palm of his hand. Then he held his had out toward Much-Afraid.

Shepherd:
Here is the seed of Love.

Narrator:
She bent forward to look, then gave a startled cry and drew back. There was indeed a seed lying in the palm of his hand, but it was shaped exactly like a long, sharply-pointed thorn. Much-Afraid had often noticed that the Shepherd's hands were scarred and wounded, but now she saw that the scar in the palm of the hand held out to her was the exact shape and size of the seed of Love lying beside it.

Much-Afraid:
The seed looks very sharp. Won't it hurt if you put it into my heart?

Shepherd:
It is so sharp that it slips in very quickly. But, Much-Afraid, I have already warned you that Love and Pain go together, for a time at least. If you would know Love, you must know pain, too.

Much-Afraid:
You have promised me, when the seed of love in your heart is ready to bloom, you will be loved in return...Please plant the seed here in my heart.

Narrator:
The Shepherd's face lit up with a glad smile.

Shepherd:
Now you will be able to go with me to the High Places and be a citizen of the Kin-dom.

Narrator:
Then he pressed the thorn into her heart.

(Silent reflection/shared homily if desired.)

Profession of Faith

All:
I believe in the God of Life, who shared life with us in the fruitful act of creation.
I believe in the God of Love, who brought Love to us in the humanity of God's son, Jesus.
In his Divinity, he made us holy.
In his humanity, he made us brothers and sisters.
In his death, he freed us to Love. In his rising, he freed us to Live.
I believe in the God of Hope.
Christ left his Spirit to build his Church,
who gave us prophets to show our failings,
who gave us saints to show his glory, who gave us ordinary,
holy people to do his work. I believe in People because God believes in People.
God gave us each other to Love, to Live for, to Hope with.
And I believe in our resurrection, the final triumph of Life and Love,
the fulfillment of all our Hope. Amen.

Prayers of the Faithful

(Some are adapted from "Order for the Blessing of Homes" in *The Catholic Source Book*, ed. Rev. Peter Klein, c. 1970, Confraternity of Christian Doctrine.)

Leader 1:
The Son of God made his home among us. With thanks and praise let us call upon him. Our response will be: *God, Hear our prayer.*

Jesus, with Joseph and Mary, you formed a holy family, remain in this home as part of this family...

All:
God, Hear our prayer.

Jesus, you taught your followers to build their houses upon solid rock: grant that the members of this and every family may ground our lives on your love...

All:
God, Hear our prayer.

Jesus, you had no place to lay your head, but in the spirit of poverty accepted the hospitality of friends. Grant that through our help the homeless may find hospitality, security and rest...

All:
God, Hear our prayer.

Are there any other prayers you would like to offer at this time?

Liturgy of the Eucharist

Reading:
Matthew 13:33

Reading:
(Adapted from *The Nonviolent Coming Of God* by Jim Douglass, c. 1991, Orbis Books.)

How does one tell a story of transformation? Jesus did it simply in his parable of the leaven... To those who heard Jesus' parable, leaven was a figure for moral corruption. In Exodus, leaven symbolized the unholy. It was banned during the holy season of Passover. For Paul, a little of this old leaven would morally corrupt the whole. Jesus' parable also assumes...we know that three measures are an immense quantity of flour, enough to make a meal for over one hundred people. Jesus' parable is subversive. It tells us that a tiny...substance, hidden in the flour by a woman, accomplished an unseen, massive transformation. Like the Reign of God.

Presentation of Gifts

Hymn:
"What is This Place?"
(Text: Huub Oosterhuis, tr. by David Smith, c. 1967, Gooi en Sticht, bv., Baarn, The Netherlands. Exclusive agent for English-language countries: OCP / Music: Dutch traditional hymn.)

Eucharistic Prayer

Leader 1:
Blessed are You, God, for You keep calling us to dwell with You in Your kin-dom of heaven. We thank You for Your constantly renewed invitations to our ancestors, to our co-disciples, to ourselves. As You have planted the Seed of Love in so many hearts.

All:
Loving God, please plant the Seed of Love in our hearts.

Leader 2:
We remember how You planted the seed in the hearts of Abraham and Sarah, Isaac and Rebekah, and Jacob and Rachel. We, like Jeremiah, often wish we could avoid the pain that comes with the sprouting of the Seed, but we thank You for being gentle in the planting of it into our hearts. May we be like Isaiah in singing Your praises, like Elijah in hearing Your voice in the gentle breezes, like John the Baptist in fearlessly preaching Your coming.

All:
Loving God, please plant the Seed of Love in our hearts.

Leader 1:
We remember how You planted the Seed of Love in the hearts of Mary and Joseph, Peter and Paul, Pope John XXIII and Bishop Oscar Romero, Dorothy Day, and all holy men and women. For all of these things we thank You, God, as we join together with all citizens of the Kin-dom of Love in praising Your glory:

All:
(sing) Holy, Holy, Holy
(Suggested sung responses: "Mass of Creation" by Marty Haugen, c. 1984, GIA.)

Leader 2:
We thank You especially for Christ Jesus, Your Son, the Shepherd. He came to dwell with us, and was so much at home here with us that not even death could take him from us. He shared all our joys and sorrows, shared our meals and prayed with us. With nowhere to rest his head, he accepted the hospitality of sinners and holy people, men and women, Pharisees and Samaritans.

Leader 1:
And on the night before he died, he faced the same fear of our sister, Much-Afraid. He drew back at the sight of the painful thorn which was about to pierce his heart. He asked that the cup of Gethsemane be withdrawn. But, asking only that Your will be done, he took it up, just as he had done earlier that evening when he shared the cup with us.

Leader 2:
Gathered with his friends at table, Jesus took bread and blessed it. He broke the bread and, just as we do here, shared it with them, saying: Take and eat. This is my body which will be given up for you. Then he took the cup, blessed it, and said: Take and drink. This is the cup of the new covenant in my blood which is poured out for you and for all people. Do this in memory of me.

Leader 1:
Here at this table, Jesus comes into our welcoming and longing hearts to dwell. He offers to plant the Seed of Love there. We see the small seed in his hands. What shall be our response?

Leader 2:
With Much-Afraid, we remember with joy the Shepherd's promise. And even though our courage falters, the Holy Spirit intercedes for us, giving us the grace and courage to say:

All:
Loving God, please plant the Seed of Love in our hearts.

Leader 1:
We thank You, God, for coming again today into our homes and hearts. As always, we recognize You most clearly in the breaking of the bread, and we proclaim together our hope and joy at this table.

All:
(sing) When we eat this bread, and we drink this cup, we proclaim your glory, Jesus, until you come again, until you come again.

Leader 1:
Let us remember those who have gone before us to live with you in your Kin-dom of Love.

Leader 2:
As Archbishop Oscar Romero reminded us before his death, they who have gone before us are present with us here in our hearts. Please call out the names of those whose spirit you wish to invite into this place to dwell here with us. After each name, as we respond with "Presente," we speak for our ancestors who have only our voices and hands to show the presence of their love.

(People name their ancestors or others who have died who have been a source of inspiration.)

Leader 1:
We ask that they pray for us and be with us always.

Leader 2:
We open our hearts to the Seed of Love within us. Help us to cultivate there a fertile place where the Seed can grow into the greatest of shrubs, where the birds of the air can come and make nests in its branches.

Leader 1:
In this spirit of praise and thanksgiving, in the unity and love to which You have called us, through Jesus, gathered together with Jesus, and united in his love, we offer praise to You, Oh God, and proclaim Your glory, forever and ever.

All:
(sing) Amen!

Leader 2:
We join hands together as we pray the words that Jesus taught us:

All:
(The Prayer of Jesus)

Sign of Peace

Leader 1:
Recognizing that the Seed of Love is growing in each one of us, let us bless one another and offer each other the sign of peace.

All:
(sing) Lamb of God

Communion

Communion Meditation:
"The Rose"
(Written by Amanda McBroom / Recorded by Bette Midler, c. 1979, Atlantic Recording.)

Closing Prayer

Leader 2:
With the grace of the spirit, we dare to pray the prayer for Hospitality of the Heart.
(By Charlotte Zalot, OSB, from *The Fire of Peace*.)

All:

Welcoming God, teach us to be generous in offering hospitality. Help us to be welcoming as You are welcoming, with reverence and care, mindfulness and respect. May our greetings be marked by sincerity and our actions be marked by tenderness. May all that we do for ourselves and others invite happiness and promise delight, seek peace and offer healing, encourage simplicity and share affection, acknowledge faith and extend friendship. Enlarge our hearts to embrace all people with love and bless our efforts to be hospitable. Amen.

Closing Song

"Joyful, Joyful, We Adore Thee"
(Text: Henry Van Dyke / Music: arr. from Ludwig Van Beethoven, by Edward Hodges.)

(Adapted from a house blessing developed by Paula Dodd-Aiello, a member of Bay Area Pax Christi, upon moving into her new home. The blessing of the rooms, also developed by Paula Dodd-Aiello, was taken from the Blessing and Dedication of Magdalene House Catholic Worker in Oakland, California.)

Vigils in Case of Outbreak of War

These vigils were created to be held at night, but can of course be adapted for use during the day.

1. First Vigil

Lighting of Candle
(Have someone light a large candle placed at the front of the church/room.)

Opening Song
"I Have Loved You"
(By Michael Joncas, c. 1979, North American Liturgy Resources.)

Opening Prayer

Leader:
God of faithfulness, we come to You troubled by the threat of war, filled with anxieties and questions. What change are we able to effect by our prayer before You, by our words, by our deeds? What can we do to bring peace to our planet?

God, we are in need of Your grace to unsettle and redirect our hearts. We are in need of Your hope to rekindle and sustain our passion for justice. We are in need of Your wisdom that we might recognize anew Your presence dwelling within us, calling us to live as children of light and of hope rather than of darkness and fear.

Be with us in our prayer this night. Help us to truly believe, not only in Your abiding presence within and among us, but in the power of our prayer to move mountains. All this we ask in the name of Jesus our brother, who shares our lives and Yours in the unity of the Spirit. Amen.

Reading from a Wartime Letter
(By Marine Corporal Craig Armstrong, Persian Gulf (source unknown).)

This is a reading from a letter written by Marine Corporal Craig Armstrong to his wife, Cris. All Marine personnel stationed in the Gulf region were instructed to send any personal valuables home to their families...

So how are you doing with all this Saudi Arabia s— that is in the papers and on the news every day? Don't believe half of the things they say. Because it is opinions and speculation. It's just a bunch of politicians that don't know what they are talking about...

We have got a new little game we play now. We wear our gas masks everywhere we go...And we will wear them until the CO says "all clear." I'm just waiting to see what games we will play next.

I've started to notice that everybody in the platoon is (getting) tighter with each other. Most of them are starting to get the point that this is serious, and not just another Panama invasion. Where we are heading now is for real.

I told you on the phone that you would be receiving my wedding ring. I sent it yesterday. It felt real weird not having it on. It felt as if my ring finger was naked. I just think about you and coming home. The first thing you will do is slide my wedding band back on my finger.

Response

Psalm 13

Side 1:
How long, O God, will You quite forget me? How long will You hide Your face from me?

Side 2:
How long must I suffer anguish in my soul, grief in my heart day and night?

Side 1:
Look now and answer me, O God. Give light to my eyes lest I sleep the sleep of death.

Side 2:
Lest my enemies say, "I have overthrown them," And my enemies rejoice at my downfall.

Side 1:
But for my part I trust in Your true love. My heart shall rejoice, for You have set me free.

Side 2:
I will sing to God, Who has granted all my desires.

Gospel:

Luke 13:34-35

(Silent reflection.)

Song

"Creator of the Stars of Night" (v.1-3) (By Marty Haugen, c. 1986, GIA.)

Closing Prayer

Leader:
God, as we enter into candlelit silence, we pray that You will share this time with us, sitting within and among us, sharing our yearning for peace, our faith in Your promise to hear us. Touch our hearts with Your gentle presence, renew our faith in Your promise of justice and lasting peace. Renew our strength for the journey that lies before us. Help us to be instruments of Your compassion, joyful proclaimers of Your gospel, faithful and faith-filled disciples of Your truth. Oh God, we pray together:

All:
(Adapted from "The Universal Peace Prayer.") Lead us, we beseech You, from death to life, from falsehood to truth. Lead us from despair to hope, from fear to trust. Lead us from hate to love, from war to peace. May peace - Your peace - fill our hearts, our world, our universe. All this we ask in Jesus' name. Amen.

Closing Song

"Stay With Me" *(Text: Matthew 26; Taize Community, 1984 / Tune: Jacques Berthier, c. 1984, Les Presses de Taize.)*

(Time for quiet prayer and reflection.)

2. Second Vigil

Have several clay pots filled with sand surrounding a large candle and smaller candles ready for people to light and place in the sand.

Lighting of Candle
(Have someone light the large candle placed at the front of the church/room.)

Opening Song
"I Have Loved You"
(By Michael Joncas, c. 1979, North American Liturgy Resources.)

Opening Prayer
Leader:
God of infinite patience and wisdom, You call us to be Your people, inviting us to the fullness of life and joy in Your presence. Let us never forget Your mercy to us throughout the ages. Make us ever mindful of Your call to discipleship, ever attentive to the working of Your Spirit, a Spirit of forgiveness, of reconciliation, of peace. We ask that You grant us strength and courage that we might always stand for truth, even when all that surrounds us urges compromise or abandonment of the path You have shown us.

Be with us as we work to bring about the coming of Your Reign, to share the gospel promise of compassion and reconciliation with a world truly in need of hearing the Good News. All this we ask in the name of our brother Jesus, who shares our lives and Yours, in the unity of the Spirit. Amen.

Reading from a Wartime Letter
(By Lt. Col. David Wood, 101st Airborne, Saudi Arabia (source unknown).)

This is a reading from a letter written by Lt. Col. David Wood to the fifth-grade class at Morningside School. He received no mail from the States - other than two bills - until these children began to write to him.

I've been in Saudi Arabia almost 40 days...My unit is an infantry organization. We move around the battlefield in Army Blackhawk helicopters. We do most of our flying at night when it's very dark.

The desert is huge...In every direction, there's only sand and hills. We have to be very careful because if we get lost it can be very dangerous...

Right now we are living near an oasis. There is a small deserted village here and it's over 300 years old. Camels, wild dogs and goats come to drink water from the well and eat the dates that fall from the trees.

Even though our soldiers and pilots, men and women, train very hard to go to war, all of us here DON'T WANT that to happen. War is not what you see at the movies; it's ugly and painful. We're here to protect people because this part of the world is very important to our economy and business. Hopefully, our actions will make a difference.

Response
Psalm 16

Side 1:
Keep me, Oh God, for in You have I found refuge. I have said to God, You, God, are my felicity. The gods whom earth holds sacred are all worthless, and cursed are all who make them their delight.

Side 2:

Those who run after them find trouble without end. I will not offer them libations of blood nor take their names upon my lips.

Side 1:

You, God, my allotted portion, You my cup, You enlarge my boundaries. The lines fall for me in pleasant places, indeed I am well content with my inheritance.

Side 2:

I will bless God who has given me counsel; in the nighttime, wisdom comes to me in my inward parts. I have set God continually before me; with God at my right hand I cannot be shaken.

Side 1:

Therefore my heart exults and my spirit rejoices, my body too rests unafraid. For You will not abandon me to Sheol nor suffer Your faithful servant to see the pit.

Side 2:

You will show me the path of life; in Your presence is the fullness of joy, in Your right hand pleasures for evermore.

Gospel

Luke 21:12-19

(Silent reflection.)

Song

"Creator of the Stars of Night"

Closing Prayer

("Peacemakers Prayer" from the Dedication Liturgy of Peacemakers Chapel at Walsh College in Canton, Ohio, on January 15, 1984, in *More Than Words: Prayer and Ritual for Inclusive Communities* by Janet Schaffran, C.D.P. and Pat Kozak, C.S.J., c. 1986, 1988, Meyer-Stone Books.)

Leader:

God of peace, sparkle our staleness and despair with Your hope. Invade the depth of our being with courage and steadfast faith. Defeat our fear and unbelief by the power of Your love.

Grant that our lives might be surprising in forgiveness and healing, abounding in joy and laughter, daring in dreams and deeds of justice. May we be do-ers, makers, prayers of peace. In Jesus' name. Amen.

Closing Song

"Stay With Me"
(During the closing chant, invite all to come forward to place a lighted candle in the sand as their petition before God in this time of uncertainty.)

Leader:

May our candles be a symbol,
not only of our individual prayers,
but also of our common prayer—
for a resolution to the current conflict,
for a renunciation of the use of armed forces in this region,
for serious negotiation,
not only in the hope of resolving this current situation,
but also to work toward resolution of the broader issues
that trouble this region, as well.

May the light of our candles burning in the darkness
remind us of the light of God's Truth,
and the power of that Truth to illuminate
even the deepest darkness of hatred, mistrust and fear.
May we believe in this light, take comfort and strength from it,
rejoicing in God's faithfulness and love.

(Quiet prayer and reflection.)

3. Third Vigil
Again, have a large candle, clay pots filled with sand and smaller candles ready to be lit near the front of the church/room.

Lighting of Candle

Opening Song
"I Have Loved You" *(By Michael Joncas, c. 1979, North American Liturgy Resources.)*

Opening Prayer
Leader:
Gracious God, maker and sustainer of all that is whole, we gather to worship You as a broken people who sit in darkness and the shadow of death. We often deal falsely with ourselves and others, healing wounds too lightly by saying "peace...peace" when there is no peace.

Through this long night, You have created within us clean, fresh hearts so that we may bring righteousness and true peace into the world around us.

Jesus, may we be more attentive to Your voice calling us to peace not war, to love not hate, to forgive not retaliate, to listen and try to understand, not to shout and close our minds and hearts. Give us the strength to drop our defenses and do away with our weapons and to encircle our sisters and brothers all over the world in understanding love. We ask this in Jesus' name. Amen.

Reading from a Wartime Letter
(By Cyrus Pringle, Quaker and conscientious objector, Civil War.)(Adapted/source unknown.)

This is a reading from the journal of Cyrus Pringle who was imprisoned with a fellow Quaker for his stand as a conscientious objector to the Civil War.

Yesterday my mind was much agitated: doubts and fears and forebodings seized me. I was alone, seeking a resting place and finding none. It seemed as if God had forsaken me in this dark hour; and the Tempter whispered, that after all I might be only the victim of a delusion. My prayers for faith and strength seemed all in vain.

But this morning I enjoy peace, and feel as though I could face anything. Though I am as a lamb in the shambles, yet do I cry, "Thy will be done," and can indeed say, "Passive to God's holy will, trust I in my Master still, even though they slay me."

I am reminded of the anxiety of our dear friends at home and of their prayers for us.

Oh, praise be to God for the peace and love and resignation that has filled my soul today! Oh, the passing beauty of holiness! There is a holy life that is above fear; it is close communion with Christ. I pray for this continually but am not free from the shadow and the Tempter. There is ever present with us the thought that perhaps we shall serve God the most effectually by our death, and desire, if that be the service God requires of us, may we be ready and resigned.

Response
Psalm 63

Side 1:
O God, You are my God, I seek You early with a heart that thirsts for You and a body wasted with longing for You, like a dry and thirsty land that has now water.

Side 2:
So, longing I come before You in the sanctuary to look upon Your power and glory. Your true love is better than life; therefore I will sing Your praises.

Side 1:
And so I bless You all my life and in Your name lift my hands in prayer. I am satisfied as with a rich and sumptuous feast and wake the echoes with Your praise.

Side 2:
When I call You to mind upon my bed and think of You in the watches of the night, remembering how You have been my help and that I am safe in the shadow of Your wings.

Sides 1 & 2:
Then I humbly follow You with all my heart, and Your right hand is my support... Whoever swears by God's name shall exult; the voice of falsehood shall be silenced.

Gospel
Luke 11:9-13

(Silent reflection.)

Prayers for Peace
(Leader invites those gathered to articulate any prayers they wish to offer for peace as they once again light a candle and place it in one of the clay pots filled with sand.)

Closing Prayer

Leader:
God of tenderness and wisdom, we, Your people, are in need of Your presence. In these days of fragile peace, we are often confused and unsure; lost in the darkness, anxious and fearful, as the threat of war looms ever nearer.

As we light our candles - visible signs of our faith in Your promise to be with us in our seeking - let the light of Your divine wisdom and love enter our hearts, that we might see the path before us more clearly.

May the holy light of our candles burning in the darkness – as the fire of Your love burns within each of us – quiet the voices of fear that confuse our judgment and cloud our heart's true vision.

Grant us the gift of divine insight, of abiding faith in Your promise of peace, so that we might step forward with renewed vigor and courage as we seek to be do-ers, makers, prayer-ers of peace, this night and always, in Jesus' name. Amen.

Closing Song
"O Lord, Hear My Prayer"
(Text: Psalm 102; Taize Community / Tune: Jacques Berthier, c. 1982, Les Presses de Taize.)

(Quiet prayer and reflection.)

4. Final Vigil

Lighting of Candle

Opening Prayer

Leader:

God, we know that where two or more are gathered in Your name, You are there also. Tonight, we pray not only for peace around the world, but peace in our hearts and in our lives. Help us to let peace fill our hearts, our world, our universe. We ask that Your spirit have power over us and put us on the path that leads to peace.

Be present to us this night. Continue to be our light. Keep our hearts and minds in the peace of Jesus, now and forever. Amen.

Song

"You Are Near" *(By Daniel L. Schutte, c. 1971, administered by New Dawn Music.)*

Reading

By Etty Hillesum in "An Interrupted Life ."
(From *Peacemaking Day By Day*, c. 1985, Pax Christi USA.)

This is a reading by Etty Hillesum, a concentration camp victim.

I really see no other solution than to turn inwards and to root out all the rottenness there. I no longer believe that we can change anything in the world until we have first changed ourselves. And that seems to me the only lesson to be learned from this war.

Sung Response

"You Are Near" *(refrain only)*

Reading

By Cesar Chavez (From *Peacemaking Day By Day*, c. 1985, Pax Christi USA.)

When we are really honest with ourselves, we must admit that our lives are all that really belong to us. So, it is how we use our lives that determines what kind of persons we are. It is my deepest belief that only by giving our lives do we find life. I am convinced that the truest act of courage, the strongest act of humanity is to sacrifice ourselves for others in a totally nonviolent struggle for justice. To be human is to suffer for others. God help us to be human.

Sung Response

"You Are Near" *(refrain only)*

Reading

(From *The Challenge of Peace: God's Promise and Our Response*, par. 337, c. 1983, United States Catholic Conference.)

Let us have the courage to believe in a bright future and in a God who wills it for us - not a perfect world, but a better one. Human hands and hearts and minds can create this better world.

Sung Response

"You Are Near" *(refrain only)*

Reading

Isaiah 2:2-5

Song

"Be Not Afraid" *(By Robert J. Dufford, SJ, c. 1975, North American Liturgy Resources.)*

Closing Prayer

All:

Let us pray for the world that is immeasurable, a society of millions of people and newspapers full of news.

Let us pray for the smaller world around us: for the people who belong to us, for the members of our families, our friends, and those who share our worries and those who depend on us. Let us pray for the leaders of governments and for those whose words and actions will influence the situation in (name the trouble spot): that they may not tolerate injustice, seek refuge in violence, or make rash and ill-considered decisions about the future of the people of (name the place), the United States and all foreign nationals in the area.

Let us pray also for all who live in the shadow of world events, for those who are seldom noticed: the hungry, the poor, the broken and the unloved.

Closing Song

"Peace is Flowing Like a River"
(By Carey Landry, c. 1975, Carey Landry and North American Liturgy Resources.)

Sign of Peace

(Adapted from a series of four vigils, originally planned during the season of Advent in response to the threat of war in the Middle East. Kate McMichael prepared the first three vigils and Janie Lee prepared the final one.)

Peace Mass

Call to Worship/Entrance Rite

(Before entrance hymn or Gloria.)

Reader 1:
We cannot be silent.

Reader 2:
We must not be silent.

Reader 3:
We will not be silent.

Reader 1:
We continue to build nuclear weapons.

Reader 2:
The poor are being trampled on.

Reader 3:
Violence abounds.

Reader 1:
We can call upon world leaders.

Reader 2:
We must call upon world leaders.

Reader 3:
We will call upon world leaders

Readers 1,2,3:
To establish peace with justice in our world.

Reader 1:
Glory to God who makes salvation known!

Reader 2:
Glory to God who reveals justice!

Reader 3:
Glory to God who lives among us!

Introduction to Penitential Rite

Reader 1:
We cannot be silent.

Reader 2:
We must not be silent.

Reader 3:
We will not be silent.

Reader 1:
We continue to build nuclear weapons.

"Let us pray not to be silent as we seek to work toward alleviating patterns of unbridled consumption that lead to unendurable poverty."

Reader 2:
The poor are being trampled on.

Reader 3:
Violence abounds.

Reader 1:
We can call upon world leaders.

Reader 2:
We must call upon world leaders.

Reader 3:
We will call upon world leaders.

Readers 1,2,3:
To establish peace with justice in our world.

Reader 1:
But first, we must be reconciled with ourselves.

Reader 2:
We must be reconciled with one another.

Reader 3:
We must be reconciled with God.

Penitential Rite

Reader 1:
Lead us from death to life, from falsehood to truth.

All:
Jesus, have mercy.

Reader 2:
Lead us from despair to hope, from fear to trust.

All:
Christ, have mercy.

Reader 3:
Lead us from hate to love, from war to peace.

All:
Jesus, have mercy.

Presider:
May God have mercy on us, forgive us our sins, and lead us to everlasting life. Amen.

Sprinkling Rite

Presider:
May God, who through water and the Spirit has given us a new birth in Christ, be with you all.

All:
And also with you.

Presider:

As we gather, we are mindful of a world that thirsts for peace and an end to violence, for equality and for love.

(If so desired, the reading from the Acts of the Apostles (10:25-26, 34-35,44-48) can be read here.)

Presider:

May this water which we now bless remind us of Christ, the living water, and of the sacrament of baptism, in which we were born of water and the Spirit. As we are touched with this water, may we believe ever more deeply in its power to heal, to give life, to forgive, and to sustain hope.

(Presider sprinkles the congregation with water.)

Liturgy of the Word

First Reading

The Acts of the Apostles 10:25-26,34-35,44-48

Psalm 99:1-4

Reader:

Sing a new song to the God of Life who has worked marvels, whose hand and holy arm have brought salvation.

All:

God's saving power has been revealed to the nations.

Reader:

God has made salvation known, revealed justice to the nations. God has remembered a merciful love for the house of Israel.

All:

God's saving power has been revealed to the nations.

Reader:

All the ends of the earth have seen the salvation of God. Shout to God, you earth; burst into music, sing praise

All:

God's saving power has been revealed to the nations.

Second Reading

First Letter of John 4:7-10

Alleluia

All who love me will hold to my words, and my God will love them, and we will come to them. Alleluia.

Gospel

John 15:9-17

Options for Liturgy of the Word:
A.) All readings proclaimed separately.
B) Reading I as part of the Sprinkling Rite, followed by Psalm, Reading II and Gospel.
C) Reading II and Gospel interspersed.
D) Gospel interspersed with music.

A Reading from the First Letter of John and the Gospel of John (Option C)

Gospel:
Jesus said to the disciples: As God has loved me, so I have loved you. Live on in my love. You will live in my love if you keep my commandments, even as I have kept God's commandments, and live in God's love.

Reading II:
Beloved, let us love one another because love is of God; everyone who loves is begotten of God and has knowledge of God.

Gospel:
All this I tell you that my joy may be yours and your joy may be complete. This is my commandment: Love one another as I have loved you.

Reading II:
The person without love has known nothing of God, for God is love.

Gospel:
There is no greater love than this: to lay down one's life for one's friends. You are my friends if you do what I command you. I no longer speak of you as slaves, for a slave does not know what the master is about.

Reading II:
God's love was revealed in our midst in this way: God sent Jesus Christ to the world that we might have life through him.

Gospel:
I call you friends since I have made known to you all that I heard from God. It was not you who chose me; it was I who chose you to go forth and bear fruit. Your fruit must endure, so that all you ask of God in my name will be given to you.

Reading II:
Love, then, consists in this: not that we have loved God, but that God has loved us and has sent Jesus Christ as an offering for sin.

Gospel:
The command I give you is this: that you love one another. This is the Word of God.

Gospel Interspersed with Music (Option D)

Sung Response:
"We Have Been Told" *(refrain only) (By Marty Haugen, c. 1983, GIA.)*

Jesus said to the disciples:
"As God has loved me,
so I have loved you.
Live on in my love.
You will live in my love
if you keep my commandments,
even as I have kept God's commandments,
and live in God's love.

Sung Response:
"We Have Been Told" *(refrain only)*

"All this I tell you
that my joy may be yours
and your joy may be complete.
This is my commandment:
Love one another as I have loved you.
There is no greater love than this:
to lay down one's life for one's friends.
You are my friends if you do what I command you.
I no longer speak of you as slaves,
for a slave does not know what the master is about.

Sung Response:
"We Have Been Told" *(refrain only)*

"I call you friends
since I have made known to you all that I heard from God.
It was not you who chose me;
it was I who chose you to go forth and bear fruit.
Your fruit must endure,
so that all you ask of God in my name
will be given to you.
The command I give you is this:
that you love one another."

Sung Response:
"We Have Been Told" *(refrain only)*

General Intercessions

Reader:
In faith and with persistence we ask God to listen as we say: *God, hear our prayer, and move us to action.*

All:
God, hear our prayer, and move us to action.

Reader:
Let us pray not to be silent as we seek to encourage world leaders to replace the politics of war with the politics of peace and say...*God, hear our prayer, and move us to action.*

Let us pray not to be silent as we seek to assist in conserving God's earth and nurturing its people and say... *God, hear our prayer, and move us to action.*

Let us pray not to be silent as we seek to work toward alleviating patterns of unbridled consumption that lead to unendurable poverty and say... *God, hear our prayer, and move us to action.*

Let us pray not to be silent as we seek to show a love that can create a more just and peaceful world and say... *God, hear our prayer, and move us to action.*

Let us pray not to be silent as we seek to urge each other to work tirelessly to promote gospel values and say... *God, hear our prayer, and move us to action.*

All:
Loving God, lead us from death to life, from falsehood to truth, from despair to hope, from fear to trust, from hate to love, from war to peace, now and ever more. Amen.

Liturgy of the Eucharist

(It is suggested that you use one of the reconciliation Eucharistic prayers.)

(General music suggestions: "Eye Has Not Seen" by Marty Haugen, c. 1982, GIA; "We Are Many Parts" by Marty Haugen, c. 1980, 1986, GIA; "Jesus, Wine of Peace" by David Haas, c. 1985, GIA; "Sing Out, Earth and Skies" by Marty Haugen, c. 1985, GIA; "I Have Loved You" by Michael Joncas, c. 1979, North American Liturgy Resources.)

(Adapted from "We Shall Not Be Silent: Peace Mass Booklet" by Marilyn Schauble, OSB, and Charlotte Zalot, OSB, which Pax Christi USA published during the Gulf War.)

Renewal of Commitment to Work for Peace and Justice

"If we listen to the voice of God, we make our choice, get out of ourselves and fight nonviolently for a better world."

Have a Paschal candle lit at the front of the room and incense burning from a clay pot with sand. Have on hand pieces of paper and pens for the "releasing of burdens" part of the ritual and two glass bowls of oil, perhaps perfumed, for the anointing for ministry.

Opening Song
"We Are Called" *(By David Haas, c. 1988, GIA.)*

Opening Reflection

Leader 1:
"I have called you by your name, you are mine." (pause) We have come together to renew our commitment to God's call to each of us to work for justice and peace in our world, to be bearers of the light, singers of a new song. We have been called by our loving God - in different ways, in different times, in different places - prompted by the many beautiful, faith-filled people we have met along the way and by the many events that have touched us, some earth-shattering, some as gentle as the still small voice which Elijah heard.

Micah summarizes well what is required of us—to act justly, to love tenderly and to walk humbly with our God, but sometimes our task is a difficult one. Dorothy Day said that we have all known the long loneliness and that we have come to know that the only solution is love - love for one another and for our world - and such a love comes only with community.

Opening Prayer

Leader 2:
So gathered as a community, let us pray. God of the Journey, God of Night and Light, God of Justice and Peace, God of the Struggle, we invoke Your holy name. Be with us now as we reflect on the challenges we have encountered thus far on our journey and as we consider those things that keep us from moving forward in our commitment to following You. Be with us, bless us, liberate us from all which holds us bound that we might freely choose to renew our covenant with You.

Reading

Dom Helder Camara
(From *Peacemaking: Day by Day,* Feb. 12, p. 17, c. 1985 Pax Christi USA.)
We must have no illusions. We must not be naive. If we listen to the voice of God, we make our choice, get out of ourselves and fight nonviolently for a better world. We must not expect to find it easy; we shall not walk on roses; people will not throng to hear us and applaud; and we shall not always be sure of divine protection. If we are to be pilgrims of justice and peace, we must expect the desert.

Releasing of Burdens/Obstacles to Peacemaking

Leader 1:
I invite you to reflect on the desert times in your own lives, on the things that have kept you from bearing fruit in your ministry, from re-committing yourselves to the struggle for justice and peace. What do you need to let go of in order to move forward?

When you have finished your reflection, please write whatever it is you need to release on one of these pieces of paper.

(Allow time for silent reflection. Play instrumental music in the background.)

Let us now release these burdens to God!

(People come forward and begin to burn their piece of paper in the Paschal candle and then drop them into the clay pot. Continue to add incense.)

Song
"I Shall Be Released" *(v.1, 2) (By Bob Dylan, c. 1974, Columbia Records.)*

Invoking the Cloud of Witnesses
Leader 2:
Freed from our burdens, from the things that keep us from following Jesus more closely, let us now invoke the Cloud of Witnesses to be with us, to strengthen us as we prepare to renew our covenant with God.

A Litany of Peacemakers
(From *The Fire of Peace,* c. 1992, Pax Christi USA.)

Reader 1:
God, creator of the universe, author of our covenant of peace, we pray to you: empower us.

Reader 2:
God, redeemer of the world, our way of peace... empower us.

Reader 1:
God, sanctifier of conscience, gift of peace...empower us.

Reader 2:
Mary, wellspring of reconciliation, mother of peacemakers...pray for us.

Reader 1:
Michael, our defender in the spiritual battle with forces of our own self-destruction...

Reader 2:
Heavenly hosts, angelic warriors for universal peace...

Reader 1:
Moses and Miriam, nonviolent liberators, architects and singers of the covenant of justice...

Reader 2:
Isaiah, critic of militarism, prophet of peace...

Reader 1:
Esther, intercessor for the powerless, emissary of peace...

Reader 2:
Amos and Micah and Hosea, voices for the oppressed...

Reader 1:
Jeremiah, doomsday seer, voice of lamentation...

Reader 2:
Magdalene, faithful witness of Christ's execution, first witness of his resurrection...

Reader 1:
Peter and Paul, prisoners of conscience...

Reader 2:
Matthew, Mark, Luke, John, evangelists of the peaceable kin-dom...

Reader 1:
Felicity and Perpetua, midwives and mothers, sacrificed in the sport of a military empire...

Reader 2:
Martin of Tours, conscientious objector...

Reader 1:
Francis of Assisi, lover of creation, poor man with nothing to fight for...

Reader 2:
Clare of Assisi, pacifier of armies with the power of the Eucharist...

Reader 1:
Catherine of Siena, mystic diplomat, skilled negotiator...

Reader 2:
Hildegard of Bingen, mystic, lover of Creation...

Reader 1:
Gandhi, the Mahatma, nonviolent warrior...

Reader 2:
Franz Jagerstatter, resister for Christ...

Reader 1:
Simone Weil, patroness of solidarity with the oppressed, fasting unto death with the hungry...

Reader 2:
Martin Luther King, prophet and dreamer of the Beloved Community...

Reader 1:
Thomas Merton, contemplative critic, mentor of peacemakers...

Reader 2:
Pope John XXIII, herald of peace...

Reader 1:
Pope Paul VI, apostle and teacher of peace...

Reader 2:
Dorothy Day, lady poverty, mother courage, witness to the radical gospel of peace...

Reader 1:
Oscar Romero, shepherd of the poor, martyr for justice...

Reader 2:
Maura, Ita, Jean, Dorothy, martyrs for the poor, handmaids of justice...

Reader 1:
Saints of the Shaker, Mennonite, Quaker, and Church of the Brethren communions...

Reader 2:
Children of light, transfigured in the fire-storms of Hiroshima and Nagasaki...

Reader 1:
Children of darkness, transfigured in the night of torture and disappearance...

Reader 2:
All you holy peacemakers, living and more living...

Reader 1:
Jesus, Messiah, Prince of Peace, we pray to you:

All:
Empower us.

Call to Recommitment

Leader 1:
Surrounded by such a powerful, prophetic Cloud of Witnesses and enveloped by God's enduring, everlasting love for us, let us now renew our commitment to be peacemakers in our world.

A Psalm of Commissioning for Mission by Miriam Therese Winter
(In *WomanWord*, c. 1990, Crossroad Pub. Co.)

Reader 1:
The harvest is ready. Whom shall I send?

Reader 2:
Send me, Shaddai, I am ready to serve You, all the days of my life.

All:
Go into the workplace and into the streets and reveal God's saving Spirit through the quality of your lives.

Reader 1:
The world is waiting. Whom shall I send?

Reader 2:
Send me, Shaddai, I am ready to speak of You, all the days of my life.

All:
Preach the Good News by your actions; heal, help, teach, touch, be of good spirit in good times and bad times, and live for the glory of God.

Reader 1:
The world is hungry. Whom shall I send?

Reader 2:
Send me, Shaddai, I am ready to nourish, all the days of my life.

All:
Feed the hungry of body and spirit, break the bread of compassion, distribute the fragments of hope, and be fed by the Word within you.

Reader 1:
The vineyard is ready. Whom shall I send?

Reader 2:
Send me, Shaddai, I am ready to work for You, all the days of my life.

All:
Enter into and love the mission and your many ministries, labor for justice, lobby for peace, and may you find contentment in the wages of commitment when the long hard day is done.

Anointing for Ministry

Leader 2:
Before us we have oil, so often used in our tradition for anointing—at our birth, our baptism, at our death, as a mark of the outpouring of the Spirit, at the start of a new ministry. Let us now anoint one another for yet another important transition in our lives. Let us anoint one another for the journey, thus sealing our commitment, our covenant with God, our rededication to our call to be bearers of peace, justice, truth and love.

Please come forward to be anointed, and if you so desire, state what ministry or efforts to which you are choosing to rededicate yourself.

(The two leaders hold the bowls of oil as people come forward to be anointed and to express their commitments).

Reading

"Reading the Torah" (Adapted from *Purify Our Hearts To Serve Your Truth*, c. 1980, Congregation Beth El of the Sudbury River Valley, Sudbury, Massachusetts.)

All:
Somewhere out of time
In the mystery of time
Somewhere between memory and forgetfulness,
dimly though
I remember how once I stood
At your mountain trembling
Amid the fire and the thunder
How I stood there, out of bondage
In a strange land and afraid
And you loved me and you fed me
And I feasted on your word.
And, yet, I can remember
How the thunder was my heart
And the fire was my soul.
Oh God, I do remember.
And here I am, once more
A witness to that timeless moment,
Present now in the light of your word
And in those Gathered here in your presence
I am reborn.

Sending Forth

Leader 1:

We stand here, loving God, freed from our bondage, filled with the fire of Your love and Your passion for peace, a fire that burns deep in our hearts and our souls. We stand here before You reborn, made new, renewed in spirit and recommitted to la lucha, the struggle for peace and justice for those who cry out for an end to their anguish. Send us forth as Your servants, Your instruments, Your Presence in our world. We ask all of this in the name of the One who walked this path before us. Amen.

Closing Song

"Strength for the Journey" *(By Michael John Poirier, C. 1988, Peartree Productions.)*

(Created by Cindy Pile.)

Renewal of the Vow of Nonviolence

Opening Song
"How Can I Keep From Singing?" *(Quaker Hymn, Harm. Robert J. Batastini, c. 1987, GIA.)*

Call to Worship
(From *The Challenge of Peace*, #333.)

Psalm Reflection
"Lord, Let Us See Your Kindness" (Psalm 85)
(By Marty Haugen, c. 1983, GIA.)

First Reading
Excerpt adapted from "Behold the Nonviolent One"
(By Mary Lou Kownacki, OSB, published in *Sojourners*, October 1989.)

The Russian mystic St. Seraphim writes, "If you have inner peace, thousands of people around you will be saved." St. Seraphim makes it sound so simple. Yet all of us know that to become a person who radiates such intense beams of redemptive peace is not a simple task. It takes, in fact, a lifetime of concentration to become a true peacemaker, a peacemaker like the one described in this story.

"It is said that when the Chinese invaded Tibet, many of the soldiers were very cruel toward the conquered people. They were especially harsh and mean-spirited toward the monks. When the Chinese invaders arrived at one village, the village leader approached them and said, 'All of the monks, hearing of your approach, fled to the mountains...all of the monks, that is, but one.'

The commander raged out of control. He marched to the monastery, kicked in the gate, and sure enough, in the courtyard stood the one remaining monk. The commander approached the monk and screamed, 'Do you know who I am? I am he who can run you through with a sword without batting an eyelash.'

The monk gently, but steadily, gazed at the commander and replied, 'And do you know who I am? I am he who can let you run me through with a sword without batting an eyelash.'"

The monk is my model of a peacemaker. Behold the nonviolent one: disarmed, centered, vulnerable, detached, unafraid of death. The question the monk poses for us is this: How do we become people of peace? How do we become a church of nonviolence? What experiences in life, what methods of prayer prepare us to stand disarmed? Jesus shows us the way to become a people of peace.

Alleluia
Gospel
John 15:1-8

Dialogue Homily
Vow of Nonviolence
(Invite those who desire to take or renew the vow to come forward.)

Recognizing the violence in my own heart, yet trusting in the goodness and mercy of God, I vow to practice the nonviolence of Jesus who taught us in the Sermon on the Mount:

"Blessed are the peacemakers, for they shall be called sons and daughters of God...You have learned how it was said, 'You must love your neighbor and hate your enemy;' but I say to you, Love your enemies and pray for those who persecute you. In this way, you will be sons and daughters of your Father and Mother in heaven."

Before God the Creator and the Sanctifying Spirit, I vow to carry out in my life the love and example of Jesus:
• by striving for peace within myself and seeking to be a peacemaker in my daily life;
• by accepting suffering (in the struggle for justice) rather than inflicting it;
• by refusing to retaliate in the face of provocation and violence;
• by persevering in nonviolence of tongue and heart;
• by living conscientiously and simply so that I do not deprive others of the means to live;
• by actively resisting evil and working nonviolently to abolish war and the causes of war from my own heart and from the face of the earth.

God, I trust in Your sustaining love and believe that just as You gave me the grace and desire to offer this, so You will also bestow abundant grace to fulfill it.

Prayers of the Faithful

Liturgy of the Eucharist

(It is suggested that one of the "Eucharistic Prayers for Masses of Reconciliation" be used.)

Communion Meditation

"Prayer of St. Francis" *(By Sebastian Temple, c. 1967, OCP.)*

Final Blessing

Closing Song

"Pax Christi" *(By Miriam Therese Winter, c. 1997, Medical Mission Sisters.)*

See music in Appendix B.

(Adapted from Pax Christi Metro DC's annual liturgy for those who wish to take or renew the Vow of Nonviolence. This service was developed by Tricia Sullivan.)

General Liturgical Resources

All Desires Known
Janet Morley
c. 1988, 1992, Morehouse Publishing
P.O. Box 1321
Harrisburg, PA 17105 (in the U.S.)

SPCK Holy Trinity Church
Marlebone Road
London NW1 4DU (in the U.K.)

Earth Prayers from Around the World
Elizabeth Roberts and Elias Amidor, Ed.
c. 1991, Harper SF, a Division
of Harper Collins Publishers
353 Sacramento St., Suite 500
San Francisco, CA 94111
415/477-4400

**More Than Words: Prayer and Ritual
for Inclusive Communities**
Janet Schaffran, CDP, and Pat Kozak, CSJ
 c. 1986, 1988, Meyer-Stone Books
714 South Humphrey
Oak Park, IL 60304

**Prayers for a Planetary Pilgrim: A
Personal Manual for Prayer and Ritual**
Edward Hays
c. 1988, Forest of Peace Books, Inc.
Route One, Box 248
Easton, KS 66020
(Also: Prayers for the Domestic Church)

Psalms Anew: In Inclusive Language
Nancy Schreck, OSF, and Maureen Leach, OSF,
c. 1986, St. Mary's Press /
Christian Brothers Publications
702 Terrace Heights
Winona, MN 55987-1320

**Seasonal Source Books
Published by LTP**
Available for Advent, Christmas, Lent (2 vol.),
Triduum, Easter, Death
Liturgy Training Publications
1800 North Hermitage Ave.
Chicago, IL 60622-1101
312/ 486-7008

Women-Church Sourcebook
c. 1993, WATER,
The Women's Alliance for Theology,
Ethics and Ritual
8035 13th St.
Silver Spring, MD 20910
301/589-2509

**WomanPrayer, WomanSong:
Resources for Ritual**
Miriam Therese Winter
c. 1995, Crossroad Publishing Company
370 Lexington Ave.
New York, NY 10017
(Also: WomanWisdom, part 1, c. 1991;
part 2, c. 1992 and WomanWord, c. 1990.)

Music
Publishers

Desert Flower Music
P.O. Box 1735
Ridgecrest, CA 93555
619/375-2320
*Jim Strathdee

G.I.A. Publications, Inc.
7404 S. Mason Ave.
Chicago, IL 60638

Gather
*David Haas, Marty Haugen, Dona Pena

Loretto Spirituality Network
725 Calhoun St.
Albany, CA 94706
510/525-4174
*Colleen Fulmer

New Dawn Music
P.O. Box 13248
Portland, OR 97213
*John Foley, SJ

Oregon Catholic Press
OCP Publications
5536 NE Hassalo
Portland, OR 97213

Music Issue
(Annual; most parishes get it along
with their *Today's Missal* order.)
JourneySongs (OCP version of *Gather*)
*Bob Hurd, Rufino Zaragoza, Jaime Cortez

Peartree Productions
P.O. Box 677
Windsor, CA 94592-0677
707/544-1768
*Michael John Poirier

The Sparrow Corporation
Birdwing Music imprint
9255 Dering Ave.
Chatsworth, CA 91311-6995
*John Michael Talbot

Two by Two
1916 Buena Vista
Alameda, CA 94501
510/523-3370
*Jesse Manibusan

Francisco Herrara
848 York St.
San Francisco, CA 94110
415/647-8619

A sincere and concerted effort has been made to contact all rights holders and to obtain reprint permissions. Due to the complicated nature of this process, some required acknowledgements or rights may have unintentionally been overlooked or omitted, and we ask for forgiveness. If notified, the publisher will be pleased to correct any such omissions in future editions.

Appendix A

EAST TIMOR, November 12, 1991
271 names of those known to be killed in the Santa Cruz massacre documented by the Catholic Church in East Timor. (The name, age and profession, if known, are listed for each of the victims.)

Abel Araujo, 20, student
Abilio Ximenes, 23, student
Adelaide M Faria, 26
Aderito, 25, student
Adolfo Matos, 28, student
Alfonso S N, 25, student
Agostino Tilma Fernandes, 18, student
Aju, 26, student
Alberto (Soares), 47, merchant
Albino Ximenes, 23
Alcino Carvalho, 23, student
Alcino Freitas, 35, farmer
Alegria Jesus Reis, 17, student
Aleixo Santos, 33, farmer
Alfredo Carmo, 15, student
Alfredo Conceicao, 21, student
Alfredo Costa, 17, student
Almeida Santos, 28
Almerio Reis Fernandes, 15, student
Alvaro Gomes, 32
Amadeu Oliveira, 23, student
Amaro Silva, 34
Amelia, 17, student
Americo Cortinhal, 20
Americo Espirito Santo, 25, student
Amo 'Bank Summa'
Amorim Rego, 22, student
Ana Lobato, 16, student
Anabela Ferreira Baptista, 22
Andre 'Manatuto,' 15, student
Angelo M., 19, student
Angelo Monteiro, 31, merchant
Anico Silva, 18
Ano Besi Tuk
Antonio Braz, 28
Antonio Carmo, 13, student
Antonio Gusmao, 23, student
Antonio Ho
Antonio Labi Rai, 18, farmer
Antonio Santos, 26, student
Antonio Soares Pinto, 19, student
Antonio Tilman, 19
Aquino Oliveira, 22,student
Aristides Santos, 19, student
Asu Txai, 44, merchant
Atay, 22
Augusto Sanches, 29, student

Basilio Araujo, 21
Bentes
Bento Jesus, 17, farmer
Bento P. Garcia
Bento Santos, 18, student
Bernardino Canhoto, 24

Caetano (Paulino), 18
Cailarano, 35, farmer
Camilo, 21

Cancio Freitas, 22
Carlos Soares, 18, student
Castelo, 21, student
Celina 'Aileu,'19, student
Celio Pascoal Cost Amaral, 22
Chico Batavia, 30, farmer
Clementino Silva, 20, student
Constancio Soares, 29
Constantino Silva, 29, student
Cornelio Costa Soares, 20, student
Ctho Ctho,18, student
Cussu Mali, 30, farmer

Damiao, 21, student
Daniel Silva, 35, farmer
Delfim, 16
Diana Sousa, 19
Dionisio Araujo, 24, student
Dionisio Mendes Goncalves, 19, student
Dionisio Santos
Domingas Duarte Pacheco, 13
Domingas Soares Pacheco, 14
Domingos, 10
Domingos Costa, 30
Domingos Frederico, 18, student
Domingos Moreira Costa, 17, student
Domingos Oliveira, 21, student
Domingos Pacheco Silva, 18, student
Domingos Pacheco Sousa, 13, student
Domingos Reis Santos, 23, student
Domingos Santos, 28
Domingos Segurado Marques, 29, teacher
Domingos Ximenes Rosario, 17, student
Duarte Acolito
Duarte Pacheco, 19, student
Duarte Silva, 22
Duarte Silva 'Adu,' 23
Dudu Oliveira, 20

Eca Soares, 21, student
Elidio Costa, 21, student
Eligio Goncalves, 17, student
Estanislau Martins, 24, student
Eugenio Martins, 20, student
Evangelino Pinto Pedroso, 20, student
Evris Madeire, 22

Fae Lelo, 37, merchant
Fernando (Nogueira), 22, student
Fernando Lato, 25
Fernando Lay, 30
Francelino Pires, 23, student
Francisca, 23, student
Francisco Borromeu Silva, 19
Francisco Carlos (Abonno), 22, student
Francisco Fatima, 33
Francisco Oliveira Cam., 21, student
Francisco Santos Soares, 20, student

Francisco Seixas, 20
Francisco Silva 'Binaraga,' 22, athlete
Francisco Silva, 18
Francisco Tilman, 17, student
Francisco Urbano, 23, student
Frederico 'Lospalos,' 22, student

Gabriel 'Comoro,' 22, student
Gil Vieira Amaral, 13, student
Graziela Bonaparte
Gregorio Santos, 20, student
Gustavo, 20

Hacobio (Recobio), 17, student
Helder C. G. Barreto, 25
Huru Fatu, 26, farmer

Ilidio Costa, 21
Ismael Araujo, 17
Ismenia Jose Reis, 20

Jacinta, 22
Jacob Silva, 17, student
Jaime Vaz Coutinho, 19, student
Joanico Araujo, 22, student
Joanico Gomes, 28
Joanico Lobato Piedade, 18, student
Joao 'Ossuí,' 35, farmer
Joao Baptista, 15
Joao Costa Sequeira, 24
Joao Garcia, 25, student
Joao Guterres
Joao Leao, 22
Joao Mau Lu, 25, student
Joao Silva, 18, student
Jojo, student
Jorge Cunha, 25, student
Jorge Rego, 18, student
Jose 'Audian,' 10
Jose Andrade, 22, student
Jose Antonio Ximenes, 23, student
Jose Bento
Jose Bibik
Jose Cortinhal, 19, student
Jose Kodok (Aleijado), 16
Jose Nuno Galhos, 18, student
Jose Oliveira, 15, student
Josefina Antonieta Silva, 18
Juliao Adalaide, 20, student
Julio Corte Real, 20, student
Julio Flavio 'Azio,' 26, student
Julio Guterres, 50, farmer
Julio Matos, 16
Julio Sarmento Borges, 18
Justino, 22
Justino Cruz, 27
Justino Rosario

Justino Santos Pereira, 17, student

Kai Laranu, 35
Kamal Bamadhaj
Kusu Malay

Leandro Isaac
Lelia, merchant
Leopolidino Amaral, 23, student
Linda, 31
Linda Sousa, 31
Lito Calsona
Lourenco Soares, 23
Lucio Sequeira Soares, 15, student
Luis Alves, 21, student
Luis Moreira, 32
Luis Paulo, 19
Luis Paulo Reis Belo, 19, student
Luis Silva Matos, 19, student
Luis Silveira, 22

M. Moniz, 16, student
Manecas Magno
Manecas Pereira, 17, student
Manuel 'Televisao,' 18, student
Manuel Cabral, 23, student
Manuel Cesario Amaral, 18, student
Manuel Jesus, 20, student
Manuel Jupiter, 21, student
Manuel Marques, 25, student
Manuel Mesquita, 23, student
Manuel Rosario Amaral, 18
Manuel Sarmento, 14, student
Manuel Tilman, 15, student
Marcelino Ferreira Santos, 18, student
Marcelino Silva, 23
Marciano Mendonca, 24, student
Maria, merchant
Maria Rego
Maria, 28
Mariano Mendonca, 24
Mariano Silva, 22
Mario Marobo, 19, student
Mario Miguel, 20, student
Mario Silva, 20
Mario Victor, 26
Marito Fatubai Mota, 21, student
Marito Vieira, 22
Martinho Costa Amaral, 28, student
Mateus (Santa Cruz), 27, student
Mateus Freitas, 16, student
Mateus Pereira, 19
Mateus Ximenes, 26
Mau Chico, 18, farmer
Mau Dua, 13, student
Mica Soares Tilman, 17, student
Miguel, 32

Miguel Monteiro, 17
Miguel Neves Reis (Miki)
Miguel Roberto, 20

Nelio Ximenes, 15
Nelson Armandino, 19
Nelson Azevedo Pinto, 19, student
Norberto Amaral, 18

Odelia Araujo, 18
Olan Dua, 13
Olandino Soares, 19
Orlando Menezes, 16, student
Oscar Santos, 25

Pancracio Marques, 20, student
Paula, 17, student
Paulo Freitas, 18, student
Pedrito, 22
Pedro Nogueira, 24, student
Pedro Sanches, 28
Pedro Soares (Apeu), 19, student
Predi Martins, 18, student

Rafael Tilman Fernandes, 20, student
Reis
Ribeiro Martins, 25
Rita Ramos, 30
Romualdo Baptista, 31
Rosario Araujo, 10
Rosario Freitas, 28
Rui Alves, 25
Rusu Malay, 30

Sabino, 25
Sabino Pereira Serrano, 21, student
Sara Zumalay, 42, merchant
Sebastiao Gomes, 20, student
Sergio Filomeno, 21
Sina Raku, 42, farmer

Taibere, 35, merchant
Tito, 44, merchant
Tito Antonio Costa, 16, student
Tobias Rego, 18, student
Tomas Mendes Pereira, 16
Tomas Pereira Costa, 18, student
Tome Costa, 22, student
Tonilio Amaral, 17, student
Txai Pere, 46

Varudo
Vasco Gomes, 17, student
Venancio Correia, 35, farmer
Venancio Fonseca, 21
Vicente Binaraga
Victor Nunes, 27

Zelio, 19, student
Zito M. Alvaro, 30

Appendix B

Pax Christi

(Words and music: Miriam Therese Winter, c. Medical Mission Sisters, 1997)

1. Through the shad - ows of the past a brand new day is break - ing.
2. From an o - cean of des - pair a wave of hope is ris - ing:
3. When com - pas - sion finds its way to all the wound -ed pla - ces
4. For a fu - ture free from war the hu - man heart is yearn - ing.
5. All a - round our wear - y world we hear the Spir - it stir - ring,

Slum - bering spi - rits are slow - ly wak - ing,
peace and just - ice un - com - pro - mis - ing,
and car - ess - es the tear - stained fa - ces,
When we wit - ness to what we're learn - ing,
keep - ing faith in the dream re - cur - ring:

call - ing us all to work at u - ni - verse - ma - king
borne on a tid - al wave of love em - pha - siz - ing
then, on - ly then will we have peace a - mong ra - ces.
peace - ful non - vi - o - lence will guide our dis - cern - ing,
heal - ing and rec - on - cil - ing peo - ple pre - fer - ring

and a un - i - ty we can see and share.
sol - i - dar - i - ty a - mong all who care.
Lov - ing kind - ness teach - es that God is there.
her - ald - ing re - joic - ing be - yond com - pare.
plan - et earth trans - formed. Good the news we bear.

Refrain

Peace on earth: this is our prayer. Let there be *pax Chris - ti* eve - ry - where.

234